SECOND WIND

one woman's midlife quest TO RUN seven marathons on seven CONTINENTS

CAMI **OSTMAN**

SEAL PRESS

SECOND WIND
One Woman's Midlife Quest to Run Seven Marathons on Seven Continents

Published by
Seal Press
A Member of the Perseus Books Group
1700 Fourth Street
Berkeley, California

Library of Congress Cataloging-in-Publication Data

Ostman, Cami.
  Second wind : seven marathons on seven continents / Cami Ostman.
    p. cm.
  ISBN 978-1-58005-307-5
  1. Ostman, Cami. 2. Marathon running. 3. Runners (Sports)—United States—Biography. 4. Women runners—United States—Biography. I. Title.
  GV1061.15.O85A3 2010
  796.42'52—dc22
                        2010018182

Cover design by Domini Dragoone
Printed in the United States of America by Edwards Brothers
Distributed by Publishers Group West

The author has changed some names, places, and recognizable details to protect the privacy of friends and family members mentioned in the book.

To back-of-the-packers everywhere.

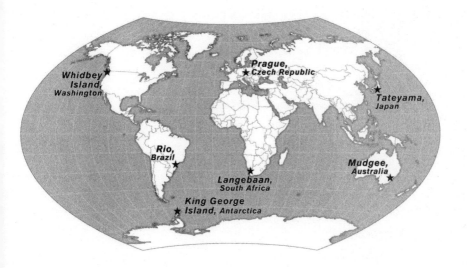

contents

Introduction 6

1 Beginning the Race 12
The Starting (Over) Line

2 Europe 25
The Prague Push—May 2003

3 Together and Alone 50
My Own Vision Quest—September 2003–June 2007

4 Australia 70
The Mudgee Nudge—August 2007

5 In My Own Back Yard—March 2008 95

6 North America 107
Whidbey Island Wonder—April 2008

7 Panama City 127
Blood, Sweat, and Tears—August 2008

8 Asia..147
The Tateyama Triumph—January 2009

9 Africa..170
The Langebaan Long Haul—March 2009

10 Cobwebs and Casseroles—April-June 2009.......................201

11 South America...211
The Rio Resolve—June 2009

12 Getting There—July 2009-February 2010..........................229

13 Antarctica..253
The "Experience"—March 2010

Epilogue..284

Acknowledgments...287

About the Author..291

introduction

I started this journey by running out on my life. On September 11, 2001, while the world was watching the devastation of the Twin Towers' collapse in New York, I was loading boxes into the back of my car and moving out of an eleven-year marriage. I was afraid of what the future held and I felt guilty for leaving, but I knew I couldn't stay.

The demise of the relationship, as is so often the case, started even before the marriage began. Flash back more than twenty years to my preadolescence. Within the space of a two-year period, my parents divorced, my father disappeared into addiction for awhile, and our house burned to the ground. My mother remarried. A new baby was born into the family, making me the oldest of four and still the only girl. And then I was in junior high—the hell of childhood for most of us. All of my structures were shattered, leaving me scared and lonely as the adults in my world focused on putting their own lives back together. By the time I was thirteen years old, I was teetering on the edge of depression and in desperate need of guidance and stability. Enter religion.

I spent a lot of time that first year of junior high writing poetry full of darkness and grief and sharing it with a few school pals who were similarly angsty and morbid. One of those poetry friends told me she wanted me to come to her church one Sunday, and, always glad to get out of the house, I agreed to go. The church I visited claimed God loved me. I needed love. They told a story of God's giving peace of mind and joy. I needed peace and joy. They didn't tell me they'd give me rules, but that was to come. And I needed rules, too. I went back week after week and finally, one Sunday, I walked down the aisle during an altar call and became "born again."

In the ensuing years, the various churches I attended gave me a structure my family lacked. In fact, the discourses I was exposed to gave me guidance for almost every aspect of life imaginable. I gave myself over to the rules, never bothering to think critically about them. Throughout my adolescence, I abstained from sex, threw out all my rock music, avoided R-rated movies, obeyed my parents even when they were unreasonable, and, most important, constantly confessed my bad thoughts (sins) to God.

By the time I left my family home at nineteen, I was steeped in a very literal, simplistic structure of religious experience, and it was still what I needed. I had a lot to be thankful for in these guidelines; they had given me a sense of security and saved me from getting into troubles unknown. But a few years later, at age twenty-one, when I met a young man and started dating, I found myself in shaky territory. I couldn't have sex, and I couldn't marry him, either, unless he shared my doctrines. Those were the rules.

My young beau converted to my way of believing—or at least he tried. We married and, mostly at my insistence, we built our relationship around my understanding of what a godly marriage should look like.

The guidelines for a young woman inside a marriage were more burdensome to me than those that had guided me through my adolescence. I sat under teachings that said a woman must always have a "covering": In other words, she is never fully in charge of herself. Either her father or her husband must be her leader and her adviser. Certainly, he must do so with an attitude of benevolence, but that did not change the fact that the state of the woman was to be one of submission. My father would have nothing to do with this; he'd long ago left me to my own devices. My young husband, likewise, found it baffling and was no more a natural "head of the house" than I was a natural follower. The marriage wasn't meeting my expectations on a spiritual level, and I felt lonely in it. I also felt I was incessantly failing God, and yet at the same time I was beginning to feel God's expectations were unreasonable. There was a very small, hidden part of me that wanted something else.

By the time I reached my early thirties, I was experiencing a growing dissonance between what I actually wanted for my life and what I thought I "should" be doing. I didn't know then that a lot of people have these crises when they have lived most of their lives according to someone else's agenda. I knew only that I was suffocating.

To address my confusion, and to find some meaningful vocation (since we didn't have children—the most meaningful thing a Christian woman could do), I began a master's degree program in marriage and family therapy. I hoped to sort out the truth about marriage and family, and to figure out once and for all what God wanted from me. I chose a program at what I thought was the most conservative Christian institution in the Seattle area, one that offered accreditation in my field of choice.

I got more than I signed up for. During my studies, I was invited to examine every assumption, guideline, interpretation, and expectation in my own life from many angles. I was being prepared to work in therapy with clients who not only didn't hold my narrow beliefs but also had lives full of unanswerable questions and mysteries that couldn't be solved. Slowly, over two years of intense study and self-examination, I started to see that I was in that boat, too, along with every other human being, regardless of doctrine. I graduated in 2000 with more questions than I had started with and fell further into crisis. I was getting ready to run.

ONE HOT SUMMER DAY in 2001, I stood in the living room of a new home my husband and I had recently purchased and looked at my bookshelves. Books had always been my great love and solace. There on my shelves were books full of religious instruction, guiding me into a life of rules and submission. They sat side by side with newer books guiding me toward questions I had only recently dared to ask. One question, in particular, I had pushed away for over a decade: Was I happy? I had refused to ask it, even during my studies, because I knew it would bring forward a flood that might drown me. The question seemed simple, and yet it was one of the most complicated I'd ever sought to answer.

I had been told for years that happiness was irrelevant, that the peace and joy of God were deeper and more sustaining than plain happiness, somehow. But that day, as I looked at my bookcase, I knew enough to be honest and say that for me this was hogwash. I was unhappy, and that mattered to me. Period. It wasn't anyone's fault other than my own. I'd been the one who'd insisted on embracing such rigid ideas for so long. I was thirty-four years old and very unhappy, in my relationship and in general. For the second time in my life, all the structures that supported me (theology, marriage, church community) were about to be shattered—this time to provide me with the opportunity to sort through the pieces and find exiled parts of myself.

I said goodbye as well as I knew how, loaded up my car, and drove into an abyss of loss, hoping to start a quest that would lead me to me.

As I floundered in isolation, separated from the church community that had kept me in place for so long and from God as I had known him, an old friend came along and encouraged me to take up running, an activity I'd dabbled in over the years but had set aside during my crisis. I wasn't keen on the idea at first, but I gave it a try on a small scale and found that while it was hard for me, running also soothed me. When I was running, I was breathing. When I ran, I centered my entire attention on my body in the present moment and got some relief from the emotional gymnastics that were the result of my shattered life. Like a prayer, but without a specific petition, running called me to quiet my thoughts. This was a good start. I kept it up, aware of all the things I was running from, and still having no idea what I was running toward.

LONG-DISTANCE (AND SPECIFICALLY marathon) running was about to provide me with a new structure that required just enough of that same dogged religious commitment to make it feel familiar, and yet its only "rule" was that I run 26.2 miles (42 kilometers in most of the world), and even that I would fiddle with now and again. As the idea to run seven marathons on seven continents morphed into a real goal and then became my midlife vision quest—teaching me about myself, spirituality, relationship, and life in general—I came home to myself, and in doing so became a real woman. No longer a puppet to a masculine god, I've built a life, a character, and a set of values that sustain me. I've done this wearing my running shoes and an iPod Shuffle.

It hasn't been easy or quick or tidy or even much fun some of the time. And yet the trials are what make the marathon the perfect metaphor for living life with the long run in mind. The marathon teaches a person to plan, to dream, to push through hard times, to admire unlikely people, to give up the penchant for perfectionism, and to accept life for the messy endeavor it is. Training for the marathon gives a person the opportunity to learn things about the self that, I would argue, can be learned only through hard physical training. How much pain can you take? Can you tolerate being alone? How long can you entertain your own thoughts and really be with just yourself? How do you feel about being dead last? How many times can you repeat the same motion with your body, the same mundane activity, and still find value in it?

Running has given me a model for how to reconstruct a life for myself. Marathon racers, just like people in relationships with other human beings, all run together and yet alone. Sometimes you have to choose whether to keep up with others, or to find your own pace at the back of the pack. Also, a race, just like a life, feels most secure when it's well organized and there's a lot of support along the course, but it is often more interesting to get lost and to have to rely on strangers to help you find your way again.

SECOND WIND IS THE story of how I decided to embrace the marathon and the lessons it has to teach by running on all seven of the world's continents. These pages hold not only tales of the races and the travels, but stories of inspiring, interesting people around our globe. I hope that once you are done reading, you will want to take a look at the "shoulds" that may hold you captive and that wherever you have gotten stuck in your life, you will see a way to break free and find *your* second wind.

The quest to live more authentically requires something unique for (and from) everyone. For me, it has required a lot of loss, a change in spiritual perspective, hours and hours of training, and the foibles of explaining "constipation" in pharmacies the world over. Perhaps for you it will mean taking on a completely different challenge than mine, but whatever it looks like, I hope you will join me at the starting line and run your races and live your life at your own speed and to the tune of your own playlist.

beginning the race:
THE starting (over) line

"The descent is characterized as a journey to the underworld, the dark night of the soul, the belly of the whale, the meeting of the dark goddess, or simply as depression. It is usually precipitated by a life-changing loss."

—MAUREEN MURDOCK, *The Heroine's Journey*

"The first step, if you'll pardon the pun, is to forget everything you have ever believed about running. Everything you think running is and everything you think runners are is almost certainly wrong."

—JOHN "THE PENGUIN" BINGHAM, *No Need for Speed*

1

On a Thursday in March 2002, I sat up in my bed and felt a throbbing in my skull, which, on this particular day, was accompanied by strange puffs of flashing light that appeared in my line of vision whenever I blinked my eyes. Wherever I turned my gaze, the apparitions floated around in the nook of the bedroom where I had been sleeping. I tried to rise, but the apartment started spinning—slowly at first, then faster and faster, until I conceded defeat, flopped myself back onto the bed, and cried for a while.

In another half hour, I rose again. The flashes of light were still there; they followed me into the low-ceilinged living room and accompanied me to the window, where I opened the blinds and looked up from my dark basement studio onto a view of the sidewalk to see if it was raining. It was. It's always raining in Seattle, where the skyline is surrounded by beautiful views of water and mountains but is also capped by rain clouds ten months of the year.

The visions of light followed me into the shower and to the kitchen, where I made coffee. I was becoming alarmed. Were these the early signs of brain cancer? Or psychosis? Was I finally succumbing to the inescapable legacy of depression among the women in my family? Mine would come *with psychotic features*, no doubt (as a psychotherapist, I even happened to know the DSM code: 309.34). Why couldn't I have followed the men of the family into alcoholism, instead of this? Maybe it wasn't too late to choose an illness for myself before it chose me. I made a mental note to buy wine after work.

I dressed and drove the two miles to my new job working with homeless youth in Seattle's U District. This was the kind of job I had pursued since obtaining my master's degree in family therapy—something that would give me the opportunity to really make a difference. With a strong recommendation from Bill, a former supervisor turned friend, I had been given the chance, and the privilege, to work with this disenfranchised population as the organization's program director. Many years earlier, Bill himself had given me my first professional job, as a teacher in an international exchange program at Western Washington University. I had been a student there at the time and had stayed in Bellingham, a small city ninety miles north of Seattle, after graduation to work for the program he ran. I had continued on and off for eight years, and we'd stayed in touch here and there.

When I applied for the job at the drop-in center, I asked Bill to be a reference. When I told him about my broken marriage, he offered me support and understanding, empathizing from his own experience with the sorrow of divorce. Connecting with him had helped me feel less isolated. He'd even called back to check on me a few times in the early weeks of my new job to remind me that he believed in me, that things would eventually come together for me. I wanted to believe him.

I was, in fact, very grateful for my new job, even if I had trouble getting through my days. It was the only stability in my life at the moment, my only anchor. Each shift, which started at two o'clock in the afternoon to accommodate the nocturnal habits of the drop-in center clientele, was filled with the busywork of making sandwiches, disposing of used needles left in the bathrooms, and reprimanding kids for pitching F-bombs at one another (not exactly work that required a master's degree). But they were also days filled with important conversations and rewarding moments of watching heartfelt connections between volunteers and young people who were typically cut off from positive adult relationships. I knew what it was like to feel isolated and alone and was gratified to be orchestrating community for others who needed it as much as I did.

WHEN I ARRIVED AT work on the day of the flashing lights, our drop-in program was in full progress. I parked my car and crossed an intersection to the big brick church building that hosted our organization. I had to brace myself on the banister next to the stairs that led down into the basement that housed the program. I scanned the room, looking for our executive director, Lisa. Lisa was a trained therapist, too, and I wanted to consult with her immediately about what I was now convinced were potentially dangerous hallucinations. Although I had been at this job less than a month and was afraid that revealing the extent of my unsteadiness could be problematic for my job security, I was more afraid of the flashing lights and the spinning.

I spotted Lisa sitting at a round fold-up table, talking to a transgendered kid with a nose ring and a tattoo down the side of her face and neck. They both looked up as I approached.

"Excuse me, Sarah," I said to the youth. "Can I steal Lisa for a moment?"

"Whatever." She rolled her eyes, rose gracefully, and sauntered away, hips swaying. I watched her go, hoping she didn't feel dismissed. I'd spent a lot of my life being dismissed; I knew how it felt.

"What's up?" Lisa asked me. She stood, her friendly but solemn face coming even with mine. Lisa was one of those knowing souls who could sniff out everything from dishonesty to a joint smoked furtively in an alley before the lie was even told or the joint lit. She knew the outline of what was happening in my private life, and I valued her opinion.

I ushered her over to a remote corner of the drop-in area and whispered, "Lisa, I think I'm having a psychotic break. I'm seeing spots of light whenever I blink, and the world's been spinning since I woke up." I waited for her to confirm my suspicions.

Lisa looked at me for a long time and narrowed her eyes before she moved next to me and put her arm around my shoulder, shuffling us both toward the exit and back up the stairs. She spoke to me warmly: "Cam, you're not having a psychotic break, you bonehead. You're having a divorce. You've been crying so much, you aren't getting enough oxygen to your brain."

We were outside the building on the busy road now, but she carefully watched the traffic and kept us advancing across the street in the direction of the parking lot. Then she started giving me commands: "Go home and don't

back until Monday. Go to the doctor and talk to her about antidepres-̣nts to get you through this. And put some ice on your face. It's bloated."
She walked me to my car and closed me into it, and I drove back to my tiny, makeshift home.

I don't know why I hadn't thought to blame the hallucinations on cry-ing. I was mourning the loss of a life that I hadn't inhabited well and yet was sad to leave. I'd spent too much of my life trying to follow rules: first the ever-shifting rules of my broken nuclear family and then the immutable, paternal-istic rules of the conservative churches I'd gotten involved with as a teenager. Finally, out of fear of repeating my parents' mistakes and a genuine fear of God's wrath, I had collaborated in creating a set of impossibly rigid rules in my marriage, and I couldn't figure out how to change them without blowing them apart. I had moved out of my beautiful, spacious two-story house and into a musty-smelling basement studio. I had left my beloved dog and cat behind, taken a risky job, and quietly said goodbye to my old self, counting on a new one to emerge. It wasn't happening quickly. In fact, I could scarcely see evidence of it happening at all.

My life was a patchwork of disorganized details: dishes that didn't match, secondhand furniture, and garage-sale linens and towels to get me by until I felt permanent enough somewhere to coordinate colors. I spent my coffee breaks attempting to collect my nerves in the restroom and wandered aimlessly through shops on the weekends, trying to decide which household items I needed to replace and what I could live without.

The questions I had about who I would become were disorganized, too, since all my old boundaries were no longer in place. I had rejected an entire paradigm that had guided me about what to believe and how to behave, as well as how to think, dress, worship, pray, serve, and speak. There had been a standard for what I should read, whom I should share deep feelings with, and even in which context my sexuality was allowed to be expressed. Did leaving it all behind make me a quitter, an ineffectual, depressed loser who couldn't bear the cross of the holy life God wanted me to lead? Or was I an adventur-ess, facing down my own version of danger, looking for new horizons? I knew, somehow, that I would get to decide what defined me. But how? I was used to looking outside myself for the answers; the prospect of looking within was dawning on me, but I was tentative. What if there was no one in there?

I was relieved by Lisa's compassion, not to mention her astute diagnosis, and followed her prescription. That very day, I got an appointment with my doctor, who put me on a low dose of citalopram, a generic antidepressant, and who admonished me against adding any more stress to my life. *Helpful advice,* I thought wryly.

When I got back to my apartment, I tidied up, taking dirty dishes from the cardboard boxes I'd been using as end tables and putting them in the sink to wash later. I didn't possess the energy to complete a task all the way through. By nine o'clock that evening, I climbed back into bed. As I wrestled to fall asleep, I cycled through my usual ruminations about what my future might hold, now that I was free to make sense of life in my own way.

I remembered an incident from a few weeks earlier. It seemed to me that whenever someone went through a divorce, other people often perceived it as primarily a failure of love. Some people tried to restore their own faith in couplehood by offering the divorcing person opportunities to recouple as quickly as possible. I myself had declined all offers from my girlfriends to set me up on blind dates, except once, when I had regrettably agreed to let a married friend invite a single man along on a group outing to the theater so there wouldn't be an uneven number (some people are afraid of uneven numbers, I was finding out). Even as the man entered the restaurant and approached our table, I could see the neon lights on his forehead announcing: "Want Wife and Children." He gave me too many compliments at dinner and tried to hold my hand during the play. After the curtain call, I quickly said my goodbyes, walked to my car, and drove away before the guy had a chance to ask me out on a real date.

I knew "dates" were not what I needed. The idea of putting myself on display to impress men brought on waves of panic. Besides, I was clearly not wife material and I didn't want children. I left that evening afraid I wasn't good material for intimacy of any kind. Even the new cat I had adopted for company kept an aloof distance. And my failure had been not the malfunction of love, but the absence of self-knowledge. My inability to know and trust myself had invited me to build my marriage on someone else's principles. This was my chance to correct that. I was just a little stuck at the moment, not to mention hallucinating. I put my thoughts to rest and finally fell into a hard, still sleep.

TWELVE HOURS LATER, I awoke refreshed. It was a Friday and, thanks to Lisa, I had the day off. The clouds in the sky were still dark, but the rain had stopped—and so had the spinning. I phoned my friend Lin, who lived in a cabin with a view of Puget Sound, and asked if I could spend the day bundled up on her porch looking out at the water. As Lisa had observed, I needed air.

There's nothing like tidal waters to recalibrate your internal compass. The light breeze and the cups of tea my friend kept placing in my hands calmed me. The day passed in a perfect rhythm of long silences and aimless conversation. Like the waves on the nearby shore, my thoughts crashed forward and receded at their leisure. I took in full, deep breaths of sea air and embraced my tentative liberation. As the day wore on, the previous day's panic quieted. I was grateful for the time, grateful for Lin's hospitality, and grateful for the job that had given me the day off to sit by the beach.

Dinnertime rolled around, and Lin had plans. She offered for me to stay and make myself at home while she went out, but I was ready to move on. I got in my car after many thank-yous, but before I reached the highway, I realized I wasn't yet prepared to go home to my cave after a day of so much fresh air. I pulled over and thought about what to do. I could drive back to Seattle and settle in with a book at a coffee shop, but I didn't think I had the focus for reading just then. Or I could try to find someone who wouldn't require much of me to spend some time with. But who?

I had lost a lot of friends in my divorce. In the religious culture I was coming from, people felt they needed to choose sides, to pick between the one left and the leaver, the right over the wrong. Divorce was a major offense against God, unless it was undertaken because one person was victimized by the other's abuse, addiction, or adultery. None of those things had happened to me. I had left because of unhappiness and general confusion, and that put me squarely in the wrong among my most conservative friends. Some of them had disappeared quietly from my life, others had been vocal about their disappointment in me, and a few had expressed fear for my eternal soul and said they would pray for (but not talk to) me. I understood all of this because I had been there myself; I'd made judgments when couples I knew had divorced in the past. Now, as the offending party, I felt a profound loss of community and was sorry I had been so unrelenting toward others at times. Friends who were willing to stand by me as I built a new foundation for myself were treasures, and also few in number. I happened to know that my three best pals in Seattle all had plans that night. I was lost.

It was getting dark. I cried for a while, steaming up the windows in my car. Such was this grief—it abated and then returned, torrential. I knew I had to take it in small pieces. Right now, I needed dinner and easy conversation with someone who could tolerate my state of mind without making me explain it. Finally, I decided I would call Bill, my former supervisor. I had been meaning to buy him dinner to thank him for giving me a glowing recommendation, but until now I hadn't been able to exert the energy for the drive north to Bellingham. Now I was halfway there anyhow, so I called him and told him where I was. Was he free? I asked. He was. We agreed to meet at a bookstore we both knew between Bellingham and where I was sitting by the freeway on-ramp.

IT WAS FULLY DARK when I arrived and got out of my car. I hadn't seen Bill face-to-face in over three years. He hurried toward me to hold my car door open for me. He was taller than I remembered. His hair had turned to salt and pepper, and his complexion was smooth and tanned. His blue eyes sparkled with kindness. Should I hug him? Shake hands? Stand at a stiff distance? I used to have rules about how to greet the people in my life appropriately (no front hugs for men—the breasts incite lust), but not now. Deciding to take a risk, I opted for the hug and felt his slim shoulders and warm arms around me. I knew I was in a safe presence.

We walked together to a small Thai restaurant nearby, and his arm brushed mine comfortably along the way. I tried not to pull away, as I would have done before. We entered the restaurant through a low door and loitered in a crowded, ornate waiting area decorated with mahogany elephants and bejeweled goddesses. When our table was ready, Bill moved aside and let me walk in front of him. When we got to our table, he held out my chair.

Thankfully, conversation during dinner was seamless, shifting from news of Bill's four children, now in their late teens and early twenties, to the sad end of my marriage and my bumbling efforts to create a new life. I shared my experience of the flashing lights from the day before and was relieved by the discovery that I could already laugh at my having mistaken them for hallucinations. This was exactly what I wanted—an easy-flowing conversation in which I had to neither entertain nor pretend I was completely fine.

As the evening trickled on, something in me began unlocking. Here I was, breaking through boundaries that felt huge to me, and yet they were boundaries that most people never would have recognized as such for themselves, or even succumbed to in the first place. I was having dinner alone with a man, I was sipping on an alcoholic drink, and I was getting divorced. No one watching me could have known how revolutionary I was at that moment. I noticed the tightness in my chest relaxing a little, my customary vigilance softening just a bit.

When we finished our pad Thai and Panang curry and were settling in with another glass of plum wine, we traded travel stories and spoke of all the places we wished to see before we died. I hoped to take my grandmother to Norway to visit relatives later that spring; Bill hoped to someday make his way to the Czech Republic for the same reason. Both of us wanted to explore South America and travel through Asia. I hadn't anticipated we would have so many things to talk about. I realized I'd never given myself permission to really get to know Bill.

Near the end of the evening, Bill introduced another topic he thought we shared interest in. "Cami, we have something else in common," he said. "We're both runners. You inspired me to start running."

"Get out!" I said. It was true I had run for a while when Bill and I worked together. After many years of aerobic dance as my only form of fitness activity, I'd taken on the challenge of running for some variety in my workout schedule. Exercise had always been important to me, not only to let off steam in my uptight existence, but also because obesity ran in my family (yes, in addition to depression and alcoholism). Running itself had been difficult for me, though, and I'd never considered myself much of a success at it. The idea that I had inspired someone to take up the sport was laughable.

"No, really!" he insisted. "You were running before you moved away, and I thought it was great. Seemed like a good way to get outside and move my body. I started it to get me through *my* divorce." He had run his first marathon in the fall of 2000 in Victoria, BC, and had continued running races of all distances over the past year and a half. I was impressed. "We should run together sometime," he suggested.

I was taken aback by this suggestion. Running with Bill would feel too vulnerable, too visceral. It was one thing to share a meal at a restaurant where I was tucked in safely on my side of the table behind my plate of food, but running would allow him to see me in a way I wasn't ready for. I might seem interesting to Bill in this dull light, but actually, I was in a perpetual state of lethargy right now. I walked alone now and again (mostly so I could cry) around Greenlake, a manmade lake in North Seattle surrounded by a three-mile paved trail. I used that time to chew over my past mistakes and worry about the future, the two topics that consumed my thoughts, but running hadn't even occurred to me.

"I don't think I'm up for that, Bill," I said.

"Well, it really helped me clear my mind and get in touch with my feelings during a difficult time," he said. "I ran until I hurt more on the outside than on the inside. You should really try it. It works." I appreciated his transparency. It was helpful to hear others acknowledge the intensity of the divorce process, but *more* pain wasn't the remedy I was looking for.

"How about getting together sometime for a movie instead?" I surprised myself with this suggestion, but I wanted to stay in touch, wanted another chance to experience myself in this way.

"Absolutely!" Bill responded enthusiastically.

As the restaurant closed down and the waitress vacuumed under our table, a polite encouragement to get out so she could get home to her own life, Bill and I made arrangements to see a movie the following weekend. Then we hugged goodbye.

I WAS AWAKENING TO some strength, some audacity inside of me I didn't know was there. Yesterday I'd crashed and burned, finally at the bottom of my hell. Today I began to rise from the ashes. I drove home in a reverie, contemplating how I had spent most of my life seized up by the sense that any wrong move could destroy me. I'd been militarily watchful against common mistakes and normal human experiences. Now that all the fears I had held my breath to prevent had come true and my life was a shambles, the world was opening. Tonight I was breathing in a life without all the old restrictions. It was the difference between swimming in a pool, where you can see the solid edges surrounding you, and swimming in the ocean, where you may not even be able to see the land. I was going to learn to turn over onto my back and float, to let life offer me gifts. I would learn acceptance, and how to say yes instead of no.

All the rest of the weekend, between my ritual crying jags (which didn't stop altogether for more than another year), I had brief interludes when, for the first time in my life since I was a child, I felt a tiny bit, well . . . not sad.

When Monday came around and I reported back to work, Lisa noticed the change. "You look better. Either those antidepressants kicked in over the weekend or you fell in love. How's your psychosis?"

"Gone," I said simply. "The rest did me good. I'm on the mend."

It was true. I had been six months in Hades (and years in Limbo). But I was getting ready to emerge from the darkness. I felt so much improved, in fact, that the next morning, when I might have typically taken my slow grief-walk around the lake, I remembered Bill's suggestion and suited up in my old running gear to take an easy jog instead. I stood for a moment in the quiet of the morning and listened to the distant sounds of the city's traffic and construction, before sliding into a slow run. I breathed in the cold March air. People and dogs and bicycles zoomed past me in both directions, the park providing a respite from the bustle of life taking place only blocks away.

So slowly that I felt embarrassed by my ineptitude, I moved forward, leaving behind the parking lot and children's play area where I had started. My lungs ached a little, even at my puttering pace. Although I had tried to maintain my fitness level during these dark times, I was obviously compromised.

I knew now, as I made my way on this born-again-virgin run around the lake, that I was giving myself permission to run away from the pain I was holding. It was okay to let go of the guilt and the fear and to take in air and light.

I watched the morning sun on the lake as the clouds parted temporarily and gave Seattle-ites a brief glimpse of those famous blue skies. My thoughts disappeared as I witnessed my breathing find its rhythm. Contrary to Bill's claim that I could get in touch with my feelings, I stopped mourning and worrying entirely and instead picked up a mantra of concentrated patience: *One more step. It'll be over soon. Breathe.* I repeated these words. Whenever my thoughts drifted to some concern or negative feeling, I easily returned, Zen-like, to center my attention on what my body was doing. My concentration funneled solely toward my movements—not toward what steps I had to take to get my finances secured, or wondering if my ex-husband would ever forgive me. *Lift your foot. Breathe. Lift. Breathe* was all I had. And I was astonished to discover that it was enough.

It took me thirty-six minutes to run the lake that morning, but at the end of the run, I realized something important: I had entirely stopped fretting and criticizing myself! Thirty-six minutes of concentrating on lifting my legs and propelling them forward had provided me with thirty-six minutes of internal relief. And I felt strong, in spite of the ache in my lungs. The focus on my neglected body gave my mind and heart permission to rest. Getting in touch with my feelings was not what I needed; it was letting them go. I would try this again (many times, as it would turn out).

I wasn't sure this was what Bill had been referring to when he had said his running had helped him through divorce, but it could work for me.

I didn't know what other people did to deconstruct their lives, but for me it was going to be critical to find a tranquil place of rest where the old definitions and stories about myself could stop pulling at me. Maybe running could give me that.

I went to work later that day. Drop-in was easy for a change (I was told to go fuck myself only once). When I got home that night at eleven o'clock, there was a message from Bill, inviting me to visit him in Bellingham the following weekend for that movie we had agreed upon. When I called him back the next morning, the first thing I mentioned was my run.

europe:
THE prague push
MAY 2003

"Synchronicities are soulful. It is the soul that knows something is meaningful… that recognizes what it loves and that it is loved, that is nourished by what we do when what we do comes from our own depths."

—JEAN SHINODA BOLEN, *Crossing to Avalon*

"The first thing is to love your sport. Never do it to please someone else. It has to be yours."

—PEGGY FLEMING

2

Spring came late to western Washington in 2002, as it often does. It was June before Seattle was able to fully appreciate the return of the sunshine illuminating the foliage of the trees. By July, four months after my initial run around the lake, I was regularly running three miles several days a week. Running continued to be a safe reprieve from my recriminating train of thoughts.

Bill and I saw each other frequently over those months. I hadn't expected the depth of friendship that blossomed between us, but I was grateful for it. Bill was warm and easy to be with. He was familiar with sadness and had space for mine in his heart. Before I realized what was happening, he and I developed a regular routine of spending time together nearly every weekend.

As I felt my energy return, I was willing to run with him. I might suggest a short run in Seattle on the Burke-Gilman Trail, the old railroad path that now serves as an inner-city refuge for bicyclists, runners, and rollerbladers. If I was visiting him in Bellingham, we sometimes ran through peaceful Bayview Cemetery, with its gravestones and monuments to grief, and then into the beautiful, woodsy Whatcom Falls Park, pausing to watch local kids jump off a rock cliff into a pool at the bottom of the falls.

Remaking a whole life is hard work, however, so there were still many days when my energy was too low for even a slow run. At these times, if Bill and I were together, we took long walks. My medication had taken effect, but from time to time I still found myself rummaging through my kitchen, looking for my favorite blender or my slow-cooker, and then breaking down when I realized I'd left it behind.

But I was making progress through the initial grief. With the encouragement of Bill and other friends, and the kind permission of my landlord, I got a five-pound pug puppy I named Jane, after Jane Austen, a famous optimist. I also bought some furniture and stopped using cardboard boxes as end tables.

Bill and I spoke by phone almost every evening. I got home from drop-in most nights at eleven o'clock and called him to regale him with stories of kids we'd had to kick out or who'd gotten into rehab or housing. We would wish each other good night just before midnight, and I would take Jane out for one last walk before climbing into bed with her to watch the late shows on TV, thankful for her little warm body.

On the days we were together, Bill was an excellent cheerleader for my new running endeavor. He may not have known what it was like to step outside of an entire belief system, but he certainly understood the healing power of running. He designed routes that kept me on flat ground and helped me avoid boredom with beautiful views. He bought me socks that wicked away sweat and took my cotton anklets away from me to prevent me from getting blisters. He made photocopies of articles about the best foods to boost energy and offered them to me for my reading pleasure.

IN AUGUST 2002, ON a rare hot day almost one year after leaving my marriage and only six months after that first dinner together, Bill and I took a hike in the Cascade mountains. As we were walking the Chain Lakes Trail, which runs in a loop around Table Mountain, Bill made me a sudden and unexpected proposal. Looking out at a green valley, we paused for lunch on a large flat boulder and dug out peanut butter sandwiches and apples from our packs. I was shuffling through my bag for a bottle of water when Bill spoke abruptly. He said my name in a way that sounded too formal for our current setting.

"Cami," he began, and then continued in a rapid monologue, as if he had memorized his lines: "I know you've been focused on getting on your feet, and you may not want to do this, but I hope you'll seriously consider what I'm about to ask."

I held my breath and looked at the sincerity in his dear face, hoping he wasn't going to make me hurt him when he finished his sentence. I was still mending. I wasn't even sure what I believed about exclusive relationships, or whether I could ever be in one again without giving away too much of my self-authority, something that was still new to me. I was in no position to offer anyone anything.

He glanced away from me and studied his hands, and then continued, "I'd love it if you would do me the honor of running a marathon with me."

I let out my breath, and with it came a sharp laugh that startled Bill. He looked up at me with curiosity. *A marathon?* He wanted me to run a marathon with him! This *was* a surprise. I reassured him with a smile that I wasn't making fun of him. It was only that I was just barely getting my running legs under me, just finding my pace. My base fitness level couldn't withstand more than three or four miles at most. Maybe I could be ready in a few months to run a 10K, but 26.2 miles was out of the question. I couldn't imagine, even with training, that I could get myself to the point where a marathon would be feasible. This wasn't unlike what I felt about my relationship with Bill: ready for a weekend now and again, but not for giving myself to it.

I opened my mouth to turn him down. I wasn't up to it. But Bill interrupted me and went on with his speech: "In Prague. I want to run the Prague Marathon this coming May, and I'd like it if you'd join me. That's nine months away. Plenty of time for training. And before we get to the Czech Republic, we could travel through Germany and taste some wine."

Now he had my attention. Wine, a formerly forbidden tonic, was a new passion of mine. I watched my consumption because of my family history, but I had to admit I loved the stuff. Also, since our dinner at the Thai restaurant, I had taken that trip to Norway with my grandmother and had been bitten by the travel bug in a big way. This component of Bill's proposal was very enticing, but on the other hand, I didn't think I could afford another trip to Europe so soon.

Bill had anticipated this objection, too, because before I could speak to the issue of money, he said, "The trip is on me. I know your money is tight. I probably wouldn't do this kind of trip by myself, so you'd be doing me a favor by coming along." This arrangement definitely wouldn't work. It would make me feel like I didn't have ownership over the trip for myself. I would have to crunch my numbers before I would know if I could come up with the funds.

I fixed my eyes on Bill's face and watched him search my expression for clues as to what my response would be. I knew he had made contact with an elderly distant relative in Prague, and that he hoped to make the trip before the old man died. I suspected we would be well suited as traveling companions. I felt excited at the idea of getting back to Europe and wandering with Bill through cities neither of us had ever seen. But even if I could come up with the money, the marathon was a huge glitch for me.

I had been at the finish line to see Bill complete races a few times in the past months and felt the excitement of his accomplishments, but I also knew that training for a marathon required a substantial time commitment. It would take many hours a week, there was always a chance of injury, and what if I just plain couldn't do it? But then again, in the past year I had stretched myself in many ways and broken through a lot of boundaries. Why not this? Why not push to find out what my limits were? Wasn't that what my life was about right now? Pushing back? Doing uncomfortable things?

I was still thinking. I turned to look out again at the valley. We were across from a rough, rocky peak. I studied the face of it, considering.

"Can I get back to you?" I asked. I liked the vision of myself as a traveler and adventurer, but I wanted to allow myself time to figure out some details.

I looked back at Bill's face. His smile fell a little. "Sure," he said, betraying his disappointment that I couldn't give an absolute yes.

"I'll tell you what," he said, rallying. "How about I tell you what our training might look like so you can make an informed decision?"

"Sure," I said.

We finished our sandwiches before packing up and completing our loop back to the car. As we hiked, Bill filled me in on all the particulars of training for a marathon. I listened carefully, because I had a hunch what my answer was going to be.

I TOOK THE NEXT week and worked on my finances. I didn't want to unbalance my tediously tight budget, but there was some room for adjusting to save a bit more. I could cut back on espresso drinks and eat at drop-in with the kids. I could wait to buy the new vacuum and set of dishes I had my eye on.

I spent another week thinking about how traveling with Bill might affect my new, precarious sense of autonomy. Three solid weeks (the length of our proposed trip) with anyone was sure to be intense, and I was still relishing my alone time. This was the first time I had ever lived by myself. I had grown up with three younger brothers in a house with one bathroom and had moved from there to living with roommates. Then I'd gotten married at twenty-three and succumbed to the religious ideology that a woman alone was insufficient, that she needed a man (husband, father, pastor) to accompany her through life and guide her. I had scarcely had an hour to myself in thirty-five years, and now I was soaking in my privacy—reveling in it.

On weekdays I spent my nonworking hours buried in a book or listening to music or zoning out in front of the television. Everything I did with my time was a result of ignoring the old "shoulds" and listening to my own newly discovered Wisdom. On weekends, even though I enjoyed the time Bill and I spent together, I was also content when we hugged goodbye and I was once again on my own. I had to consider what constant companionship, albeit for an abbreviated period of time, would feel like.

I took a third week sketching out a training schedule (according to Bill's thorough description of the process) just to see if I could realistically fit it into my life. My weekday calendar was already chaotic. I didn't have regular work hours, so all the long runs would need to happen on the weekends. I did have nearly nine months to work with, however. I could spread out the training as much as necessary.

In the end, though, my considerations really came down to whether or not I would take the chance and push myself beyond all known limitations. By the time Bill made his proposal, I was certainly ready to stop feeling sorry for myself. I needed something to take up the hours I had been spending in regret, reviewing the failures of my marriage and my life. Perhaps training for a marathon was just the thing. Maybe a goal like this could get me over a hump.

I phoned Bill on a Sunday night three weeks after he made his offer and said, "Okay. Let's do it. Let's go. I want to pitch in by paying for all of our accommodations, though. And I'll train with you for this marathon."

IT WAS EARLY SEPTEMBER 2002 when I said yes to my first marathon, to the teacher that would introduce me to many forgotten parts of myself over the next several years. In November, we walked the Seattle half marathon at a moderate pace. I was sore afterward, but encouraged that I could walk thirteen miles without much consequence. Then, in January 2003, I started my training schedule in earnest. I continued my short runs during the week by myself and did increasingly longer ones under Bill's tutelage on the weekends.

On my four- or five-mile jaunts alone along the paved trails that wound through the Seattle area, I had plenty of opportunities to engage in fantasies about my future and about the trip we were planning. If you train for a long race, you find out that you have to learn what to do with your mind. Some people meditate; others work out problems. Bill "cleared the cobwebs." When I wasn't simply counting my breath and being patient with my pace, I visualized. During the last few years of my marriage, I had restricted myself from imagining the future, feeling that it was fruitless to imagine myself happy without the ability to make my dreams come true. So many of the things I had wanted when I was younger seemed to be closed doors once I was a married woman. Other than the dream to pursue education, something no one in my immediate family had ever done before me, I had stopped dreaming about my larger goals: missionary work, writing, joining the Peace Corps, and other cockamamie ideas I'd had of changing the world.

But here in Seattle, with the Space Needle as a sentinel over my process and Lake Washington as a symbol of baptism, death, and rebirth, I was in training for dreaming my life anew. The future seemed like a blank slate at the moment.

Now, when I ran, my reflections were not about the guilt and the grief I had found relief from in that first run the year before. Thanks to the meditative stance I'd been taking on my runs all these months, now I was able to reflect on my history in a new, less judgmental way, and to realize that my dreams of traveling and changing the world had been altered since the earlier days of my youth. I was no longer living under the pressure of an evangelical mandate to save other people's souls. Although I was pleased to be making an impact on others' lives through my work, I was also giving up some control and letting the world change me. All the years I had spent preaching to others about what they needed to change had brought me to a place where I was discovering that it was me I wanted to change. I wanted to let life flow through me without trying to stop it. True, I wanted the agency to trust my own Wisdom and live out my own dreams and paint my own colors on my walls, but I also wanted to give myself up to whatever the universe might have to offer. I didn't want to miss the opportunity to love deeply, to see other ways of living, to stretch myself beyond what I thought I could do.

In my fantasies, I imagined this trip to Prague teaching me something I needed to know about my innate power as a woman: that I could do anything I wanted if only I set my mind to it. I imagined touching the Divine in some new way that was distinctly feminine and located inside my own self, instead of "out there," somewhere out of reach. I imagined breathing in adventure and wonder. And I imagined sailing across the finish line of my first marathon, strong and victorious and wiser than when I started it.

Unfortunately, although it was the alone time in my training that gave me these fantasies of a perfect European experience, the training process would also be the vehicle for their downfall (only to provide a totally different lesson, of course). Without realizing it was happening, I began to approach training with the same perfectionist stance with which I had approached my spirituality in the past. The desire I had to follow the training schedule and to come through the experience stronger than when I went in morphed into a demand by my old inner critic that I "succeed," and that I do so faultlessly.

Religiously, every Sunday, I added a mile or two to what I had run the weekend before. I knew it would be a major milestone for my confidence if I could get past the half-marathon point. Beyond an eight-mile training run, however, I was having trouble keeping my energy up. I'd lost some weight during my depression in the last year and truly wasn't at my physical or emotional peak. Bill tried to introduce me to energy gels during my runs, but I refused them; their consistency and flavor were too objectionable to me. I tried to carry some nuts or nutrition bars with me when I ran for more than an hour, and those helped a little, but after a few tries I still couldn't sustain a run for longer than eight miles.

My disappointment over this plateau I'd hit was growing. Running was becoming my real-life symbol for creating a new self. If I couldn't make it through a long run, would that mean I wasn't going to be able to build something good for myself in the long run of life? Just as in my religious experience, when how much time I spent in prayer or worship was a symbol of my devotion to God, my success or failure on my longer runs grew to symbolize whether or not I was going to make it in my new life. I didn't recognize that I was exchanging the rigorous legalism of my previous faith for a rule-bound experience of running. I began to feel I *had* to do this marathon, had to run the whole thing, and it had to mean only one thing: that I was a success, and not the failure I feared I was. I was also afraid of letting Bill down. He was putting a lot of his own energy and time into coaching my training.

One weekend, Bill and I were in Bellingham and were just setting out for what was to be my third attempt at a ten-mile run. We jogged at my slow pace on one of the old railroad routes that had been turned into a recreational trail. We'd been going for about three miles when I got a sudden, forceful pain in my chest. I stopped running and clutched at my heart. Bill stopped and looked back at me, worried. I was seized by an acute squeezing sensation. Nothing of this sort had ever happened to me. The pain was so sharp and continuous that it could only be something dire. I was certain my heart was bursting open.

"I'm having a heart attack, I think," I said to Bill as the tears came. The pain was pulsing through my chest and back and arms. All breath left my body. No matter how I twisted my trunk, I could get no air.

I could see worry turn to fear in Bill's expression, which further frightened me. I watched him groping in the pockets of his sweats for his absent cell phone. Then, realizing he couldn't call for help, he looked around on the trail to find someplace I could sit. He helped me over to a large moss-covered rock.

"Sit here and breathe," he said, kneeling beside me, stroking my back.

As I settled myself on the rock, Bill's touch soothed me a little, but the moment I got one full gasp of air, my body began to tremble. And then, coming as a complete surprise to me and out of my control or volition, wracking, violent sobs gripped me. I began to cry with vehemence, as if some archetypal emotion from the collective unconscious, the grief of all who had ever worked too hard for something they weren't sure they wanted, had possessed me. I hadn't even been aware of feeling sad when the pain first took hold of me, but here I was, shaking with a lifetime of—and this was the crucial moment of recognition—anger! I wasn't sad. I was angry. But why? As the moments ticked on and my crying continued, it came to me.

I didn't want to be perfect anymore. There it was, simple as that. I didn't want to be a perfect wife or a perfect daughter or a perfect employee, sister, therapist, driver, credit card holder, or Christian. I didn't want to believe perfectly or speak perfectly or be perfectly kind and generous. And I didn't want to run a perfect marathon! I didn't want to be careful anymore—careful to say the right thing, think the right thing, handle things right, run the right number of miles. I'd had enough of deciding I was insufficient, of feeling less than adequate for my own life. I'd had enough of trying to meet standards or morals or expectations or training schedules that someone else had set up for me.

This all came tumbling forth, somewhat incoherently, as Bill sat beside me and nodded and held me when I would let him. To his great credit, Bill did not try to fix my anxiety with a new, less demanding set of rules. He did not defend the training program he had laid out for me. He sat quietly with my anger and waited, almost an hour, for the flood to run its course and tire itself out—for the moment, at least (for once you find your anger, it will be at your disposal when you need it).

No one passed us on the trail that day for the entire hour, a welcome anomaly for that stretch of path. Eventually, when my weeping subsided and the panic attack (my doctor later reassured me that's what it was—my heart and lungs were fine) gave way, Bill and I took an unhurried walk back to the car and drove to his house. That evening, over pizza, I was ready to talk about what to do regarding the marathon. I didn't want to give it up, but I did want to find a way of doing it on my own terms, in a manner that allowed me to accommodate my actual ability and readiness.

My body had told me that afternoon that I needed to get honest and take charge of myself. No more relegating decisions to others, even the experts (even to an expert I was growing fonder of with each passing day). The marathon course would be open for six hours. I could walk some of it and relieve the pressure I'd taken on to run the whole thing. Bill had never done that, but he was willing to take it slow on my behalf so we could finish together. I felt I could build up to running at least half of the race in intervals, so I suggested alternating every four minutes between running and walking for the whole 26.2 miles, and Bill agreed.

That night I made a pact with myself: No more perfect. No more careful. From then on, everything I did with my whole heart would be enough: good enough, close enough, well enough. Enough was enough. And even that I would allow myself to do messily and imperfectly.

Through March and April 2003, we trained with a stopwatch to mark our four-minute stints, and I was finally able to complete a nineteen-mile training walk/run about two weeks before our departure date. When the time finally came for us to pack and board the plane, armed as I was with a new and budding commitment to imperfection, I was as ready as I could be for this first foray into marathon life.

WE STARTED OUR JOURNEY in Germany. In the beginning, the trip was exactly as I'd imagined it would be when I'd dreamed about it during my training runs. As Bill had promised me in his incentive package, we floated down the Rhine River and tasted the sweet white wines of Germany. We spent a night in the romantic medieval town of Rothenberg and walked along its ancient fortress wall arm in arm. We visited Dachau and stood silently inside the memorial chapels there. We wandered through Munich's churches and drank gallon-size steins of beer at the Hofbrau Haus and ate round, cream-filled, donutlike pastries at a local fish festival. In Berlin, we saw a beautiful ballet with costumes by Versace danced to the music of Queen, and we touched the remnants of The Wall. We drank Starbucks coffee right in front of the Brandenburg Gate.

On a Thursday afternoon after ten days in Germany, we boarded a train to Prague. We arrived on Friday, two days before the marathon. We'd taken the sleeping train in from Berlin to save money on a hotel room, but the movement of the train prevented us from getting anything you might call sleep.

Our plan was to spend a day in the city before the race. The day after the marathon had been reserved for meeting Bill's distant relative. While for me this trip was about reaching toward the future, for Bill it was a pathway into his past; he had done some genealogical research to locate the branch of his father's family that had not made their way to America.

I understood the importance of Bill's pilgrimage here because of the trip I had taken to Norway with my grandmother. I hadn't felt particularly connected to the homeland, but sitting on a stone fence my grandmother's father had helped build and watching her face as she put the backs of her hands up against the cold rocks gave me a deep appreciation for how making this connection to the past could fill in some pieces to the puzzle of one's identity. For Bill, the Czech Republic was the place that could connect him with his history, and with his own recently deceased father. All of this, on top of the marathon, was placing a lot of expectation on this particular trip.

By the time we arrived at the train station, we were desperate to get a nap and anxious to organize our next few days, but we would have to navigate Prague's metro system first.

We were in over our heads as soon as we disembarked the train at the Prague station. We consulted our guidebook for directions to the Lida Guest House, where we had reservations, obtained maps of the city and the public transportation system from the information kiosk, and then found a bench to sit on and study our situation. We chose a seat just outside the station to catch some of the morning light. Posters advertising the marathon hung along the walls of the ramp where pedestrians exited onto the city streets. The ads featured thousands of fit runners sailing past the thirteenth-century Powder Gate, one of the remaining gateways letting citizens into the city. That was going to be us!

We studied the map of the metro system at length without comprehending it. The map we had picked up was in English, but the signs on the inner-city train quays were in Czech. Unable to match the words on the map with the signage in the station, I finally came up with the idea that I should get a map in Czech so we could cross-compare the locations with their Czech names.

This method helped us locate the line we thought we needed to take to get to the south side of town. We purchased metro tickets from a machine and climbed aboard the train, fairly confident that our stop would be the ninth one on the line. We sat in battered vinyl chairs bolted to the floor and watched out the window as we passed between ancient buildings and into dark underground tunnels. Unfortunately, the train took us only six stops before turning back in the direction from which it had come.

Bill and I sat opposite each other, luggage piled on our laps and between our legs.

"We're going backwards," I said, concerned.

"No, no, it probably just feels that way," Bill said, no doubt unwilling, tired as he was, to believe we were on the wrong track. I was annoyed that he'd dismissed my concern.

"Yes, we are. Look!" I demanded, shoving the unintelligible map into his hands.

We waited for the next stop, and then the next. Sure enough, we arrived shortly back at the Prague train station where we had started. We rose to our feet.

"Should we get off?" Bill asked. Exhausted, he was fumbling slowly now with the metro map, trying to see how we had made our mistake.

"I think so. We're on the wrong line." But no sooner had I said this and hoisted my backpack over my shoulder than the automated sliding doors of the train car closed, trapping us inside.

"I guess we'll do the ride again," Bill grumbled.

When the train finally pulled to a halt back at Prague Station the next time, we were ready. The doors opened and we got off the train. I was barely able to keep awake at this point, but back on the platform, we needed a new strategy to get to our accommodations. Bill was feeling compelled to hurry up and keep moving, even if not in exactly the right direction. He asked several non-English-speaking passersby how to get to our stop. No one was able to help. I wanted to park myself on a bench with the maps and further scrutinize them until they made sense to me. I wanted to slow time down and get all the information in some kind of order.

Bill was showing irritation at my sluggish pace, and his irritation irritated me.

We had never argued before. But now that there was tension between us, an old, familiar fear rose in me. Would I have to swallow my own feelings and scurry to take care of Bill's anxiety at the expense of my own need to collect my thoughts? Here, at the edge of our first conflict, I remembered my new commitment to be just enough and no more.

What I did next may strike no one as especially interesting, but it was, for me, a coup against the people-pleasing voices inside my head. It was a silent protest against a cultured pressure to be "sugar and spice," a reckless abandonment of the "others first" theology of my young adulthood. What did I do? I sat down.

I plunked myself down on a bench and closed my eyes. I heard Bill sigh and stride away. I heard him call, "I'll be back." I breathed in the liberty of knowing and honoring my limits. In a few minutes, I opened my eyes and saw Bill coming toward me with a new map in his hands and a smile on his face.

"Any luck?" I asked.

"Yep. Follow me." He helped me up, hefted his own backpack onto one of his shoulders, and lifted mine onto his other. We made our way to the train.

WE FELL ASLEEP EARLY that evening, grateful to have a bed that didn't shake and lurch. I was proud for the way I had been able to let the moment of conflict between Bill and me be what it was, two tired people in a strange place, instead of following the old patterns of pleasing others or trying to be right. I was holding true to my promise that I would eschew my old, careful stance and be a little untidy in my dealings with the world.

The next day we woke early, excited to explore Prague's city center. This time, with the help of the brothers who owned and operated the guesthouse, we took the metro to the Old Town Square (or Staromestske Namesti). If you stand in the square's center, you can see the Old Town City Hall, which houses an astronomical clock where the twelve Apostles make an ostentatious appearance to announce each new hour of the day. You can also see Saint Nicholas Church, where Jan Hus's followers preached the principles of the Reformation. Small cobblestone streets spidered out from the square in all directions.

Prague took my breath away. Unlike other European cities we'd each visited, World War II had kept its dirty mitts off this one. The buildings in Prague maintain their original architectural integrity. They are not replicas constructed to replace bombed-out structures. There are no bullet holes on the Tyn Cathedral, as there are on most of the buildings on Museum Island in Berlin, for example.

WE WANTED TO BE certain we knew where we needed to go the following morning, and so, because each street looked much like the rest, we made our way to the race center, tagging landmarks on our map and memorizing street signs along the way.

At the event center, a number of large tents had been erected to house vendors and volunteers. We picked up our race packets and some extra water. We asked questions about the course. Our walk/run regimen was enough to get us across the finish line in five hours and fifty minutes, ten minutes shy of the six-hour limit. This meant we had to be fairly precise about our completion time, and it would behoove us to know the hills and aid stations that might slow us down.

After meandering through the race expo for an hour, we took a five-minute walk to Wenceslas Square (Vaclavske Namesti) and sat down in front of the statue of St. Wenceslas on his horse. The statue honors the death of the favorite Good King Wenceslas and marks the location of the victory of the Velvet Revolution against communism in 1989, which brought democracy to the Czech Republic. Here, we sat amid the newly renovated shops and the thriving entrepreneurial spirit catering to tourists and shoppers and looked over our packet materials.

As a first-time marathoner, I was surprised by the contents of the race packet. Samples of health foods, energy gels, pain relievers, and two T-shirts each, along with brochures for marathons to numerous possible exotic locations, fell out of my plastic bag.

"There's a marathon on the Great Wall of China?" I asked Bill, holding up a brochure.

"Yep. Shall we do that one next? How about one on every continent, while we're at it?"

"Sure," I replied glibly. I would be wise to wait and see how I did here in Prague before booking tickets for a world tour. I still had no idea what I was getting into.

We located the map of the course and studied it, noting where we would cross the river and where we would be entertained by music. We took particular care to locate the start/finish line in relation to a McDonald's that marred the ancient ambience of the Old Town Square. When we were satisfied that we were well oriented to Prague's downtown, we strolled through a few churches, picking up flyers about upcoming concerts, and then headed back to our guesthouse to carbo-load and get some rest.

Settling into bed that evening, I watched Bill get ready for the next day. I noticed with curiosity the care he took laying out each piece of clothing and all the supplies he would need: He placed Vaseline, safety pins, a water bottle, and a digital watch in a tidy pile on top of his bib number. I felt slightly amused by Bill's meticulous approach to these preparations as I sipped on a glass of wretched Czech wine I had purchased from a street vendor on our ten-block walk from the metro stop. Observing this almost sacred ritual he was engaging in, I recognized again how important running had become to Bill. I formulated a question for him.

"Bill," I interrupted his concentration. "If tomorrow really lived up to your dreams, what would need to happen?" I was acutely aware nowadays of how unspoken hopes or expectations could spoil an experience (or even a whole relationship). I wanted to get them all on the table.

He looked at me and then away, thinking. When he finally answered my question, I was surprised at the simplicity of his response. "We would get to the starting line forty-five minutes before the race begins," he said. I supposed this made sense, given that we had rushed all through this trip, sometimes to no advantage, to catch trains and buses and tours. This hadn't been one of those vacations where you squander time sipping drinks on the beach. It had been a full-on exploration of castles, museums, and political history. A little safety margin before the marathon would feel good, and seemed easy enough to pull off. I promised I'd do my part to get us there early, and we went to bed.

In the morning, we awoke and dressed for the race. We clothed ourselves in our marathon attire. Having not laid out my outfit the night before, I had to rifle through my suitcase to find a mutinous sock. Bill gave me a look of concern, but it disappeared when I held up the sock. We coughed down some woefully insufficient coffee. The start time was 10:00 AM, so we left our lodging at 8:45, and by 9:05 we were downtown. We knew we were close to the event center when we could finally see the steeple of the Tyn Cathedral jutting above the buildings. Feeling easy because of the wide margin of time we had left for ourselves, we dawdled and used the McDonald's restrooms to avoid the lineup at the port-o-potties we'd seen at the starting line the day before.

After exiting McDonald's, we paused on the street to take off our sweatshirts and stuff them into Bill's duffel. As we ambled toward the starting line, we laughed about how effortless the morning had been compared with our train station experience two days before. We were figuring this city out.

But our leisurely attitudes were brought to an abrupt halt. Suddenly, a horde of runners dashed passed us. We both froze. I turned to Bill, trying to keep the pitch of my voice even. "Who are those runners?" I asked. Bill looked at the numbers on their chests and dropped to his knees to rummage through his duffel, until he dug out his own race bib. The design was identical. "Did they have an early start for the fast people?" I inquired. He didn't think so—I could tell by the way his eyebrows furrowed and he flushed red. I looked at my watch. It was nine fifteen.

Panic completely impeded the previous look of anticipation on Bill's face. With frantic urgency, he burrowed more deeply into his bag, excavating a wrinkled paper with race instructions on it. I leaned over his shoulder. "The race starts Sunday, May 21, at 9:00 AM," it read. Nine o'clock? How had we missed that? Instead of arriving early, we now found ourselves fifteen minutes late!

As the athletes descended upon us, I began to sweat, my heart pounding to the sound of their collective pace. "Shit! We have to find the starting line—fast," I said.

"It's too late," Bill moaned and collapsed further onto his knees.

"It isn't," I argued, pulling him to his feet. "We've got our timing chips, so our time is all that matters." I was calculating the time in my head. If we had fifteen fewer minutes than the other runners, we would have to make up those minutes somewhere along the way to finish before the course closed. We could do this! After all I had been through in the last year, after the ridiculous number of hours I'd spent training, I needed to do this. We only had to find the starting line.

I was inexperienced enough with marathon culture to think that missing the starting gun was just a little snafu. I had come to blows with my lifetime nemesis of perfectionism in training for this thing. I didn't have to do this marathon perfectly, but I did need to do it. Against his better judgment, Bill acquiesced to my naive optimism and determination, and in a flurry we found our way to the start. The square was packed with spectators, but a volunteer, seeing us holding our bibs in our hands and understanding what was going on, snatched our bag from us and ran ahead, signaling where we could retrieve it after the race. Someone else waved us through the crowd toward what we could finally see was the banner above the starting line and the chip registry. We kept on running through the starting hatch and heard two faint beeps as we crossed the electronic tracking strip. I breathed a little easier for a moment.

We had done it. I was starting my first (and possibly only) marathon. True, it wasn't happening as either Bill or I had hoped, but it was still thrilling. True, it would have been more exciting to be among the mass of runners who had started with the gun at nine o'clock, but here we were. Better late than never.

I was settling into my reverie of personal victory a few blocks into the run, proud of myself for persevering, when a crowd of spectators closed in in front of us and left us no open path to run in any direction. We'd lost the route. There were no signs or arrows pointing us in the right direction. Tourists and fans were now milling around on what must have been the course. The temporary fences that had been put in place to show participants the way had already been removed to allow foot traffic through.

We arrived at a crossroads, with no indication of which direction to bear. I began asking bystanders if anyone spoke English and was met with a sea of void stares. I pointed to my bib number and then held up my hands, asking, "Where?" One man shook his head and pointed back in the direction from which we'd come—to the starting line. I gave a weak smile of thanks and turned to find Bill. He was standing a few feet away in the midst of a small group of people looking as lost as we really were. I approached him.

"Now what?" Bill asked me, as if I knew. But even I was beginning to suspect we might be defeated. Had I trained all those hours and come all this way for nothing? Bill, who saw this marathon as a way of anchoring himself to his history, looked forlorn. There didn't look to be any way through this. We stood, looking at one another, anonymous, surrounded by hundreds who could not help us. This just wasn't our day.

We were reaching a decision to give up, when we saw a pack of runners one street over from where we were standing. They were coming around what we later discovered was the turn that was about the two-mile mark on the course. The course was, we knew from the map, the shape of a lollipop, with a little loop at the beginning, followed by a lengthy out-and-back along the shore of the Vltava River. These runners had just completed the first loop.

The crowd turned to watch the athletes. Applause and cheers of encouragement erupted. I looked up at Bill's face and saw the same question on it that I was asking myself. He returned my gaze and we communicated silently. In concert, Bill and I pushed through a wall of fans and stepped into the flow of these passing racers, entering their throng, aware that we were cutting off the first two-mile loop of the race that took the route through the city center before it crossed the Charles Bridge into the outskirts of Prague. The cheering turned to outraged shouts and boos as the fans saw what we were up to, but we were quickly absorbed by the pack. Here we were. Without much deliberation, we had decided to follow the runners we could see, rather than forfeit the experience altogether. But this made us cheaters.

For me, the decision was remarkably easy. Although I had always been known among my friends for my compulsive honesty (I had once even driven five miles to return a pen I'd inadvertently taken from a bank teller), I had some unexplainable but blessed absence of guilt about these stolen miles. Twenty-four miles was still a long way to run, by any standard. It would have to be "enough." I had no real proof I could complete a marathon anyhow—only calculations in my head and a reliable level of physical fitness. Under the circumstances, I was doing the best I could, and this was the new focus of my life: to be content with my own personal best.

Bill, on the other hand, was immediately overtaken with shame and regret. I looked at his face as we jogged side by side and remembered his excitement from the night before, how he had prepared so carefully. I knew he loved the purity of the marathon. He felt it was a special distance, both historically and personally significant. Historically, the marathon represented the distance Pheidippides, a Greek soldier bearing news of an unexpected Persian defeat, was able to run from Athens to Marathon without stopping (though he's said to have dropped dead upon arrival); personally, for Bill, the marathon marked the end of his divorce process and the beginning of new hope in his life.

We ran without speaking for about half a mile. I was beginning to see the remnants of a dream disappearing for him. The Czech Republic was his Old Country. This was his first trip to Europe and his first international marathon. The race was the whole reason he'd coached me through weeks of slow training. Skipping part of the course was sure to be a huge blow to Bill. I felt sad for him.

"We're gonna have a great story to tell," I offered, attempting to bring some levity to the situation.

His response was uncompromising. "There's nothing to tell," he said. "We aren't running a marathon."

"Yes, but it's still a really long run," I said.

"But it's not a marathon." And then he said, "I don't think I can keep going."

My thoughts were fluttering around like butterflies over the open ocean, looking for somewhere to land. We were silent. Another mile came and went. Here was exactly the kind of circumstance that would have sent me into a tailspin of anxiety in the past. My old pattern would have been to feel I should do something to make the other person feel better, to invest more deeply in my partner's feelings than in my own, to follow his lead in whatever he needed to do, and to ignore my own internal process in order to keep peace. But here was also another chance to own my own choices. It seemed the universe was giving me many opportunities to flex my new emotional muscles. This marathon wasn't going to live up to anyone's prerace expectations, but as for me, I was going to do what was left of it and embrace it fully. I needed to learn how to make the best of an imperfect life, with or without a partner, and I would start here.

"Well, I'm going to finish it," I finally said. "If I'm disqualified, that's okay, but I'm going to do the Prague Marathon. It's what I came here for."

Bill considered this, looking at me in disbelief. "You wanna finish this?"

"Sure. Why not? It's the best I can do at this point. In fact, screwing it up takes all the pressure off." These words sounded powerful coming out of my mouth because they were true—they were coming from my own internal Wisdom! Only a few months earlier, I hadn't been sure I had any.

Bill looked away from me, confused. He had, after all, gotten me into this. I waited, hoping he would agree to keep running. I didn't want to do the race by myself, but I would if I had to.

I looked up and studied his expression, reading his struggle. Then his eyebrows raised and a slow smile replaced his scowl. The light was coming back to Bill's face.

"I know what I'm going to do," he said.

"What?"

"I'm going to cross the finish line, and then I'm going to get the map for this damn race and go back to do the two miles I missed. Want to join me?"

It's brilliant, I thought. We could make a game of it. It was a great compromise. We could eat and stretch before we went on to do the missing miles. "Yeah," I said, adding rules to the game, "I won't let them put my medal on. We'll put them on when we're done."

"Excellent!" he said, brightening even more. "And we'll stop for beers along the way on those last two miles." Now we were in the spirit!

THE MARATHON ROUTE WAS spectacular. Along the Vltava River, all was green and smelling of earth. The river was flowing steadily within its banks. Just the year before, the river had overflowed and raging water had pulsed through the city, seeping into buildings, ruining ancient artifacts, and destroying homes. But now, as we ran alongside it, the water was calm. I couldn't believe we were in the Czech Republic.

Once Bill and I made the decision that we wouldn't wear our medals until we had completed every step of the official course, we relaxed for a while. The temperature was perfect, seventy-ish. We ran steadily for our first eleven miles, up to the official thirteen-mile marker. We ditched our well-practiced intervals and ran to catch ourselves up. Adrenaline kept me going somehow. At ten, twenty, and thirty kilometers, there were strips laid down on the ground to read our chips as we passed by. Our first six miles were going to look ridiculously fast, I realized.

At one point, we got a glimpse of those beautifully sculpted, arrowlike

Kenyan runners going the opposite direction after the turnaround point, and we slowed down to watch in awe as they sailed past us. The muscles flexed in their legs as they kept some kind of internal beat that made them breathe and stride in a perfect rhythm. I'd never seen anything so beautiful.

When I saw mile marker fourteen and still felt pretty good, I was thrilled and fooled into thinking I wasn't in over my head. It was at about mile sixteen, when we hit the turnaround point, that I decided I needed to adopt our walking-and-running routine. I really had never run—straight—for more than eight miles during our training. Bill kept a careful eye on his wristwatch to make sure we could still make it in before the course closed.

At mile seventeen, my legs were still in good shape. Right around mile twenty-one, however, which for us would have been nineteen miles into the race (the same distance as my longest training route), my legs started aching. Then, at the twenty-two-mile marker, I began to feel shooting pains in my thighs and calves. Every step made my quadriceps tighten and yank hard on my hips and back. Everything ached.

"I really hurt," I said to Bill.

"Yeah, I know," he said, a little too dismissively, I thought.

"No. I mean, I really, really hurt. This isn't a normal kind of hurt."

He looked at me seriously, put a gentle hand on the small of my back, and pushed me forward. "Yes, I know," he said. "It's okay, Cami. That's how it's supposed to feel."

I couldn't believe that. I'd never felt such physical pain. My legs were burning, searing like the worst sunburn I'd ever had—only on the inside. Had I honestly not believed that running a marathon would be this hard? The brutal truth was setting in. This fucking hurt! A lot! I started to cry softly. Why had I worked so hard over the past few months in training, been so determined this morning to do this stupid race, when I could have given up five hours ago at the starting line?

Now it was my turn to say, "I don't think I can do this." We passed the twenty-three-mile marker. We would end up running only twenty-four miles. What if we had run the whole thing? I wouldn't have made it. By the time we reached mile marker twenty-four, I just incorporated my whimpering into the tempo of my breathing. My face was snotty and wet, my shoulders and neck were cramping, but I kept going. There wasn't much else to do.

As we expected, we found ourselves toward the back of the pack. The crowd of cheering fans along the route was dwindling. By this point, the traffic cones on the highway had been removed to let another lane of cars go by, and a steady stream of impatient traffic began zooming by us. I was running nearest to the traffic and fighting irritation with the thickening exhaust. My sight was blurry from my tears, and my eyelids were heavy.

I didn't see the car sail by me, too close for Bill's comfort, so when Bill grabbed me by both shoulders and yanked me to the right, out of the way of the traffic rocketing past us from behind, I was startled and then perturbed. I screamed impulsively as my heart rate quickened, and I shouted, "What the hell are you doing?"

He looked at me, shocked. He was surprised by my admonishment. He thought he had just saved my life and probably expected a grateful response. My reaction was involuntary, an instinct. When I saw his face, I softened and settled back into my painful pace. I was a mess.

But this was what I had wanted—imperfect and messy! Somehow, at the back of my mind, beneath the pain and crying and near misses by little European automobiles, a deep knowledge was settling in. Taking over where previously there had been an illusion of reality as dualistic (everything as black or white, right or wrong, good or bad) was an emerging center point, an experience of "both/and": I was a mess *and* I was okay. I was fragile *and* I was strong. I was a cheater *and* I was running this race with integrity.

We ran the whole of the last two miles before the finishing hatch came into view. By that time, I could scarcely manage to lift my legs. Bill insisted we switch places. He judged that I was in no condition to prevent myself from getting killed by an oncoming car. He kept his hand on my back and urged me onward to the end.

At the finish line, as we had agreed, we refused our medals. I didn't let the volunteer handing them out place mine around my neck. I took it in hand

and thanked her. I didn't allow myself any feeling of triumph. We hobbled back to the guesthouse, where we showered, dressed, and took a heavy dose of pain relievers, and made our way back to the subway. There were several other marathoners staying at the same guesthouse; they called us crazy as they watched us limp down the stairs to head back to Prague's downtown. Their only plans were to eat, rest, and celebrate. We opted not to tell them that we had yet to complete the race.

After eating sausage and goulash in the Old Town Square and fortifying ourselves with our first pilsner, we tracked the course and, step by throbbing step (I could barely stand now, let alone walk), we started and stopped Bill's watch with each pub we patronized, until we had officially completed the Prague Marathon course.

It was late afternoon when rain began pouring down on us; the clouds had accumulated above and the sunshine had taken its leave. Finally, at the exact spot where we had cheated our way into the race, Bill and I awarded each other our medals. I fingered mine and rubbed its coldness against my face, before insisting that we pose for one of those arm-outstretched self-photos travelers take when no one is there to snap a shot. I leaned in a little closer to Bill and we shared a gentle kiss. We slowly made our way to the metro station. We would need to rest and get ready for the walking tour of Prague that Bill's distant cousin had promised us the next day. We didn't talk much, so I had a chance to consider what this day had given me.

Things don't always go as planned in life. I already knew that, but now it was certainly confirmed. Also confirmed was the way in which listening to my own internal Wisdom, rather than external rules or expectations, would lead me to my own version of triumph. I was coming to know that even my mistakes were gifts if I was patient and observant. I was learning to trust myself more than anyone else. And, most surprising to me, I was learning to love again.

together and alone:
my own vision quest

SEPTEMBER 2003–JUNE 2007

"A woman must practice calling up or conjuring her
contentious nature, her whirlwind, dust-devil force."

—CLARISSA PINKOLA ESTES, *Women Who Run with the Wolves*

"Mental will is a muscle that needs exercise,
just like muscles of the body."

—LYNN JENNINGS, long-distance runner

3

Four years passed between Prague and my next marathon. I hadn't given much thought to the idea that I might do another one. During those years, a number of things happened. First, my life began to settle into a stable routine. Part of that routine involved reading. I'd always been an avid reader, but now I was reading for resonance instead of instruction. What struck me? What stimulated my own Wisdom to come forward? I read about the feminine face of God, about Buddhism, about sexuality. And I read every memoir I could get my hands on about the lives of other women awakening into midlife and living into their own truths. These texts, as I began to think of them, helped me make sense of what was happening inside of me.

In a woman's midlife journey, I read, there could be a number of stages or states in her process. Some of these stages fit for me. There was, for example, often a sudden awakening to the effects of an ill-made bargain, such as in the fairy tale of the handless maiden whose father sold her into marriage with the devil. For many years, the innocent maiden was blissfully unaware that a bad bargain had been made on her behalf back while she was but a child, but then one morning she woke up and her parents broke the news that she was scheduled to marry the devil himself. She'd been promised to him years before, they said. The maiden had to do some quick thinking to get out of her bondage. She was indeed eventually freed from her betrothal, but not without acquiring some serious battle wounds along the way (she lost her arms).

No one had sold me into the constraints under which I'd been living, but I'd made some bad bargains in my adolescence (conforming to religious legalism) and in my young-adult years (getting married before I really knew myself) that had felt rather poor to me by my mid-thirties. I had finally awakened and taken action to change my life.

I read in my books that sometimes, after a woman realizes she has lived her life according to a patriarchal system—be it church, culture, marriage, or a combination of them all—she may go to a dark place (in some myths, she even goes underground) where new truths can germinate. I'd been in that dark place during the first year and a half after my divorce—literally living in a basement.

But in the years after Prague, I began working through another important stage I'd been reading about: creating a sacred space where I could safely heal and test out the new self-knowledge I was gaining. I was ready to create a home for myself above ground.

EVER SINCE MY CHILDHOOD, I'd been obsessed with owning my own home. It started when I was ten and the house my family lived in burned to the ground in a house fire. We lost every item we'd ever owned. Just before Christmas 1977, every photograph, every childhood toy, every homework assignment, every document proving who we were was incinerated and we were left homeless, dependent on the generous support of extended family. These losses instilled in me a keen longing for permanency that sometimes ached in my heart to the point of causing me physical pain.

When I left the house to my ex-husband in the divorce, I was devastated. It was a house I adored. It was open and inviting and bright, but it was also a misguided attempt at keeping a dying relationship intact. When I moved out, I again lost almost everything I owned—left it all behind to atone for my guilt because I had been the one to officially break the vows. This time, however, I at least salvaged some key symbols of who I was—books and family heirlooms that belonged to me.

By late summer 2003, I was ready to find a home of my own to house those few possessions. I needed to restore my sense of place. Everyone has different needs in terms of finding a safe retreat. I wanted to create a space that would function as a symbol of belonging, to make a home to shelter the self I was discovering. I didn't want to belong to another person or a set of theological doctrines. I wanted to belong to myself alone and invite others into my circle because I had something to offer while still having enough for myself.

After a couple of months of searching, I found a condo in a beautiful old brick building with a two-bedroom unit for sale close to my work and to one of Seattle's urban villages, where everything from groceries to sushi to haircuts would be within walking distance. I fell for it immediately and, after an inspection, put in an offer, which the seller accepted.

I was the proud owner of a home with new walnut-colored hardwood floors and a neatly tiled blue bathroom. Best of all, I would be moving out of the basement. I would have a real bedroom, ceilings I couldn't reach, even on my tiptoes, and space to invite friends over for dinner.

I was excited. And a little sad. Even as I packed up my things and did the final cleaning of my studio apartment, I began to realize that I would be further entrenching myself in Seattle, ninety miles away from Bill. I was determined to be true to the individuation process I was engaged in, to embrace each stage of this journey toward more conscious knowledge of self, but I was doing it while falling in love. Love had never been my intention the night I'd called my old friend. I'd wanted only to be with someone who could hear me in my pain, but love has a sneaky way of crawling into your heart when you're not looking.

I was going to need to embrace the learnings that love was offering me, along with the lessons I was gaining through my readings, by creating a home for myself and continuing on with my commitment to running. I would take this chance to do love differently. I would love in a slow, considered way, paying careful attention to the voice of Wisdom inside of me that was looking out for my own needs.

Bill was respectful of my processes, and yet he was in a different stage than I was. While at thirty-five I was finally at the beginning of my career, Bill was closer to the end of his. While I was filling my home with animals and friends, his children were leaving home and he faced an empty nest. He was many years out of his first marriage and ready for a long-term relationship; I was ambivalent about committing, even though I felt the pull to see him more frequently than Saturday afternoons and part of every Sunday. Could we work around this complexity? I didn't know it yet, but we were getting glimpses, even then, that making space for different needs and paces in life was to be the hallmark of our relationship.

MOVING DAY WAS IN October 2003. Bill and several friends helped me unload all of my belongings onto the center of my living room floor. I delivered on the pizza party I'd used as a bribe to get people to spend an entire day lifting and loading. After eating, my friends trickled away one by one, waving their well wishes at my impending unpacking process. Bill and I settled down on my new floor amid heaps of clothing and boxes, and uncorked a bottle of celebratory wine. Bill toasted to my new investment and to the making of a new home, yet he was subdued.

I asked him what was bothering him, even though I knew.

"You're sort of permanent here in Seattle now, I suppose," he said.

We sat silent for a while, listening to the traffic on the street behind my complex. We sipped our wine under the stark light emitted by a shadeless floor lamp I'd plugged in to illuminate the room. We understood the reality of our situation: We were two people—in different parts of the life cycle, with different needs, living in two different cities—who cared deeply about each other. That evening, in the middle of the chaos of my boxes, was when we first conceived of the idea of running seven marathons on seven continents. Bill reminded me of the race along the Great Wall of China, a flippant comment back in Prague that I had laughed off. But we had had a good time in Prague in spite of (or because of) the unconventional way we'd completed the marathon. Bill was building a case that traveling and running marathons together would be a way for us to partner around a common goal.

I remember his eyes and the playful yet utterly sincere suggestion. "Let's just do it—a marathon in a different country every year until we've done one on every continent! At least I'll get to see you once a year that way."

"You'll see me every weekend, like you always do," I bantered. But I was intrigued. He had recognized our incompatible sets of personal needs and had invented an improbable scenario wherein we could imagine a meeting point. I liked this kind of creativity. I would join in with the dreaming, though I still very much doubted that I could complete 26.2 miles straight through without a push. I had always thought I'd travel to every continent someday. Why not imagine myself as a marathoner while I was at it? "I like the way you think," I said, joining the vision. "Would you run every race with me?"

"I would!" he answered. *He'd have to*, I thought. Prague had taught me that the marathon was hard, both physically and emotionally. I still couldn't believe I'd done it, and here I was agreeing to do at least six more.

"I think I could count two halves as one full marathon on North America." I was already trying to wriggle out of the running part of the deal.

"That would be cheating," Bill said.

"So what? We cheated in Prague," I reminded him.

And so we played the Seven Marathons game. As I unpacked that night, we talked about the places on each continent we'd like to visit, and wondered which countries hosted the best marathons. I lobbied for the most exotic locations, and for races without hills.

A few more years would pass before we finally made our dream a reality, but I did keep running. Both with and without Bill, running was central to my daily commitment to breathe and be present and honest with myself. I became a very committed 5K-er, keeping my three-mile runs on flat ground and retaining a steady twelve-minutes-per-mile pace. My condo was three blocks from the Burke-Gilman Trail, and I found my way up to it almost every day. I ran for fitness, and for time to visualize possibilities in life. I wasn't zealous or fanatical about it. I did it on my own terms.

Over the next year, I started a private counseling practice and worked with about ten clients per week, in addition to keeping my full-time job at the youth center. I decorated my home with bright colors and invited friends and colleagues over frequently. I focused my energy on recuperating from the huge financial upset I'd suffered by leaving so much behind in my divorce. Time passed in exactly the way I needed it to. My life was full of peace and love, and I slowly climbed into a more secure place monetarily, emotionally, and spiritually. My home gave me a gift of healing, just as I had hoped it would.

During that same period, the loose, informal arrangement I shared with Bill tendered some confidence in me that I might not be a dismal failure at romantic relationship. I dared to hope I could hold on to the healing I was gaining and be my own messy self without shame or apology, and that that might be enough, along with love, to build on.

ONE FALL DAY IN 2004, Bill and I were walking through Stanley Park in Vancouver, BC. The air was warm and the leaves on the ground were orange and red and pale yellow. Somehow, going over the border signaled permission for both of us to leave our busy lives behind and to think outside of our usual boxes. It was like a mini–foreign vacation, even though it was less than an hour from Bill's house.

We sat down on a bench to take in the beauty of English Bay on what was turning out to be an uncharacteristically clear day for that time of year. Bill and I held hands as we talked, and I felt full of love and joy. I savored the moment, and as I did so, I realized that I wanted to fill my life with a million moments just like this—with Bill.

"We should celebrate our relationship, Bill," I said spontaneously. He looked at me with the patient, studying expression I had grown accustomed to. He was not one to respond impulsively.

"Like with a wedding?" he finally asked.

"Kind of like that. But not exactly," I said. I actually did want a party, and my ambivalence about our relationship was all but gone. I definitely wanted a partnership, but I didn't want to call our relationship a "marriage" or throw a "wedding," just in case those words were jinxed. They were words too easily misunderstood or taken for granted. They were words that carried roles and rules in their meanings, and they made me feel I would be joining an institution, rather than participating in a unique relationship. I was determined that Bill and I would be the ones to define what our relationship meant—not cultural, familial, or religious expectations, and certainly not overused, misconstrued words.

"We should," he said. "I'd like to celebrate, too."

We told Bill's children about our decision at Christmas. They were supportive and happy for us, if a little confused at the absence of the word "marriage"—until we told them we would indeed be filing a certificate at the courthouse. In January 2005, we flew to Arizona to share our news with his mother. We planned to run a race while we were there. Some people exchange tokens, like rings. We would run an engagement race to symbolize that we were on a dynamic journey, that our relationship was about deciding to run the race of life together.

We chose to run in the Lost Dutchman half marathon, a small event held in Apache Junction, Arizona, about one hour east of Phoenix. I was excited to be there in the sun with Bill, celebrating our intention to blend our lives in a new way.

Those 13.1 miles wove through neighborhoods that lay in the shadow of the Superstition Mountains, a series of jutting, craggy, red-rock formations. The route started at Prospector Park, named for a Dutch prospector who was purported to have found gold in the mountains. We were looking for treasure, too—made of hope, rather than gold. We hoped to transcend our previous failures and to create a partnership that would make room for continued growth and changes in each of us.

The course took us past spectacular adobe-style mansions sprinkled here and there among otherwise modest Southwest homes. Unlike the green and gray of the Northwest, the Arizona colors blazed with reds and browns and yellows, the colors of bricks and soil and sunshine. At a crescendo on the route, we reached the top of a hill on a tightly packed dirt road where the race organizers had placed a faux-brick archway through which the mountain peak was framed perfectly, proclaiming idyllic mystery and majesty.

The dry heat felt good to me as we ran the rolling roads, a reprieve from the winter happening at home. As I had trained for this run, I had forsaken the four-minutes-running/four-minutes-walking schedule we had implemented in our training for the Prague Marathon, but I still stubbornly insisted on walking the steep hills. Bill humored me, staying by my side the whole way. We crossed the finish line hand in hand, smiling. I hoped this was an omen for our lives together.

That summer, we threw our "celebration" at a boathouse in Bellingham. We honeymooned in Japan, without a race to entice us, although we did climb Mt. Fuji, sing karaoke, sip sake, and eat lots of noodles.

OVER THE COURSE OF another two years, our lives gradually melded. Eventually, I quit my job at the youth center, sold my condo, and moved my furniture to Bill's place (our place now) in Bellingham. I cut my practice in Seattle to two days a week. I commuted on Wednesday mornings from Bellingham to Seattle, stayed with friends or family overnight, and came home on Thursdays. This kept me in the Seattle world just enough to nurture my business and my community there. I didn't know many people in Bellingham anymore, and I was afraid I would be lonely if I dropped out of Seattle altogether. I grieved when I said goodbye to the condo that had given me a space to heal, but I had to trust that I could carry my healing with me to Bellingham or wherever I went.

In Bellingham, we grew our family, adopting a beautiful female Boston terrier we named Fuji, after the other formidable Fuji we had recently encountered. She was a joy to everyone in the family except for our cats, though they gradually came to tolerate her.

We kept up our running. Bill became more and more competitive in his age group. Our refrigerator accrued a collection of blue, red, and white ribbons for races of all distances. I ran several organized races during those two years but kept mostly to the trails in Bellingham, running alone or with Bill for fitness. We ran together less often as Bill's race times improved. His knees began to hurt at my slower pace, and my pace simply didn't speed up.

I felt I kept my postdivorce commitment to imperfection intact during the two years following our celebration, but I suppose I did get a little lackadaisical about pursuing my journey to bring forward the deep Inner Wisdom

I now knew I had, or to really nurture the aspects of myself that had been ignored for so long. In short, I got busy and distracted with my new life.

I still liked to imagine Bill and me running marathons on all seven continents together, crossing finish lines holding hands, but it was mostly a romantic fancy. On a Wednesday in April 2007, almost two years after we'd gotten married (by now I idly used the word "married" to avoid quizzical looks when I referred to my "partnership" or my "friend") and one month before my fortieth birthday, I received a call from Bill that jerked me out of my complacency.

I was seeing clients in Seattle on a packed day. I had seven sessions scheduled, with only one break for eating elbowed in at two o'clock, when I intended to find a quiet place to eat lunch and read my travel guide on Spain and Portugal. Bill and I were planning a summer trip. There was no marathon on our agenda; I just wanted to go to Europe to celebrate turning forty and to do some wine tasting and museum hopping. As I was getting ready to leave the office for lunch, my cell phone rang. Bill was on the other end.

"Now hear me out," he started. *This is not a good sign,* I thought. It was the kind of statement that prefaces either a confession or bad news.

"Okay."

"I know we've been planning to go to Europe this summer, but . . . " He paused. My anxiety rose. Some people generally like to keep their options open until the last moment so they can remain flexible for a better offer, and some like to settle plans quickly. Bill is the first sort; I am the latter. I had changed everything in my life a few years ago, and nowadays I was feeling less pliable, enjoying how predictable my life had become. I didn't want to change plans. I'd lived for years entrenched in a very organized way of understanding the world. I maintained a certain affinity for tying up loose ends and closing the door to surprises.

But I took a breath. I was still in my dark, cozy office, the lighting and decor designed to comfort the traumatized and help along the telling of difficult stories. "Go on," I said in my most patient therapeutic voice, more for my benefit than for his.

"I found a marathon through the wine country in Australia, in a little town called Mudgee." He waited for my response.

"Hmm. Australia?" I asked. My heart raced a little. Why couldn't we just go with what we had planned? I'd already sketched out an itinerary and a budget. I really had my heart set on Madrid and Lisbon. And it was *my* fortieth birthday, after all. Shouldn't I get to say what we did to celebrate?

I was quiet as tears sprang to my eyes. Bill and I had been together for five years by this point. We were good friends and partners, but we were both recovering pleasers in relationships. If I wanted something different from what Bill wanted, I sometimes became confused. I loved him and wanted him to be happy, but I knew from experience that swallowing my voice was not being true to myself and ultimately didn't work for our relationship. I sat with the phone to my ear, managing my feelings, trying to figure out how to respond.

"I've already checked on the times in the marathon. Looks like it's open for at least six hours. This would be our second continent. We'd only have five more to go." I could hear him smiling on his end of the line. Bill and I had amused ourselves for years with this fantasy of running a marathon on every continent, but now I confessed silently to myself that part of me preferred the fantasy to any real possibility of having to do the hard work to make the game into a reality.

"Okay, well, let me give it some thought," I said. I'd learned to give myself time before reacting to even small challenges.

I hung up the phone and looked around my office. Here was where people paid me to help them take on the challenges life provided, to support them through important transitions, and to grieve significant losses. Here was where I worked with clients to help them change damaging or painful definitions of themselves. I'd spent many hours in my own therapist's office doing similar work on myself these last years. I hated to admit it, but I was ready to float for a while without planning any new major challenges into my schedule. I was ready for a long stretch of serenity (or apathy—call it what you will). Still, I'd told Bill I'd think about his idea.

I skipped lunch to sit in my little sanctuary of an office and sort through my feelings. I put my travel guide back in my bag, threw my feet up on my sofa, and closed my eyes.

I could push to keep our original plans for Europe. I knew Bill would give up on Australia if I didn't want to do it. Or I could go with Bill to Australia and cheer him on from the sidelines as he ran the marathon. Sipping shiraz and snorkeling off the Great Barrier Reef wouldn't be torture. Australia would be an adventure, with or without a marathon. No one would require me to run the whole 26.2 miles; I could do the half, or the 10K if they had one.

But as I ruminated over what amounted to a fairly insignificant decision in the big scheme of my new, happy world, what would become one of the most significant thoughts I'd ever have began to formulate. Up until I had left my first marriage, nearly six years earlier, I had meandered through my life, a hapless victim of whatever "God" saw fit to drop in my lap. In these past few years, I had made a commitment to live more consciously and to heal, but in the last year I had definitely begun to let complacency seep in. I liked my routine and the solidity of the safety I'd created for myself.

Don't get me wrong: My happiness was well earned and carefully crafted, but after moving in with Bill and settling into our conjoined life, I was lazy about attending to my search for a new experience with divinity and continuing the awakening that had been so poignant and fresh to me in the aftermath of my divorce. I remembered saying to myself in those early difficult days that although I wanted my life to be stable, I never wanted to lose the awe I felt at each of my new discoveries. I'd heard some of my clients say the same thing during and after their divorces.

I had grown and changed immensely since then, but what would keep me growing now that I felt so safe and healed and accepted? I could easily slip into the old smug self-satisfaction and decide that I wouldn't bother to push myself toward deeper truths and discoveries. This complacency was what I had feared would happen if I got "married." It was so easy as a married woman to slide into roles, to give away power to the other person and fail to attend to oneself with as much focus as conscious growth requires.

As I sat on the psychotherapist's couch in my own office, it dawned on me that I had an unusual opportunity most women long for. I had the chance here and now to distinguish myself, to take on a challenge, to go on a vision quest, to craft a grail search for myself, complete with tests and trials. I could embrace the adventure I had joked and dreamed about: run a marathon on every continent and learn whatever they had to teach me. The grail at the end would be more self-knowledge, a deeper Wisdom, and maybe some reconnection with the divine in a new way that would make sense to me.

I thought of all the books I'd read about women coming alive to the sacred feminine, the different states of awareness. Many of these books talked about a journey or a quest. Some women climbed mountains. Some visited sacred sights in Europe. Some stayed in silent monasteries, waiting for illumination or enlightenment. Others searched out and contemplated important works of art, followed the Black Madonna or Tara, the female Buddha. I needed a quest, too. Prague's race had turned out to be a faithful teacher, giving me the information about myself I needed at the time. Maybe I had just the right quest directly in front of me.

I came to a conclusion: Not only would I agree to go to Australia that summer and run a marathon, I would get serious and run them all around the world. I'd saved a little money. I ran my own business and could flex my schedule. Bill had plenty of vacation time reserved. Why not do it? I would open myself to what the race in Australia could teach me about my relationship, my body, my Wisdom, the world—whatever! Somehow, I suddenly understood that if I didn't do something large, all of the hard work I had done in these last years would one day be just a memory of a nice but useless, one-time "aha" moment, instead of a permanent change in my way of engaging in the world that could sustain me through the second half of my life. I'd be right back where I'd started in 2001.

I couldn't believe what I was thinking. I called Bill back and told him I'd be home late. I was going to stop at the bookstore and pick up a travel guide to Australia.

IF ONLY WE COULD decide to embrace a lofty challenge like a marathon on every continent and then dictate both the circumstances and outcomes so that, at the end, we'd feel happier and stronger and have glorious stories to tell our friends. Alas, running can bring out the worst in us, as well as the best.

I had almost forgotten that the freedom from perfectionism I'd gained while training for Prague had come on the heels of a very painful panic attack. As I began training for our marathon in Australia, I imagined I would experience something transcendent, like an ethereal sense of being party to the Divine Feminine in the world, or perhaps really learn to love and accept my body. But apparently I had some other things I needed to understand about my relationship first, before I could really get going on my vision quest. Or maybe I was about to receive my first vision quest challenge.

I wanted to find a half marathon for Bill and me to run together to start the training process. Bill suggested we run the Scotia Bank Vancouver half marathon, a route that begins on the University of British Columbia campus in Vancouver, BC, and runs along Point Grey, a peninsula that protrudes into the Strait of Georgia. The course then circles English Bay and ends in Stanley Park, where we sat when we first decided to throw our celebration. The race was in late June, when it was supposed to be warm and hopefully clear, so we could enjoy the magnificent scenery.

I was looking for a couple of things from this run. First, I needed to build confidence in my physical endurance. It had been a while since I'd run for longer than two hours (since our engagement race, actually). I had worked my way up to a nine-mile run, and now I was looking to be reassured I could push to 13.1 miles.

I was also looking for some clarity about how Bill and I would negotiate our different paces. Bill had been enjoying the progress he'd been making as a runner lately, but we had agreed that we would do our intercontinental runs together, which meant doing them at my pace, since I was the slowest common denominator between us. I needed to know how we'd work that out. As it turned out, I would get what I needed in the Scotia Bank race that day, but not how I'd imagined it.

ON RACE DAY, IT was no more than fifty degrees in the great Northwest. The sky was ominous as we drove the twenty-five minutes from our house to the border. The crossing was clear. We cruised through it without a problem and made our way to the parking area just off UBC's campus, where it started to rain. At the start line, we stretched and rubbed our hands together to keep the chill at bay. We were both feeling stressed about running the entire race in the rain, but we were here and committed to doing it.

The gun went off. Our chips beeped us into action, and three thousand runners began to seed themselves. We moved rather quickly to the back of the pack. Runners pushed past us in their haste to find open space where they could run abreast of their friends or partners. Bill and I made our way in the crowd. By the time we reached Point Grey, we should have had a view of the sea, but the fog was thick and we could scarcely see the beach. We were socked in.

All we could see were people's asses as they shot ahead of us – asses of all shapes, attached to people of all ages and sizes. I was not bothered by this, focused as I was on my own stride and breath. But for Bill it was unbearable to watch these runners pass us, especially in conjunction with his own increasing physical discomfort caused by the slowness of our pace. There was about to be trouble. "This is miserable," Bill said.

"I can't think about it." The rain was coming down hard. I had to concentrate. I was miserable, too, but I needed to be successful that day. I needed to focus all my thoughts into a mantra that would keep me moving.

"Can you move any faster?" he asked.

"I can't," I said. I glanced over at him, sorry to be holding him back. I'd come a long way in my life, but my people-pleasing tendencies could still exert a powerful pull. I would have given anything in that moment to move my body faster just to make Bill happier. But I couldn't. I felt guilty and inadequate, but I really was doing the best I could.

At mile six, the rain became a full-blown storm. Large pellets of icy water pummeled us, head to toe, in a sideways arc. "I'm cold," Bill said. "I don't think I can do this whole race at this pace." I'd never heard Bill complain about being cold.

"So go ahead," I told him. I felt fine about finishing this miserable race alone. But his chivalry and stubbornness would not allow him to leave me behind. Instead, he stayed by my side and urged me to run faster. My guilt began to give way to vexation. I was trying to hold on to some compassion for him, but my whole body was fighting for every step I took. I wasn't experienced yet in pushing through all kinds of conditions to keep running.

By now, Bill and I had had plenty of arguments, but sometimes you have a disagreement that alters or defines something in the relationship, one that clinches a deal or brings something to light. They're hard, but they're important. We were about to have one of those.

I watched Bill from the corner of my eye. His energy was darkening, and he began directing it toward me. My normally supportive, gentle partner was turning increasingly gloomy and melancholic with every raindrop that fell.

"How can you run this slowly?" he asked. My last strands of empathy were weakening. I wanted to warn him he was in danger of going too far, that I was getting angry. I could feel some nasty self-righteousness brewing in my belly and rising up to my throat. Words I might wish I could swallow were stringing themselves together in my mind. Bill was asking exactly the wrong question. He was pawning off his misery on me. I made one more attempt to stay grounded.

"Bill, if you need to run ahead, just go. I can finish this alone. If you're miserable, take care of yourself. Just go ahead to get done as fast as you can."

"And what? Wait for another half hour in the rain for you to finish? Besides, what would be the point? I can't get a decent time now."

"Well, this is as fast as I can go." I said this in a low growl.

"It's as fast as you *can* go or as fast as you *will* go?" he snorted. He'd crossed the line. I snapped.

"Dude, you're fucking out of line," I yelled. I was livid. "Do whatever the hell you want, but quit talking to me! I need to concentrate." I stared straight ahead and ignored him. I willed him to disappear as I seethed. Inside I was cursing him and planning a bitter tirade to unleash if he tried to speak to me again.

I started shaking more from the anger than from the cold. How dare he disrespect me, throw his pompous contempt in my direction, and blame me for his unhappy state of mind? The words I had lined up for him if he said one more word to me would be designed to give him a taste of his own rancid medicine.

The grail search had begun. Here was my first test. The ugly parts of myself that I'd kept under wraps in the interest of exhibiting good Christian behavior or being ladylike were awakening, stretching, and yawning, brought to life by a cold, hard rain and a cranky man with aching knees.

We all have these parts of us: bitter, coarse, vindictive. I had known this journey would bring me face-to-face with my inner self. I had just hoped that I would dig deep and see the divine or more of that satisfying Inner Wisdom shining its light on my beauty and strength, and not an Inner Bitch ready to crush the spirit of the man she loves. But the Bitch in each of us has her rights, too, and she deserves a little airtime once in a while.

Bill slunk back a few paces and ran about ten yards behind me. We ran this way for a couple of miles. I could feel his eyes on my back; I sent telepathic warnings to him not to approach me. I was prepared to hold this against him for the whole day, even after we'd gone home, and to fly off the handle at his least little offense.

Just as I reached the lip of the bridge, Bill sped up to catch me.

I opened my mouth to deliver my well-rehearsed diatribe, but before I could speak, he grabbed my hand and kissed my palm, running awkwardly beside me and holding it to his cold cheek. "I'm sorry," he said. "I was totally out of line. Please forgive me." He was repentant. My anger melted. I forgot everything I had meant to say.

"So am I," I said. "Sorry I yelled at you." A tentative peace between us was quickly restored, and my Inner Bitch took a breath and settled in at the back of my psyche for the moment. But I knew something in me had changed. I'd realized something. Our fantasy of running a marathon together on every continent was not going to be possible. We weren't compatible as runners. It was a blow.

Until that moment, I hadn't seen that I'd been idealizing our relationship. I had tried so hard to be iconoclastic as I'd entered into formal partnership with Bill, but I was seeing now that I'd fallen into a sentimentalized idea of marriage in spite of my best efforts. As much as I was committed to spitting in the eye of perfectionism, part of me still imagined that Bill and I were somehow going to be able to join and become one happily congruent unit jogging side by side in the marathon of life. I was being shocked out of this by a storm that raged in equal measures outside in the elements, inside my relationship, and in my mind. What did it mean?

Our feet were soaked through our shoes and our hair was drenched when we reached mile twelve. We happened to see the winner, a Kenyan runner who had completed the course more than an hour earlier, walking in the opposite direction. I caught his eye and he waved and shouted, "Looking good!" I gave him a faint smile. Then he pointed at Bill. "Not looking so good," he said. The argument had depleted Bill, while my anger had oddly energized and strengthened me.

At long last, we passed the thirteen-mile marker and then the anti-climactic finish line. In an ironic twist, the rain stopped briefly just as we crossed, at two hours and thirty-four minutes. All that was left were the cold air and our solemn attitudes.

We shivered on the bus that took us back to the parking area. Once we finally got to our car, which was still another mile from where the bus dropped us off, we cranked up the heat and drove silently toward the border. We stopped for coffee. I held the warm cup, nuzzling it with my nose and my cheek to stave off the numbness I still felt from spending the morning in the rain. And I was thinking.

I didn't know if I could run a whole marathon by myself. I was scared at the prospect of doing it alone, but I wanted both Bill and me to be happy. I'd been afraid of doing other things alone—leaving a marriage, starting a business, buying a home, raising a puppy—but had done them anyhow. Then again, you never actually do anything entirely alone, even if you don't have a partner. Someone is always around to help a little: friends, family, even strangers. Maybe I could find companions in a marathon on the other side of the equator.

And the challenge was mine now, after all; it was no longer just the silly notion of holding hands with my partner across a proverbial or literal finish line. We were registered for our next marathon, the second of my life, and I wanted it. I wanted to know my body could do it, wanted to upset my own status quo, wanted to celebrate the accomplishment and to earn a medal I could hang on my bathroom light fixture. I knew Bill was supportive, but I wanted him to run his best, not just be there for me at the expense of his own goals.

After this race today, I knew Bill would have to choose between running the best race he could or running at a painfully slow pace by my side as little more than my cheering squad. Moving forward in our life together, I wanted us to cheer one another on, certainly, but I also wanted us to each engage at our own pace, according to our (very different) capabilities. Just as I had learned in my divorce that I needed to construct a life that allowed me to explore who I was, I was learning in this new marriage and in my commitment to running that I needed to construct a balance between connection and independence—togetherness, tempered with individuality. I wanted a way we could have it all.

"We have to run the marathon in Australia separately," I declared. It was the only answer.

Bill shook his head slowly, but he remained silent.

"It will be better. And it's what I want," I added.

"It's not what we agreed," he finally said. I watched the rain resume and hit the windshield; the rapid wipers tried to wick it away.

"But it's better. We'll be happier." I waited as Bill watched the road. Finally, he nodded and reached for my hand. Running and marriage have a lot in common, I was realizing. Sometimes in running, you find yourself on your favorite trail, the wind gentle, the perfect song playing on your iPod; your muscles are strong, you have a companion at your perfect pace, and you fancy yourself the fastest Kenyan soaring over the finish line at record speed. Other times, salty and sweaty and cramping, with mucus dribbling out of your nose and the rain pouring down and mud splashing up, you hate your companion and you complete your run simply because the only way back to where you want to be is the way you came. You finish only because you started. But I could see there is a third way, too: You run some of the way with your ill-fitted companion, whom you love (but who makes you mad), at a pace that is roughly your own but maybe a little faster than you'd like to go—until you realize you can meet your partner at the end, rain or shine, angry or happy. You can accept your Inner Wisdom and your Inner Bitch and let them run together.

australia:
THE mudgee nudge
AUGUST 2007

"What are we to make of what seem to be different personalities within people? Are they merely sets of cognitions and emotions, or are they something more? How did they develop? How do they relate to one another and other people? How are they affected by the person's past, family or culture? How can they change?"

—RICHARD C. SCHWARTZ, *Internal Family Systems Therapy*

"Everything you have done has led to this very day. It's all quite dramatic. And it all has quite a way of messing with your head."

—DAWN DAIS, *The Non-Runner's Marathon Guide for Women*

4

There are things we can know about ourselves only when we are utterly, totally, completely alone. Not alone just until the phone rings or alone until we flick on the television, but alone long enough to see ourselves clearly and to follow our internal dialogues down all of their various paths and rabbit holes. I had relished the solitary time in the years after my divorce, but moving in with Bill meant that I rarely had time to myself. I'd settled into our new partnership so smoothly that I hardly noticed the loss of the private time that had been so critical to me a few years earlier.

Having let those secluded moments of reflection slip away so easily, I wasn't even aware of how unexamined I was in danger of becoming. I was fond of telling clients who worried they would get lazy and stop growing, "The Process is more committed to you than you are to It." By this I meant that we will grow whether we set our minds to it or not. Even if we hide from self-examination through various avoidance behaviors (overwork, serial relationships, television), life has a way of offering opportunities for growth. Sometimes they even sneak up on us, as I was about to experience.

ONCE I DECIDED TO run the Mudgee Marathon without Bill by my side, it only made sense for me to do most of my training on my own as well. I needed to practice depending on myself. I had a little less than three months (from late June to mid-September) to transform myself into a marathoner, and since the Mudgee race was going to have few participants, it was critical that I get ready—body and mind—for long stretches of solitude.

Vancouver's half marathon had given me the shove I needed to take complete ownership over my decision to become a marathoner. It had also given me a glimpse into my Inner Bitch, part of myself I had successfully avoided for many years. I'd been raised to be a nice, sweet girl, but ever since my panic attack during the Prague training, I hadn't been able to stomach "nice" when I didn't *feel* nice.

The Inner Bitch I had contended with in Vancouver wanted her due. Over the years she had been ignored, pressed into silence, belittled, and delegitimized by religious and cultural forces invested in shutting her up. So many women get caught in a "too nice" dungeon where the bitchier, angrier parts of us never see daylight, at least not honestly. We call it depression. I'd spent too much time there; I never wanted to go back.

My commitment to myself after Vancouver was not to silence any of the parts of me, but to learn to better manage my contradictions and to tolerate the tensions that existed among all the different voices inside my head. I intended for this to happen in a very reasonable manner, with each of those voices speaking up in turn and growing to respect one another. This training period, I figured, would be a good time to let my Inner Wisdom—that core, deeply reflective aspect of myself that reminded me I was a manifestation of God's love—and my Inner Bitch get to know each other.

Unfortunately, as my training progressed, I found these two wouldn't make easy friends. Wisdom, in true feminine form, was open-minded and willing to get chummy and compromise for the greater good; the Bitch was critical and loud, and complained at the drop of a hat. She wouldn't quiet down long enough to be reasoned with. Having been let out of her cave, she seemed to want to be the leading lady in every scene. Wisdom encouraged me to run with a peaceful heart and to be thankful for the strength of my body and for the personal growth I was achieving. The Bitch was critical, dissatisfied with everything.

The more hours I spent alone running, the more complicated the dialogue between these two parts of me became. I quickly realized that running alone, though allowing me to move my body at my own pace, also meant wrestling with myself for hours at a time. This wasn't how I had imagined my new personal commitment playing out. I had been looking forward to time without Bill at my side, complaining about my pace. I'd thought I would experience peace, a return to that healing solitude I'd so cherished. Not so. The inner dialogue became a burden I came to anticipate on every run.

The longer my weekend runs became, the more my discontentment grew. Irritation with the weather, my shoes, my hair, my route was ever-present. I reran old arguments in my mind that I'd never actually gotten to have (or allowed myself to have) with the people who'd hurt and betrayed me or had disagreed with my recent decisions. I made lists of offenses I'd already "forgiven" back when not forgiving people had been a sin and held the threat of hell.

But worst of all was the boredom I felt. It would set in moments into my training runs, and then I'd fight it for fifteen, seventeen, or twenty long miles. The Bitch invariably won out. Gone were the moment-to-moment breathing and the fantasizing about the future I'd previously enjoyed during longer runs. The ongoing monologue in my mind now was dominated by boredom: *I have better things to do than this. Oh my god, I have eight miles left? #&%$! One two three four five . . . seven hundred and twenty-one . . .*

I didn't know how common this kind of intense boredom and restlessness was among runners. I'd never read a book about running or been to a seminar. I started to worry I wasn't cut out for this running-a-marathon-on-every-continent thing. It *was* a crazy idea for someone who had never run a full marathon without someone pushing her along. When I told nonrunner friends about my struggle, they usually made a good point: "If you hate it, why are you doing it?" I couldn't explain it to them. I loved it, or at least the fantasy of it, *and* I hated it.

I was too embarrassed to talk to any of my runner acquaintances about my boredom, except Bill. He couldn't understand my dilemma, though. He said he never felt bored when he was out in the fresh air, moving his limbs and absorbing vitamin D. Still, he took pity on me and surprised me with an iPod Shuffle to help me drown out the voices in my head. It helped some, but even with '70s disco music blaring through my earbuds, I battled—I just did it to a beat.

AS IT TURNS OUT, when you're by yourself, it's not so easy to shove off the responsibility for your unhappiness onto someone else. You can't get your misery to be someone else's fault if no one else is there. I was now in the position of having to really sort through the complaints and criticisms the Bitch was throwing my way. Some of her points were valid (I did need to branch out and find new routes, rather than recycle the same three miles over and over), but some were just plain mean (like the suggestion that I looked stupid and that passersby were laughing at how slow I was). It was very taxing to weed out the helpful from the unhelpful.

When it was time for me to take my twenty-two-mile run two weeks before leaving for Australia, I persuaded Bill to meet me for an isolated portion of the run. It was for my safety, I claimed. Really, I would have given anything to have company that might edge out my own thoughts at that point.

On a Saturday morning in mid-August, I drove down to the boathouse, where Bill and I had celebrated our nuptials, and parked my car. Bill had mapped out a twenty-two-mile out-and-back route for me, starting at the boathouse and turning around at the parking lot just above Larabee State Park, eleven miles away. He was out for his final training run as well and had agreed to my plan to meet up, at my pace, for a five-mile isolated segment in the woods. I was grateful for what I could get.

Bill joined me as we entered the forest and very obviously put on an encouraging face for my sake. Even with views of Puget Sound and the San Juan Islands to distract him, I caught him wincing in pain now and again. Each of his strides was shortened and stunted to match mine, and I watched him flick his leg on occasion to loosen his knee joint. He frequently drifted in front of me by several yards, and then, noticing he'd left me behind, slowed again so I could catch up. A mile after we had convened, Sam, a local runner, breezed blithely by us on the trail, shirtless and muscular, making me feel like an oversize slug. He seemed to be floating, as if his feet scarcely touched the ground. I glanced over at Bill to see if watching Sam sail by us would make him restless. He kept a neutral gaze straight ahead.

I noticed again, as I had in Vancouver, that I couldn't find my pace with

Bill running beside me. His company tempered my boredom, but during the five miles we ran together, I felt like there was a taut rope between us. Whenever Bill ran ahead, he pulled me along too quickly, and I reacted by slowing down even further to emphasize the fact that I needed to run at my own pace.

It was clearer and clearer that Bill's pace had come to represent a standard for me, one that I tried to either keep up with or rebel against. As we ran on, I noticed that the Bitch and Wisdom were having a discussion. For once (though they had different approaches), they were on the same side.

For crying in the mud, don't give in to this stupid power struggle! It shows a weakness in character. Get a grip and stick to your own lazy pace. Who's the boss of your body, anyway? complained the Bitch.

Wisdom chimed in: *I have to agree. Where is your groundedness? Who are you, really? Someone who defines herself in contrast with someone else, or your own person? Find your own truth here, Cami, and live it out, stride by stride.*

When we came out of the woods, Bill said goodbye and went on his merry way. As he left, I cemented a new intent. I had to become my own standard somehow—and learn to trust myself. If I was going to listen to all the voices inside of me, that meant that my Wise, centered self and the Bitch were both going to get their say, and I would have to figure out how to referee and pick through what they each had to offer.

WE ARRIVED IN SYDNEY on Friday, August 24, 2007. We flew in over Sydney Harbor and marveled at the reflection of the sun sparkling on the tiled roof of the opera house. Bill reached over to hold my hand as the plane descended and the wheels finally touched the ground on the landing stretch.

"We're here!" I said.

"Yep. Here we go," he replied.

It had been a twenty-hour plane trip, so our first order of business would be to freshen up and rest. We'd reserved a room in a hostel near the train station in downtown Sydney. We were only going to stay overnight, before catching a train and then a bus to the little town of Mudgee, which lay nuzzled in the Blue Mountains a few hours west of Sydney, in a region of the same name that's famous for the fruity, full red wines made there. A few days after the race, we would come back to experience Sydney, fly north to Cairns to snorkel at the Great Barrier Reef, and then rent a car and drive as much of the Australian coast as we could in two weeks, stopping for a visit in Bellingham's sister city, Port Stephens, along the way.

We had found the Mudgee Marathon on the Internet and chosen it because of its proximity to Sydney, and because we would have the opportunity to visit several wineries after the race. Mudgee is a tiny little hamlet surrounded by forests of eucalyptus trees, situated along a major highway between the small cities of Gulgong and Lithgow. Its beautiful, rolling land and quaint brick, turn-of-the-twentieth-century buildings welcomed us as it came into view through the windows of the bus we rode into town.

Once we were off the bus, we easily negotiated Mudgee's streets, with our suitcases in tow, to our $30-a-night room above a steakhouse and tavern. Downtown was all of ten square city blocks; only crossing the roads gave us some trouble. Since there were no stoplights or crossing signals, we had to rely on our good senses and watch for traffic, which was coming the wrong direction. Several times we looked left instead of right and stepped out in front of oncoming vehicles. We had a few near misses before arriving at our lodgings, and I made a mental note to be careful during the race to run against the traffic by staying on the right side of the road.

After unloading our luggage in our room, the first thing we needed to do was to find Lynn, the race organizer, who would help us register for the race. Our hotel was across the street from the park where the registration was taking place all afternoon. As we made our way over, the unusual wildlife caught my attention. It was like nothing I'd ever seen. Bright red and orange insects called out from a distance and drew me to study them close up on tree trunks or blades of grass. There were pink and green parrots and yellow-crested cockatiels flying free and wild, too. I'd only ever seen birds like that in cages. I stopped every few yards to exclaim, "Would you look at that?" Bill joked that I would never finish the marathon if I kept stopping to examine the wildlife. I was enthralled, though, and as it turned out, I would end up needing these new feathered friends during my race the next day.

We reached the registration table and finally met Lynn, who'd helped us make special arrangements to pay and register after our arrival. We paid our fees in Australian cash and picked up our race numbers. In contrast with the Prague Marathon and many of the other marathons I'd attended with Bill in recent years, there were no race packets containing samples of running-related products and advertisements for other races; here, we received only a bib number and four safety pins.

Also, at all the races I'd ever attended there had been "expos," little fairs where vendors set up booths to sell special running gear and paraphernalia. Here there was nothing, just a picnic table with Lynn and a three-ring binder organizing runners' information. Only two or three other runners milled around Lynn's table. Bill chatted with the group amiably as I studied the tiny registration setup. It started to dawn on me just how small this operation really was. There was a good chance there weren't going to be many runners in this race. It was obviously a local event organized by and for the athletic club in town, not intended for foreign participants like us. Just as I was considering this, I heard Bill ask Lynn how many runners there would be in the morning.

"Oh, I believe we have ninety-eight runners in all. Thirty-one of those will be in the full marathon," she said, and then added, "It's a few more than last year." I felt a lump form in my throat. It looked likely I was going to be alone for the whole race.

We ate at the pub below our hotel room and got ready for bed at about seven o'clock. I drifted off immediately, dreaming all night that I was lost in a maze and couldn't find my way out. I awoke unrefreshed at six o'clock.

I had learned by this point to lay out my clothes the evening before an event. I no longer mocked Bill for his fussing and organizing, now that I understood how early race mornings came and that forgetting an important element in the arsenal of accoutrements could make for a difficult run. My clothing, gloves, iPod, energy gel, and running belt were in a neat pile at the end of the bed when I got up. We tried to dress, drink our instant coffee, and make our breakfast quietly so as not to disturb the other residents at the hotel, but every move we made was registered by the old building's squeaky floor and creaking doors.

The starting line was only a seven-minute walk from our hotel. The morning was thick with wet fog, and it was chilly—maybe forty-seven degrees Fahrenheit. We came into view of a cinder block building at the top of a smooth knoll surrounded by soccer fields where the finish line and time clock had already been erected. The clock read 00:00. It was ready to go. A couple of volunteers were bustling behind a table nearby, dividing refreshments that would be distributed to the aid stations. The ninety-eight participants were standing around, clutching themselves to stay warm, stretching, or snapping pictures.

I'd never been to such a small running event. I sized up the athletes. It was impossible to tell who might be at the back of the pack (if you could call it a pack) with me.

"How're you doing?" Bill broke into my observations. "Feeling ready?"

"No. I'm worried I'm going to be alone this whole race," I said.

"Somebody will be running your pace, I bet." His optimism was unconvincing.

"And what if I can't finish?" I fretted. I'd been thinking it seemed crazy to go a whole week before a marathon without running, and it had been over two weeks since my last twenty-two-mile run. What if I'd lost my fitness level? What if sitting on the plane for one whole day had turned my legs to mush? What if my muscles had shriveled up during the "taper," that baffling but widely accepted practice among runners when the number of miles they run is drastically reduced in the few weeks leading up to a long race? I felt panicked.

"You will finish," he reassured me. But I wasn't a seasoned marathoner. I didn't know that Bill was right, and that two or three weeks of very little running did not threaten my ability to complete my race. I didn't know that once I'd done the work to prepare myself the best I could, faith in my ability was well placed. I didn't know yet that I could trust my body to do what it had been taught to do, and that the taper was really my friend, allowing my muscles to repair themselves before the race.

Instead, in those moments as I waited for the race to begin, I found myself wrestling with a nasty, niggling mixture of self-doubt and fear. I stood shivering in the fog with only a handful of other athletes, terrified of being alone for the next several hours and mortified at the thought that, having come halfway around the world for this event, I would fail. What was I doing here? How was I going to run 26.2 miles all alone with my difficult, discontented self? Every long training run I had done had been a major mental effort, an exercise in sparring with my every thought. Now I had that to look forward to, as well as the emerging panic that my body wasn't really ready, wasn't strong enough for this challenge. I'd have no one to push me along in the last miles if I wore out!

Bill interrupted my anxious trance to kiss me goodbye. It was time to seed ourselves in our little group. Even though it was a small pack, he wanted to be up at the front of it. He wended his way toward the starting line, drawn in chalk on the edge of the road. He was giddy as he abandoned me. *He loves this*, I thought. I doubted I could ever get to the point of really loving standing at a starting line, knowing I had a whole day of plodding in front of me. I yelled after him, "Have a good race!" but he didn't hear me.

A moment later the race began—poof—without any fanfare. There was no horn or gun or even a megaphone. But someone at the starting line must have yelled, "Go!" for everyone began running. Some things, even some of the most life-changing experiences, start that way. No one says, "This [fill in the blank] is going to be one of the most radical rites of passage you will ever travel through, so pay attention." Someone just says, "Okay, go ahead now," and you find yourself in the middle of an unexpected lightning storm with your life flashing before you.

I took a breath and began. I pushed the start button on my watch and saw the seconds begin ticking away. We ran back in the direction of our hotel and then took a left turn over a small bridge. The first couple of kilometers after the bridge ran on a slight incline beside neatly ordered rows of grapevines. Off to the edge of the road, lurking in a ditch, was a photographer in dark clothing with a large-lens camera. I grinned in his direction and waved. Why not at least start off on the right foot with a smile?

Beside me, three other runners chatted away in their heavily accented (to my ears) English. It looked like they might be running at a pace I could keep up with. I listened in on their conversation, wondering how I could interject myself into it. Finally, I just sidled up next to them and introduced myself. They told me their names: Brenda, Sally, and Jared. It was the first marathon for all of them. Brenda and Sally said they had agreed they would kick off their fifties with this race; it was their tribute to menopause setting in. I told them I had just turned forty and had decided to run a marathon on every continent.

"Good on ya!" they all responded.

They told me what their pace would be, but translating their numbers from kilometers to miles proved to be more than I could handle as I ran alongside them. My best hope was that we'd stick together for as long as I could keep up with them.

Bill had used a complex formula to calculate my finish time. He took my half-marathon pace, multiplied it by two, and then added 10 percent to adjust for slowing in the second half. Five hours and forty-two minutes was his prediction.

I used a different formula. I multiplied my one-mile pace (still a *very* consistent twelve minutes) by 26.2, added on an extra fifteen minutes to account for hills or wombat sightings, then rounded up to the nearest quarter of an hour. I predicted five hours and thirty minutes, give or take. But the finishing time was less relevant to me than my state of mind during the hours on the course. Brenda, Sally, and Jared gave me hope that I might have company.

Jared's Aussie accent was quite thick, and I wasn't able to catch the whole story he was telling, but it seemed he had been chided into running by his coworkers, who had bet him he couldn't do it. Through his training, he had lost thirty kilos. I congratulated him on his accomplishments and internally hoped his remaining heft meant he was as slow as I was.

I was in good company with these three. They were all running for deeply personal and noncompetitive reasons. They were my kind of runners. But, as it turned out, they were faster than I was. I relished every moment of the forty-five minutes we had together, but eventually I needed to slow my pace. Graciously, my three new mates wished me luck and forged ahead. I bid them goodbye, sadly, and watched them disappear gradually into the fog.

NOW I WAS BY myself without another human being within shouting distance. I was well aware that I hadn't spent many easy moments alone during my training, and I wondered what was in store for me today.

I looked at my surroundings. There were vineyards on either side of me. I noticed a road sign indicating a kangaroo crossing. For the time being, I was still on a paved street, though soon enough that gave way to a gravel road covered by large, loose rocks that jiggled underfoot. I kept my eyes focused on my feet and stepped carefully, slowing to a walk on the worst of it. I didn't want to turn an ankle out here by myself. There seemed to be no one behind me, but I wasn't sure. I noticed the kilometers were marked by orange traffic cones, known in Australia as "witches' hats," and that seventy-five minutes into the race I was finally passing kilometer ten. This was going slowly.

The negativity that had plagued my training started to seep into my consciousness. I tried to stay in the moment by taking notice of the landscape. A gray hare hopped out from under a fence and crossed the road, the only sentient being in sight besides the birds, the ever-present vivid reminder that I was not in Kansas anymore. I watched them flutter from the trees to the power lines overhead and back. I said, "Hi there," but they remained silent.

Flitting like the birds, my thoughts began bolting from topic to topic. I was losing my battle to stay in the present moment and enjoy the experience. The Wise, centered part of myself that once could breathe through my running slipped into internal obscurity. My thoughts became restless, until I finally settled on a question: Why was I doing this? Why had I put myself in this position where I would spend half the day all by myself in a foreign country, repeating exactly the same motion with my body ad infinitum?

Was it all because I had some view of myself that I could conquer my limitations and define myself along the way? Back on the sofa in my office a few months earlier, I had resolved to take on this vision quest. What did that mean, anyhow? Wasn't a vision quest supposed to be a time alone in the wilderness while you wait for an epiphany? By getting out of my comfort zone and setting this high-minded goal for myself, what did I hope for? A revelation about life or self? At the moment it sounded absurd.

The only major revelation I'd had so far over the course of my training for this race was that I was a miserable, slow, lonely person who hadn't yet found a pace in life that worked for her. This wasn't useful information to move forward with. I decided to offer up a prayer to the universe. I no longer believed in a distant male God "out there" who gave presents to the people he liked best. I didn't know what I believed, but here I was, alone in the wilderness (or at least the wine country), plugging along at a grueling rate, waiting for some kind of message. I might as well ask for one.

"*What?!*" I shouted into the air. "What do I need to know here?" The green birds overhead twittered at the sound of my voice. That's when I had my first flashback.

I recalled two parakeets I'd had as pets before my parents' divorce. I must have been about nine. Times were troubled in my family as my parents' marriage disintegrated; I remember being preoccupied with sadness over the constant fighting in the house. School had been my refuge, and after school I'd quickly go to my neighbor's house to spend the afternoon there until I was called for dinner.

I came home one day and found both the birds dead at the bottom of their cage, starved. I guess in my efforts to avoid being at home, I'd been forgetting to feed them—for how long, I didn't even know. This was unforgivable to me, and I'd pushed it out of my mind for years.

Now, as it came back, I felt a fresh sting of guilt. I shouted up at the birds keeping me company. "I'm sorry! I didn't mean to do it." The more time I spent alone, the more the contradictions of my life flooded me. I was a good person, even an animal lover, who had killed her own pets. What someone does with these moments of seeing her own contradictions so clearly has everything to do with her maturity as a person—I knew that. I could keep my head in the sand, trying to see life through simplistic lenses, or I could find a way to hold the guilt of my mistakes beside my belief that I was a good person. I used to think I was simply a sinner (as in Calvin's idea of total depravity—nothing good inside without God's redeeming it), but now I felt the human situation—my situation—was much more complicated than that. What was I supposed to do with this insight? I watched the birds.

Now you're starving your soul, I thought I heard one of the birds shout back. Great! The birds were talking now.

"What?!" I shouted again. But there was no answer.

True, I was pretty empty, as revealed by my boredom with myself on my training runs. I had a pretty steady diet, when left alone for hours, of negative, impatient thoughts. I wasn't much of a perfectionist anymore, but I hadn't taken a whole lot of responsibility to replace perfectionism with a more conscious philosophy, either. I knew everything I *didn't* want to be or do: I didn't want to be perfect, to repeat mistakes, to work at jobs I didn't like, to run faster than my authentic pace. But even after all my reading and self-evaluation, did I know yet what I *did* want to be? Do? Believe? And if I knew, could I have the courage to do it no matter who or what disagreed with me or did things differently?

I'd lived a pretty compliant life for the first thirty-four years, doing almost everything I'd been told to do by the authorities in my life. Then there had been six years of rejecting the rules. Now, at forty, maybe it was time to look carefully at everything—all I had rejected and all the new possible ideas and beliefs I was encountering—and build a genuine, deeply held belief system that I could live by. That's what this quest was about, after all.

But before I could get to a definitive epiphany, a fork in the road yanked me out of my stream of consciousness. One direction veered a little to the left and continued to run parallel to the farmland. There were more vineyards, more cows, in that direction. The other direction took a sharp right onto a dark avenue overgrown with trees. I could see only perhaps fifty yards down that route before it disappeared into shadows. There was no indication as to which way to go.

I took a stab and made a decision to bear left, since it would mean a less drastic change in the route, reasoning that if a whole new direction had been required, the road would have been marked. I had run maybe a hundred yards, when my doubts got the better of me and I turned around, went back to the intersection, and pulled out the map I had folded in my running belt. I didn't want to get lost. The worst thing I could imagine would be to extend this race beyond its forty-two kilometers.

I studied my map and looked at the roads, trying to place myself. Unfortunately, there weren't any visible road signs anywhere—and the map indicated only major streets. For a few minutes I stood looking in all directions, hoping another runner might come along to join me in solving the dilemma, but I didn't even know if there was anyone behind me. I waited. No one came.

These are the kind of moments when self-trust can really come in handy, but I was a little short on it right then. As I stood there, I had another strong recollection—the second flashback—of an event that had occurred when I was eighteen years old.

I had joined a missionary group that sent me to Paris to proselytize street kids—a precursor to my later, more practical work in Seattle. I arrived in Paris with nothing but an address to get to my hostel, where I was to meet the rest of the evangelism team. In the days before cell phones, and with no more than a few phrases of French, I found myself thousands of miles away from home, lost. Kind of like what was happening right now.

Back in Paris, more than twenty years earlier, I sat down on a curb and tried to "listen to God's voice," hoping he would give me a hint about where to go. In the religious context I was coming from, hearing the voice of God was common. When without a phone, listen for voices. What could make more sense? I imagined I heard a voice in my head say, *Go left*. I went left and I found my hostel.

At this moment, standing at a crossroads in Australia, waiting for someone to tell me where to go, I had another contradiction on my hands. I had been hearing voices again. I even needed a voice in my head to help me make a choice. And yet I didn't believe in the voice of an authoritarian God in the same way I once had. Still, when no one is around to offer instructions or show the way, what can you do but listen to the voices inside? I could correct a mistake if I made one, but standing around in indecision and paralysis was only creating a sense of helplessness. I had to make a decision *on my own*. I threw up my hands. What the hell, I'd go left again.

Whether it was instinct, common sense, or God whispering her secrets in my ear, I would find my way. Trust was obviously going to be the primary nutrient in my new internal diet. I decided I would run for ten minutes and if I didn't see another kilometer marker, I would know I had made a wrong turn. Every K had been marked so far, so I could count on at least that small indication that I was on the right route. And indeed, 21 K showed up very shortly thereafter, moments before a hill that appeared out of nowhere.

This hill's grade gave me a serious challenge. I bent over at the hips and leveraged my body weight on my right thigh until I could stand up straight, and then did the same on my left side. The hill seemed interminable, and because the fog obscured its peak, I had no idea how long (or high) it actually was. My legs began to burn.

I heard the Bitch complain. *My God, only halfway into this race, it already hurts like a mother. Only halfway?! What a stupid course. Thirteen miles left. You won't make it.* I'd found my way to this hill by trusting my own Wisdom, but that hadn't quieted my irritation and discontentment.

Here, I had my third and final flashback. I saw myself sitting on the stairs of the house I owned with my ex-husband, just before I left him. I was complaining, telling him all the ways he wasn't meeting my emotional needs. His face was crinkled into a perplexed, hurt expression, and he was studying me silently as I talked. I felt guilty. I knew from the Scripture that it was "better to live on the corner of a roof than to live with a complaining wife." I finished my final sentence and waited for him to speak.

Finally he said, "Why can't you *just* be happy?"

Indeed! It was a question I'd asked myself a million times. Why can't a person just be happy?

This question came back to me now as I forced myself up this Australian hill. Was it that easy? Why couldn't I have been happy with that one marathon in Prague? Why did I always have to have more? More self-knowledge? More insight? More Wisdom? But was I happier now than I was when I used to just believe what I'd been told at church or what I'd read in the Bible? I knew the answer was yes. Though this was hard work right now, physically and internally, I was free to come to my own conclusions.

Suddenly I emerged through the fog at the top of the hill. I'd made it. There, resting peacefully, as if waiting for the prodigal child to come home, was a shiny, ruddy-cheeked Australian man in a chair at a little folding table, offering aid. He had water and jelly beans, a huge smile, and directions for the next, brief portion of the race. And for a moment I was *just* happy. It was that easy. Just the very presence of another human being, the knowledge that another *Homo sapien* existed who cared enough to offer me sugar and hydration, elated me. Sometimes it takes everything to be happy; sometimes it takes almost nothing.

He directed me to turn right, go straight down a hill as steep as the one I'd just conquered, turn around at the point indicated (there would be someone there to show the way), and come up again toward him.

I obeyed my guide and started down the hill. I wasn't thrilled about another change in elevation, but as I descended, to my great, growing delight, other runners, perhaps five of them, began passing me on their way back up. I feared they were a mirage, but they turned out to be real. Brenda and Sally panted past me. Brenda cracked a meek smile and said, "It's a grand hill. Hope you make it." But I was not daunted now, only happy to see her. Even nearly stumbling over the body of a dead wallaby that had obviously been hit by a car several days earlier could not curb my pleasure at being in contact with other humans. I did have to jump out of the way to avoid tripping over the rotting carcass, and it was a quicker movement than my legs wanted to make at this point in the run. They protested with a sharp ache, but I didn't care.

The last runner to pass me shouted, "Heya! The turnaround isn't marked. Turn back at the big witch's hat."

Next, a white truck drove up beside me. The volunteer, another real person, opened his window and called out, "Turn around here, love." I was basking in this sea of humanity—or if it wasn't a sea, it was at least a puddle. It was enough at the moment.

I turned at the large orange traffic cone and made my slow way back to the man at the top waiting for me with jelly beans. The Bitch was quiet for now. I had been noticing that she took to hiding when strangers were around. It's not so hard to pull ourselves together now and again to look good in public, even during a marathon, but once I was alone, I knew the voices would let loose again. I knew I'd have to have a heart-to-heart with her when I was alone next, so when I reached the aid station again, I lingered to chat.

"How're ye going, love?" the man asked me. It was the Australian way of asking how I was. I liked it.

"Well, it's been pretty lonely," I said truthfully.

"Yeah, but isn't it lovely, darling?" he asked.

"It is," I conceded, though I really hadn't been watching the landscape. I'd been missing the beauty of Mudgee.

This suddenly seemed tragic. To run a marathon in Australia and to battle so intensely within myself that I missed the scenery and the scents of the land I'd traveled twenty hours to get to was calamitous. I now saw that spending one more moment bitching would prevent me from living fully into the remaining experience available to me here and now. Wisdom told me I couldn't allow this to happen.

"Have a little sugar and get on your way," the aid station attendant commanded.

I grabbed a handful of candies and left him. I was on my own again. I knew it was time for a confrontation. I'd had enough of epiphanies for this race. And I was weary of myself. You can handle only so much revelation about yourself in one sitting, or one run. At this moment, I needed to muster that centered Wisdom, the part of me that *did* know how to trust and how to be happy. I needed that knowing, wise-woman part of me to put the Bitch in her place for the remaining miles of this event.

I WAS RUNNING NOW on a country back road. I took the time to go back to my old, steady mantra: *One step at a time. Breathe.* I made a conscious decision to let the land help me find my center. The valley was full of green and smelled of cut grass, and the road was flat. The street had a marked camber, so when my ankles began to ache I moved to the middle of the road and ran on the center line. There hadn't been any traffic to speak of. So I was centered for the moment, both literally and inside my mind. I was ready. I took a breath.

"Listen, Bitch," I began. "Here's the thing. You've been a great help to me. Discovering you has been liberating and eye opening. You've put me in touch with some of my complaints and with my anger. Thank you." She was listening.

"Now I'd like to make a proposal, or actually, I'm laying down the law. I'm working out a more conscious way to manage the contradictions and conundrums in my life, and although you have valuable contributions to make, I don't think you're the one to lead the way. So here's the deal: I'll call on you when I need you. Or you can even speak up when you feel the urge, but you don't get to be my main running companion anymore. And you have to back off when I tell you to. That's all." I listened for a response.

She didn't say anything. I waited a while longer. Nothing. Good.

Then I heard something. It was a car, coming from behind me. I was still on the center line in the middle of the road and knew I'd better get out of the way. Instinctively, I stepped to the left to let this lone car pass me from behind on the right. The problem was, I was in Australia, where the cars drive on the left. There was a honk and a swerve, and my heart stopped ever so briefly and then jumped into my throat. The car missed me by an inch and flew down the road. I'd nearly just gotten killed!

"Shit!" I yelled. "Don't you know there's a marathon going on, you moron?!" Ah, there she was. Right on cue.

But that was the last I heard from her for the rest of the race. Shortly after my near miss, I came upon another aid station, this one attended by a tall, tanned man with a Crocodile Dundee hat camped crookedly on his head. I jogged up to his table and took a cup of water and a few gummy worms.

"How're ye going, love?" he asked me.

"Okay," I said. "It's turning into a beautiful day, isn't it?" The fog had vanished and the sun warmed my face. The temperature was perfect now.

"It's gorgeous. How're your legs?" he asked.

"Not bad yet. But I almost just got hit by a car," I said.

"Well, stay out of the road, love," he advised. I nodded and continued on my way. Every few kilometers held similar interactions with the aid station volunteers, who sat patiently waiting to greet and encourage each of us thirty-one runners, of which I now figured I was the last. These Mudgeeans really knew how to throw a marathon! And since I was free of the Bitch for the moment, I was present enough to realize that I would never have another marathon like this again, where I would be called "love" by volunteers who anticipated my needs with such attention. It was good to be able to settle in and soak up an experience! It was good to be out of my head and in my body.

I now took in the Mudgee countryside. Turning off my iPod, I let my senses absorb my surroundings. There was a gentle, welcome breeze. The birds still flapped above me, as if applauding. I waved at them. I turned onto a dirt road and breathed in the dust. The desertlike soil and the green fields to either side of me provided a striking contrast from one another. The fog had wetted the eucalyptus trees in the nearby hills, and now, as the sun evaporated the moisture, a minty scent filled my nostrils and refreshed me.

I kept my eyes open for kangaroos. I wanted to see a live one in the wild. Because I didn't know they showed themselves only at dusk and dawn, I spent most of my remaining hours on the course trying to identify specks in the distance.

The witch's hat with the number 34 on it materialized at the same time as another unmarked fork in the road. This time I decided to just go ahead and trust my gut. I took a turn without stopping and never looked back. Soon enough, I passed the 35 K marker and the 36.

Now my legs began to burn. I had six kilometers to go, around four miles. This was really my first time running the full length of the marathon. The Prague Marathon had been truncated for us, and I'd trained up to only twenty-two miles for this race. My quadriceps were rubbery, my calf muscles felt tight and short, and my shoulders and lower back were throbbing. I remembered what Bill had said in Prague: "That's how it's supposed to feel." And I kept going, confident that although I hurt, all was well.

A little bubble of excitement was settling in my belly. I'd set a goal and fought hard for it today. Even when challenged by some negative internal elements, I'd held on to my intent. I couldn't help feeling overjoyed, but I had to keep my energy focused to finish strong. I couldn't let go yet. I finally knew for sure that I was bigger than this task I'd set for myself, but I still had the final push in front of me, the last few miles. And the final push in everything (whether it's the end of an illness, or a divorce, or a major transition at work, or a marathon) can be both significant and exhausting. I knew I could finish, though.

I began to look for Bill now, who should have been coming in my direction. We had agreed that he would complete his race, recover, and then come back to find me. We'd run the last mile together. When I passed the 40 K marker and still didn't see him, I got worried. He should have finished almost two hours ago. He should have stretched and have been at least walking toward me. Now that I'd gotten my inner grumbling under control, I had the space to wonder how Bill's race had been. Had he gotten hurt? Had he turned an ankle on the gravel road? Tripped over the dead wallaby? Why wasn't he within my view yet?

Then I saw him walking slowly. He wasn't limping, exactly, but there was a tired slouch to his posture. His head was bent toward the ground and he sort of shuffled his feet, unwilling to move any faster than he had to.

"Hi!" I yelled and gave a stilted little wave with both hands, keeping my tired arms in front of my chest.

"Hi," he said weakly and raised his head to meet my gaze.

As I lumbered up next to him, he turned around and jogged listlessly beside me. I could see it was an effort. "You doing okay? You look great," he said.

"It's been a crazy race," I said. "I didn't have good company for the first half. What about you? You look tired. What happened?" For once, Bill seemed to be having trouble keeping up with *me*.

"Well," he started. "I'm all right. But you know that big hill with the turnaround at the bottom?" I nodded. I knew the spot. It was where my race had turned from an internal sparring match with old memories into an actual marathon. "I didn't turn around," he said. "I just kept going. Never saw an arrow or any sign that I was supposed to come back, I guess. Some Australian guy caught up with me about two kilometers beyond that point and told me to turn back. I figure I ran an extra three miles, maybe. And I ran them fast."

I winced. "Ooh. That can't have been fun."

"No. And just before I finally turned back, I caught four giant kangaroos hiding in the trees, spying on me."

I looked at him to see if he was joking. I'd been watching for kangaroos for hours. He was serious.

"That's cool," I said.

"More like creepy. But what about you?" he changed the subject. "You're almost there. Almost done with your first marathon on your own. You still look strong." I doubted this. I felt happy, but not strong. "I'm going to get a picture of you." I watched him hobble to get in front of me, faster than his tired body wanted to go. *He must love me,* I thought. I kept putting one foot in front of the other, more than ready to be done. I felt excited and more collected than I had in several weeks, but I was also achy and tired. Every step was an effort.

I turned one last corner, and there it was! The large FINISH was raised high above a short chute with the time clock hoisted in the air, ticking the seconds away. I was here, at the end of my second marathon, my first individual marathon, my own lonely victory. There's a moment at the end of a trying experience when all the struggle is peeled away and strength and rapture get their due. I was there. My shoulders were too sore for me to raise my arms in the air, but I smiled for the camera and let out a hoot of celebration. The time clock read 5:14:36 as I crossed the finish line by myself, with Bill cheering on the other side. Done!

I stopped running just as unceremoniously as I had begun more than five hours earlier. Someone placed a cup of water in my hand. I walked a few yards. And then I looked around for whoever might be passing out the medals.

The most amazing part of the marathon, of any major victory you fight for, is the reward—whatever it is—at the end. I wanted my medal. In Prague, Bill and I had both felt we hadn't really earned our medals when we crossed the finish line. This one, I had earned. I'd fought with myself and my memories and with hills and carcasses. I was eager to put that medal around my neck. I planned on wearing it all night, even to dinner.

There were very few people remaining at the race center. Someone bustled up to me and foisted a canary-yellow cotton T-shirt with an off-center green design into my hands. I didn't get a look at the woman because I was so focused on trying to find the person with the medals, but I heard her say, "Congratulations. Here's your T-shirt, darling."

Bill was beside me now. I tucked the T-shirt under my armpit and continued to look around the field. Bill read my thoughts and put his hand on my back. "There are no medals, Cami," he said.

My breath caught in my throat. "What? No medals?" I repeated. I could feel my face turning red and tears springing up in my eyes. Twenty-six miles. Forty-two kilometers. Five and a quarter hours by myself. Sore muscles. Unpleasant flashbacks. Dead animals. And no medals!?

I could feel the Bitch itching to take the floor. *What the hell?* I heard her start. I can't say I blamed her, but I didn't want her to be in the lead in this moment. Not now. I was disappointed, but, medal or not, I had just run my first real marathon. By myself. In Australia. It took some effort, but I quietly said, *No. Not now. This is my time to shine.* And she acquiesced, grudgingly.

Bill insisted I put my yellow T-shirt on so we could have a picture taken under the finish line. I posed and then, with a little help, settled down onto the grass to stretch. Sally, Brenda, and Jared were just climbing into a car when they spotted me and waved, bellowing, "Congratulations, Cami!" I waved back.

THAT AFTERNOON, BEFORE DINNER, Bill and I sipped wine on the veranda outside of our hotel room. The sweat was dried on my face in salty lines. I'd shower later. Now I just wanted to catch up with Bill, to tell each other our marathon tales. I watched the colorful birds on the lawn in the park across the road and gently rubbed my sore calves as I told him about the emotional roller coaster I had been on that day. When I finished my story, Bill rose from the table and disappeared into our room for a brief moment. One of the pink crested birds landed on the rail that ran the length of the porch. "Well, thanks for your help today. I couldn't have done it without you," I said to him. He cocked his head just a little. I thought I saw him nod, and then he flew away.

Bill returned and came around in front of me with his hands behind his back. "Who are you talking to?" he asked.

"No one," I answered. "The birds, I guess."

"Hmm. Well, close your eyes," he commanded.

I obliged him and felt him slip something over my head and around my neck. When I opened my eyes, I saw he had given me a medal.

"Had it made before we left home," he said.

I held it up and read it: FINISHER, MUDGEE MARATHON, NEW SOUTH WALES, AUSTRALIA, AUGUST 26, 2007.

Though it wasn't easy, I rose to my feet and put my arms around his neck.

"We did it," I said. "Thank you."

"You did it," he said.

"Yes, I did." All of me.

A FEW DAYS LATER, I sat in the hot sun on the bow of a large catamaran, my hair drying into tangled wisps. We were in the middle of the Pacific Ocean, over the Great Barrier Reef, heading back to land after a long day of snorkeling. The cool salt water felt reinvigorating after a marathon and then hours of sightseeing following our return to Sydney. We'd flown up to Cairns the day before, and now we were really resting. Bill sipped an Australian beer, and I a glass of white wine. These were the first moments I had to really reflect on the long haul that had been this voyage.

The marathon turned out to be more than I had imagined it could be. It had pulled me out of a self-deception I'd carried with me for years. It—

and by "it," I mean the hard, lonely physical training, the burning muscles during a race, in short, the running—had refused to let me go on living a divided life wherein I could cut off parts of myself so I could pretend to be whole and together.

As people, we have aspects so ugly and unhappy that we exile them into silence and obscurity. This serves us for a while, I suppose, as long as we are content with not knowing ourselves well and not being known well by others. For me, once I had moved away from a canned definition of myself provided by church and culture and started to really desire to be known by Bill and by others in my life, it became evident I'd have to know myself, intimately. I'd have to get to know my own pace in life, on the trail and off; I'd have to get to know the unappealing parts of me and learn to let them into the light without letting them destroy me; and I'd have to learn to make peace with my memories.

I'd turned myself into a tentative marathoner and had labored my way through my first real race. I didn't know what was next, but I did know, with five continents left to run on, there was a long way to go.

in my own
back yard
MARCH 2008

"Fear is the loud pounding of our heart, the racing of our pulse. Fear constricts our breathing, making it rapid and shallow. Fear tells us we are in danger, and then urgently drives our mind to make sense of what is happening and figure out what to do. Fear takes over our mind with stories about what will go wrong. Fear tells us we will lose our body, lose our mind, lose our friends, our family, the earth itself. Fear is the anticipation of the future."

—TARA BRACH, PHD, *Radical Acceptance: Embracing Your Life with the Heart of a Buddha*

"Eventually you learn that the competition is against the little voice inside you that wants you to quit."

—GEORGE SHEEHAN, runner

5

As soon as we got back from Australia, I started looking for a North American marathon to run. Having beaten even my best estimate for time, I was very enthusiastic about my new quest. Back when Bill and I were just toying with the idea of running the continents, I had quipped that two half marathons could count for one full race on my home turf. Now I realized that was my lazy self talking. That was me before I was committed, trying to find ways to bypass the hard work of the marathon and still get the credit. Now I knew that two halves didn't necessarily make a whole—in marriages or in marathons.

I was quickly learning there was nothing like the full marathon to break a person down, to test what you think you know about yourself. My particular brand of getting broken down involved reshaping who I was allowed to be, how I was to behave, and what I should think. The marathon was proving to be just the right catalyst, forcing me to sort through all of this, to examine what had once been taken-for-granted "truths," and to let banished parts of myself find their place in my life.

The Mudgee Marathon had further convinced me that although Bill and I would live and travel together, I was meant to fly solo on the marathon course. Upon arriving home in Bellingham, I was surprised to find that I craved that combination of solitude, introspection, and physical discomfort I had experienced in Australia. It was the only thing that could push me to the brink of my limitations, which I now felt I needed in order to make these deeply personal discoveries. Long, lonely, hard physical challenges don't allow for apathy or self-ignorance. It wasn't self-abuse I sought, though; it was self-knowledge.

Bill, who constantly perused national and international marathon schedules, found a local marathon for me on Whidbey Island, only two hours southwest of Bellingham. It was to take place in April 2008. That would be eight months after Mudgee and would give me plenty of time to recuperate before stepping up my training again. Bill wasn't planning to run this race at all. He'd qualified for the Boston Marathon—a huge accomplishment—which was happening the week after Whidbey. For me this was an added bonus, since it meant he'd be available for extra support along the course in my race. The Whidbey Island Marathon has a reputation for being a very difficult, hilly course, and, as we both knew, I wasn't big on hills.

I wasn't about to refuse Bill's help, but I was eager to be participating in this next race all by myself. Even though I'd completed Mudgee on my own, I still felt I was letting Bill carry the bulk of the enthusiasm and expertise for our running endeavors. It was time to change this. You can only ride another person's coattails for so long.

Since I'd completed a whole race without anyone next to me urging (or pushing) me on, I thought I knew what this personal commitment to the marathon meant. It meant showing up on the trail whether I felt inclined to or not. It meant altering my life to fit in my training. It meant spending many hours alone (something I was less worried about now that my Inner Wisdom and Bitch had a truce). I had made peace with all of this. By early February, I was actually impatient to get started again.

Marathon training, I was discovering, is something of an art that each runner has to master for him- or herself. There are innumerable details you need to manage in a very deliberate way, and it's a rather structured process that involves a lot of time, commitment, and energy. Just a few of the specifics of this process include what part of the day you like to/have time to run; what kind of fuel you need and how often you need to ingest it; how much water you need to carry; what pace you're comfortable with in your training; how quickly you want to build up your miles; and how you want to taper. I was finally learning that there were an optimal number of miles I needed to run during the week. Then, on the weekends, I liked to alternate my runs by pushing myself hard one weekend and resting the next. Without Bill's guidance, I sketched out a schedule that would have me doing a final training run of eighteen miles a couple of weeks before the race. I was still meeting clients in Seattle for two very long days of therapy, but this left me with ample time in Bellingham to run on the other three weekdays.

This time around, my training schedule was like a well-choreographed dance. It had to be—the late winter days were still short, which left very little light to work with. Distances and routes were carefully thought out in advance. We had a map of all the trails in and around Bellingham taped to the side of our refrigerator, nestled among Bill's ribbons. I still wasn't confident in my ability to pull off some of the longest runs, so I studied the map and planned the routes taking into consideration the hills, water fountains, and toilets along the way. Once my plans were in place and February rolled around, I began implementing my runs with a faithful (although not perfect) commitment, until the first week of March.

On March 3, the television news reported the rape of a jogger on one of Bellingham's trails by two men driving a pickup truck. The rape had allegedly happened on the previous Sunday at ten in the morning on a path I sometimes ran. I'd been training at precisely the same time as the victim who'd reportedly been abducted and assaulted (and left tied up on the side of the road), but on a different route. Since Bellingham is small, just a few miles from end to end, I knew without a doubt that it was only luck that prevented me (or any other female runner in town) from being in that wrong place at that wrong time.

When I lived in Seattle, and felt the vulnerability of being a single woman in an urban area, I'd followed with a vengeance all the safety rules women hear from the time we are little girls and throughout our lives: Don't talk to strangers. Don't ever get in a car with someone you don't know. Don't dress too seductively. Don't look men directly in the eye. Look them directly in the eye to show that you're strong. Don't walk alone at night or in secluded places. Don't wear earphones when you're out alone. Stay in well-lit areas. Don't park too far from the mall/school building/grocery store.

Pay attention to sounds coming from behind you. Carry your keys forked through your fingers. Carry pepper spray. Think about getting a gun. Look in the back seat before you open your car door. Learn self-defense. The list was unending and burdensome.

I had, as most women do, restricted my mobility and tied myself in knots to take into account how dangerous the world was. I had bought into the widely accepted myth that if I were really careful and especially watchful, I would be safe; if I weren't, I was fair game for the crazies.

But here in Bellingham, I felt safer and was, therefore, looser about following all of these restrictions. Directly after the reports of the attack, however, I went through a period when I resurrected the old restrictions and gave in to fear in a way that harkened back to my predivorce years.

I wasn't a stranger to fear in its many forms. As a little girl, I'd felt afraid to hear my parents fighting in the room next to mine. I learned to hold my breath and put my pillow over my ears. I learned to be very good and sweet and small and not to make extra trouble during the day, when everyone was tired from the tirades the night before.

Shortly after my parents divorced, when I was ten, a new man came into the picture with new expectations and new rules and new gripes. There wasn't much in the public discourse on the effects of divorce and blended families in those days like there is now, and, consequently, there also wasn't much conversation about how we children felt and what scared us about our new situation. I learned to be afraid of making mistakes, to take up as little space as possible, and to be watchful of the unpredictable moods of the adults in the house. I remained constantly on edge, lest I be banished to my room or from the fragile circle of acceptance that existed in my family. If one family member could be divorced and replaced, why not the rest of us?

When I found religion and sank into the metaphorical lap of my new church community, I was grateful to have people so attentive to me, so willing to be involved in my life. Unfortunately, I also quickly discovered the fact of God's wrath and learned to be afraid of going to hell. Ending up there was quite a literal possibility in my mind. The way I understood it, without exactly the right beliefs about the Heavenly Father, Jesus, and the Holy Spirit, I'd be spending eternity burning and suffering. This particular fear consumed me and prevented me from taking risks, from experimenting with philosophies and ideas. I was afraid of telling—or even listening to—my own truth, for fear that it might not agree with The Truth. If I didn't actually believe that my gay friend was sinning through his attraction to the same sex, or that rock music was morally corrupt and inspired by the devil, or that God was a Republican, I'd never say so out loud—that was for sure. I couldn't risk losing the church community I was a part of, and I certainly couldn't risk going to hell.

Fear of hell impaired me for years. By the time I went to college and got married the first time, I was terrified of making mistakes. You might even say I was phobic. I was afraid of being corrupted by the world, afraid that bad things would happen to me on Earth *and* in eternity. I was separated from my own truths and all the aspects of myself that didn't fit into the mold set for me by other people and God. Like a lot of other individuals I've since met in my practice who've been frightened of taking their heads out from under their respective pillows and saying, "This isn't fair. It doesn't jibe. I object," I was stuck in fear's tight embrace.

But in the past few years, I'd been brave. I'd told my truths, faced myself, some of my demons, and even hell itself. I had launched a campaign to take my life back from all the forces (human, institutional, or psychological) that had controlled and restricted me. As a result, fear had dissipated, dwindled in size to a manageable entity. Meanwhile, my skill set for dealing with it had expanded, and, in the past few years, I'd been relatively fear-free.

Which was exactly why this new threat of danger was so disconcerting. I didn't want to restrict my movements and shrink my world so that I could keep an eye out for perpetrators. But that is exactly what I found myself doing.

FOR ABOUT TWO WEEKS after the incident, I ran only on well-populated trails near my house where I knew I would feel protected. The trail that ran in a straight line from one public park to another was a ten-mile run round trip.

I ran and reran this route, sometimes starting at the western park, sometimes at the eastern, sometimes starting in the middle and running back and forth. But this became duller than I could bear. I could hear the Inner Bitch complaining again about being bored, but I couldn't help her out much.

Bill suggested I get a running partner, hoping that company might ease fear's stranglehold on me, but I doubted the likelihood of finding a partner who would be able to match both my pace (slow) and my endurance (better than most people's). Besides this, I'd just reached a stage in my running life when I *wanted* to run alone. I stubbornly refused to post an ad on the Internet for a partner who could match my abilities.

The worst route I came up with was a seventeen-mile run around Lake Padden. Lake Padden is surrounded by a park with playgrounds and a golf course and has a well-used 2.6-mile trail circling it. Unhappily, I ran around the lake six and a half times to get my miles in. It was like running seventeen miles on a high school track. Each time around on either side, I passed another woman who was running the opposite direction. She wore dark clothes and a scowl, similar to mine, no doubt, and I started noticing the way her eyes darted into the woods just as mine did. On my fifth lap, I finally spoke to her.

"How far are you going?" I shouted from a distance. She startled at my voice, but then visibly relaxed when she settled her eyes on me.

"Twenty-one," she said, slowing to a walk. "You?"

"Seventeen for me," I said. I offered her a sympathetic smile.

"This is a killer boring route, but what are you gonna do?" she sighed.

"Tell me about it." We waved and ran on, meeting each other a few more times before I finally knocked out my last loop. We hadn't spoken about the rape, but I could see fear at her heels, as well. And it made me mad.

All I really wanted was to belong to myself and not to some taskmaster, not to institutions, gods, or rules—and especially not to fear. I didn't want to go crazy, throw caution to the wind, or ignore common sense. It wasn't that I expected to be exempt from following reasonable and widely accepted guidelines. I just wanted to belong to myself. And since, for the moment, I didn't, since I was firmly clenched in fear's hold, I felt a bubble of repressed anger surging through me. Instead of empowering me, as anger sometimes had, this anger was turning against me and making me tired, keeping me from reaching out to others and insisting I be strong enough to carry fear on my back as I ran. But I wasn't that strong. No one is. I wanted liberation from this burden. I wanted to run without terror of being victimized.

After that exhausting, repetitive run around the lake, I stood at home in the shower and tried to soothe my rage. I turned my face up toward the showerhead and let the warm water rinse away the lines of sweaty salt that had formed on my face. My legs hurt and my neck and upper back were tight and stiff. I tried to hold still and let the warmth seep into my bones. Gradually, the heaviness I was feeling lightened up a little. I remained in the shower until I'd drained the hot-water tank and the stream had turned lukewarm.

I wrapped my body in one towel and my hair in another and climbed into bed.

Bill came into the bedroom and sat down beside me. He asked, "You okay?"

"Not really. I'm discouraged and frustrated. I feel constrained." Fear had even begun to overflow into other areas of my life. I'd started to worry about dying in a car accident on my way to Seattle, and about Bill's getting cancer. If I were successful at staving off horrible fantasies of rape, they'd only be replaced by other imaginary catastrophes. I told Bill all of this. Then we sat without talking for a few minutes.

I continued to think. All the spiraling "what ifs" I could usually bat away were sticking to me nowadays like I was a magnet. I couldn't even get enough space from them to reflect that fear's strategy was actually flawed, if I really studied it. The crazy-making thing about fear is that it loops itself around somewhat unlikely outcomes and poses them as real threats. The outcomes of my either going to hell or getting raped on the trails (or breaking an ankle or having a stroke or anything else that *could* happen) were threats precisely because I did not know they *wouldn't* happen. Everyone knows that two negatives make a positive, so this added up in my mind to "could happen." From there, it wasn't much of a jump to "probably will happen."

When I slowed down, though, it became obvious that since nobody knows what will or won't happen in the future, wonderful outcomes are just as likely as tragic ones. Unfortunately for me, I had been in a mental paralysis. Now, these new thoughts came like the flip of a switch. The answer was in the now, in living what *is* rather than what might or could be.

Beside me, Bill studied my face. I could see the lifting of my own burden reflected in his expression as he watched Wisdom gently blow away the dark cloud that had been hovering above me for weeks.

Bill patted my hand. "I think you're on to something," he said. "I'm sorry this is so hard. They'll catch these guys soon."

I couldn't wait for that. I had to get my life back right away.

I HAD ONE MORE long run planned. There was a thirty-kilometer race (18.6 miles) happening up north in Birch Bay the next weekend, and I'd decided to use it as my final training route before my taper.

On the way up to Birch Bay the following Saturday morning, wet snow pelted the car and melted quickly on the windshield. Snow at the end of March was almost unheard of, but there it was. I wasn't looking forward to running in this weather, but I'd push through it. With a little space from the intense fear I'd been feeling, I had the psychological energy to pull it off. And I was grateful for that.

This thirty-kilometer run would take us along the bay and give us peeks of Point Roberts, that little peninsula of America that you have to cross into Canada to get to. We would run through Birch Bay State Park and pass Drayton Harbor and the resort homes that surround it. If the clouds lifted even a little, it would be a gorgeous route. Birch Bay is one of the most picturesque towns in our county.

Bill and I parked and collected our bibs and then hustled up to the starting line. When the race organizer gave the signal for us to start running, we waved goodbye to each other and set out individually, he near the front and I at the back of the pack.

As I commenced, I pushed the start button on my stopwatch and settled in for three-plus hours. I jogged behind two women, one dressed in bright pink, the other in yellow (they reminded me of the birds in Australia), who talked for much of the first hour about the very situation that had been keeping me feeling restricted. I eavesdropped on their conversation. Since I hadn't been talking to anyone about the rape, I really didn't know how the situation had affected other people—especially other women. I was eager to hear their thoughts.

I decided to join the conversation. Their pace was faster than I usually ran, but I was so eager to be able to talk about the incident that I pushed myself to keep up.

After we'd been together a mile or so, I asked, "How have you two handled staying safe these past few weeks?" I asked. I wanted to know how other women had coped with knowing the attackers had not been caught.

"I have a running partner," the woman in pink said. "We've just made sure to schedule all our runs together." She hadn't carried her load alone as I had. That was smart.

"I didn't let it get to me. Didn't change a thing," the other woman said.

"Really? How come?" I wanted to know.

"Because it's my life. I probably can't stop someone from attacking me if he's really got a mind to do it. I just took all my usual practical measures and kept running." This woman, I reflected, had really stayed out of the realm of "what if" and kept to the present moment. This sister runner already knew what had just been brewing inside of me: Living in the "now" is the enemy of fear.

In my ever-growing awareness that I needed new skills to make a happy life for myself, I'd been reading about mindfulness and living in and paying attention to whatever the current moment brought. I wasn't great at it yet. Early in life I'd focused on eternity, to the exclusion of real life. Then, during my first marriage, while I had avoided planning for the eventualities of the near future, I'd hardly ever let go into the moments of life. Mostly I had tried to control them. Real attention on the current moment, the one I was in right now, was a fairly new concept to me, but one to which I had a growing commitment.

I couldn't keep up beyond mile seven, so I said goodbye to my colorful friends and drifted toward the tail of the little pack running that day. But I took something with me. I wanted what those women had. I was going to change my relationship with fear permanently and conclusively. I would take concrete steps to be safe and then to say, "That's all I can do. This is my life. Period."

JUST AS QUICKLY AS the news of the rape had plunged me into a fearful struggle to stay safe, another report came as a huge surprise. In fact, all of Bellingham was astonished and bewildered when, on April 16, a startling article appeared in the newspaper with the headline JOGGER MADE UP RAPE STORY, POLICE SAY!

"What?!" I said when Bill presented the newspaper to me as I arrived home from Seattle that evening. "Are they sure?"

"Read it for yourself," he said.

The article contained an extensive statement from the police about how they had been unable, despite great efforts, to find evidence of an attack. New reports from the hospital suggested the victim's wounds were probably self-inflicted. She was now in "protective custody" and was getting "help," but the article did not say what kind.

People were livid, Bill told me. He'd been following the editorial stream on the Internet. Some people in town demanded the woman be prosecuted. Others saw her extreme efforts at creating the falsehood as evidence of mental illness and advocated for further compassion.

I sat on my overstuffed sofa, curled up under a blanket with a cup of tea and the newspaper, processing the situation and my own reaction. Of course, like many others were doing, I tried to parse out what the woman's motivations might have been for telling such a violent narrative complete with descriptive details about her attackers. I wasn't above feeling angry at her, but in that moment I also distinctly remembered being present during numerous conversations at the drop-in youth center back in Seattle a few years earlier in which young women reported "dueling rape" histories, one after the other, escalating the details to almost impossible proportions. When our volunteers asked what to believe in the face of some of the more outrageous stories our young people told, I always said, "Believe the feelings in the story, and always remember that although the account may or may not be strictly factual, these kids have been through hell." Maybe this woman lived with some kind of hell and the best she could do was spread it around. I certainly understood the way hell could infect a person.

Mostly, as I sat with the article in my lap, I thought about how her fabrication had elicited a brief but potent resurgence of fear in my life. Fear is definitely a power to be reckoned with, able to alter the shape of our lives and rob us of rationality and independence while isolating us from help. It can prevent us from entering or leaving relationships. It can make us hate people who are different. It is both very real and very false at exactly the same time. I was appreciative to have found a reprieve from it for the moment, and I was, of course, glad that no rape had actually taken place (though that certainly didn't mean there were not rapists on the loose). Nothing could justify the woman's lie, but the whole fiasco had forced *me* to take one more look at how to continue toward wholeness and healing, so I couldn't hate the "victim" for what she had done. All I could do was look forward—or, more aptly, stay in the present.

north america:
whidbey island wonder
APRIL 2008

"Mindfulness is attention. It is non-judging and respectful aware-ness. Unfortunately, much of the time we don't attend in this way. Instead, we continually react, judging whether we like, dislike, or can ignore what is happening."

—JACK KORNFIELD, *The Wise Heart*

"Running has given me the courage to start, the determination to keep trying, and the childlike spirit to have fun along the way. Run often and run long, but never outrun your joy of running."

—JULIE ISPHORDING, marathon winner

6

When you're in your twenties, you can't fathom shedding your old skin and starting a second life. Most of us are totally blindsided by our need for one. I certainly was. In the six years since my divorce, I had opened up a trunk full of unhealthy ways of thinking, knowing, and being and had tossed out what didn't fit anymore. Running had become an integral part of my psychological and spiritual transformation process.

Now it was April 2008, and in May I would turn forty-one. In just the last few weeks, I had finally understood that I needed to stay out of the realm of scary "what ifs." I'd come to realize that I was better off living in the present moment with whatever arose. It had taken me a long time and many, many miles to get this message.

Whidbey Island Marathon race day arrived. Like every other day, it would be another chance to plod along on my journey toward greater self-knowledge. It was also a chance to tick off one more continent, my home continent, from my marathon list.

"Do a stretch. I'll get a picture!" Bill bellowed from the sidelines of the starting chute.

I rolled my eyes at him in exaggerated exasperation before posing and flashing him a cheesy smile. I checked my watch. Five minutes till start time. I switched it to stopwatch mode and then jumped in place a few times in a futile attempt to get warm. Here I was at the starting line of my third marathon. I felt renewed after my victory against fear, and was as ready as I could be for this race.

Looking around at the sheer number of runners here, I knew I wouldn't be as isolated as I had been in Mudgee. About four hundred people were assembled with me in the chute. Dean Karnazes, the famous ultrarunner, was among them somewhere. Though I couldn't spot him from where I had seeded myself at the back of the group, I hoped to meet him at the awards ceremony after the race and shake his hand.

Right now, especially after the last month of difficult training, I was grateful—even giddy—to be among so many runners and to have Bill there as my pit crew. His presence in my life and at this race, ready to support and encourage me, was significant and precious. I looked over at him and swelled up with love and appreciation for his commitment to me and the way he accepted me as the somewhat neurotic, hyper-introspective, often confused work-in-progress I was and would likely always be.

I looked up at the clouds overhead. The sky was a low, solid blanket of gray, with even grayer billows blowing underneath the principal cloud cover. I wasn't surprised. Weather like this made me wish I could pick up and move to someplace tropical. But I was determined to stay in the moment, and right now, it wasn't raining. That was good.

The starting line was near the water's edge, at a beach called Cornet Bay. If all of us had held our breath at once, we might have heard the lapping of gentle waves on the shore. Instead, there was a racket of nervous laughter and talking among the runners. I looked beyond where Bill stood behind the taped-off holding arena into the greenery. Although it was technically spring, the deciduous trees wouldn't have their leaves back for at least another couple of weeks. Only if you studied them at close range could you see the little buds that portended green shoots. At least there wasn't frost on the ground today, though.

Just as I was taking one more breath of air deep into my lungs, the horn went off and the crowd started to scoot forward. I walked from my place at the rear up to the starting line and then sped up to a dawdling jog until I could get enough elbow room among the other runners to pick up a comfortable pace.

I knew I was in for a long day. Bill and I had driven the course the day before, and I had been shocked at how tough it looked. The course went up, up, up, with little downhill or flat land, before heading up, up, up again. As he put the car into second gear up the mile-long hills, Bill tried to calm me by saying, "It's not much worse than Mudgee. You'll do fine." I saw with my own eyes, though, that this race was a totally different kind of marathon. This one would be about lots of elevation gain. I realized as we drove the route in a cool mist that I'd have to be prepared to add and subtract layers of clothing as I sweated up a hill and froze on the way down.

Today, however, as I made my way up the small incline out of the park drive and took my first turn onto a long, straight two-lane road, there was actually a spring in my slow step. I'd trained through fog, rain, and fear to prepare for this day, and here it was. I hummed a song softly beside a little group that had formed within the first mile. *Take each moment as it comes,* I reminded myself, and fell into the rhythm of the group's pace.

The athletes around me seemed to breathe as one, our breath making petite puffs of steam as we panted. We came alongside a series of grassy fields where cows grazed serene and unperturbed. Watching their big bovine eyes follow us gave me unexpected delight, a feeling I was only beginning to associate with running. Synergistic vibes seemed to be transmitted through the air among us, and I was feeling good.

It was odd that after two marathons, hundreds of hours of training, and perhaps two dozen other organized races of various lengths, I was only now beginning to *like* running. I had seen the value in it for years and had even appreciated its effects on my life and on my body, but as for actually enjoying the feel of the wind on my brow or the sounds of other runners' footfalls near mine . . . not so much. Today, as I tried to focus on feeling my aspirations come and go through my nostrils, I felt peace. Or maybe even merely the absence of suffering. And I liked it. I'd pushed through some invisible barrier. By sticking with my commitment to run, I was over a hump. Running was becoming a part of me, rather than just a means to an end.

I looked around me to see who my compatriots were. Just behind me was a woman running with a big black dog. Given my love of dogs, it made me happy to see one on the course. Although the woman's pace was faster than mine, she trailed me because of her frequent stops to tip her bottle of water into her pooch's mouth. Beside me was a small group of runners, two women and one man, going at my exact pace. It was rare for me in a race of any distance to be running alongside others I didn't have to push to keep up with. I considered this small crew a kind gift from the universe.

Without introducing ourselves, we began to chat, running four abreast. One woman was visiting family in the area and had flown in from Wisconsin early to run in this event. She called the hills on the course "mountains," which made the rest of us laugh. The single man in the group had an outgoing demeanor, like an attention-starved golden retriever. He was talkative and eager to keep conversation flowing. The other woman's husband was doing race support, following her in his car. He joined us every mile or so to take her windbreaker off her hands or to give her a piece of banana. He was shadowed by Bill, who was equally attentive to my progress and cheering, "You're doing great! You look strong." I felt it. I was having fun for the moment, which, I was growing to realize, was the only moment I had.

A little over an hour in, we faced a winding two-mile hill. It was gradual at first, and then the grade sharpened, plateaued, and climbed again. My clique stuck together and continued running, albeit at a much slower pace than we had started out at. The road was heavily wooded, so the pavement was dry and the temperature was cooler under the trees.

"My quads are burning," the woman from Wisconsin complained.

"I'll tell you a story to keep your mind off your legs," the man in our group puffed. Through breathy huffs and with long pauses to catch his air, he began a story to keep our minds off our pain.

His wife raised horses, he said, and one morning, when he had gone to the foot of his driveway to pick up his newspaper, he'd discovered a horse tied to his mailbox with a note. Someone had decided the horse was too much to care for and so had dropped him off at the family's farm home, abandoned like a newborn baby left on a church stoop. The horse still lived with this man and his family and became a favorite among their equine brood. I waited for some sort of moral to the story or connection to this race, but there was none. He was finished.

I took in the moment for what it was and realized that there didn't have to be a message. I loved that this runner was simply pitching in to entertain us with a directionless story without much of a punch line. I'd spent my last weeks in training obsessed with fear, looking for perpetrators that didn't exist and holding my feelings close to my chest. Now, sharing in shallow, meandering conversation and running with others, even strangers, was like finding new life. I felt like I was Lazarus being released from the grave, coming out of the deep crypt into fresh air.

I didn't have the capacity to pull off telling a whole story while on the hill, but when we got to the top and I'd recovered, I took my turn to distract the group. I told about the time my neighbor became hysterical when her cat suffered cardiac arrest. I was called upon to provide first aid, complete with shouting, "You, call the vet! You, get a blanket!" while I performed kitty CPR. The poor, ungrateful cat passed away in spite of my efforts, but my neighbors thanked me with a bottle of wine on my front step the next day.

Everyone laughed at my tale. The glee we felt at having mounted one of the worst hills on the course was visceral. Time was passing more quickly than it had for me in Mudgee. I *almost* wanted it to slow down. I definitely wanted to soak in the pleasure I felt. I couldn't believe the change in me, from a complaining, frightened, reluctant trainee to a giggly back-of-the-packer full of frivolity. Was this the runner's high I'd always heard about but never experienced?

At about mile eight, the women ran ahead and the man and I continued on side by side. We finally introduced ourselves. His name was Stuart. Stuart and I had been together for a couple of hours now and had conquered almost a third of the marathon. We had encouraged one another and swapped energy gels for flavors we preferred, and I'd nearly hit him with one of my inept snot rockets. It wasn't exactly intimacy, but it was on the edge. On this basis, we moved beyond chitchat to more-substantial conversation. I asked him if he'd been running for a long time.

"Few years," he said. "You?"

"I've tried to be a runner for a long time, but it's only been the last few years that I've really been committed to it. I started in earnest during my divorce. It was cathartic." This was true, but even in the last couple of weeks, something had changed, and so I added, "Now I can't do without it for more than a day or two."

"I believe it," he said. "I started because I couldn't take the stress of my job without some way to let off steam, and now it's my mainstay. I'm a lawyer," he added.

"I bet that's a stressful job," I said.

"It's a lot of pressure for me. I'm not sure I'm really suited for it. I have clear ethics in terms of how I like to practice, and it's like I'm always being asked to fudge them."

"That sucks. So how does running help?" I asked, always the therapist.

"It's where I turn things over in my mind. Sometimes I lose my equilibrium, and running helps me get it back." We both grew quiet and took some time to breathe in the damp air.

I related to what Stuart was saying—how the mind needs the body's cooperation to get relief from its pain, be it grief, stress, anger, or confusion. I was almost at the point where I couldn't remember how I'd coped without running. How had I breathed? Or thought? How had I listened to myself? How had I healed my wounds or released my anxieties? Had I? I knew emotionally balanced people who didn't run, but they all maintained some kind of mind-body practice, like yoga, walking, or dancing.

Eventually, Stuart and I arrived at another steep hill and our conversation dwindled. I needed to slow to a walk, and he needed to keep running. I shouted, "Good luck!" as he ran ahead. I was alone now, but I was okay. In an effort to take each moment's offering, I let my mind rest from conversation. I picked up my pace at the top of the hill and listened to the pattern of my own breath. In. In. Out. Out. My mood was cheerful; my legs were strong. This was good.

Just then, I saw Bill pull up in front of me and park the car near a little cemetery. He got out and stood waiting until I reached him, and then he jogged alongside me. "How're you doing?" he asked.

"I'm good. Almost halfway," I said. "I've had a lot of company. It's been nice."

"Yeah. Looks like you're having fun. We don't talk so much up in the pack where I run. We're breathing too hard." I was sure that was true. Bill and I were completely different kinds of runners. He pushed for time and personal bests, trying to beat the guys in his age group. I was still new and figuring out what was important to me, but at this point, I strove more for feeling content than for time.

"See what you're missing with all that competition business?" I joked.

"No doubt," he said. "Listen, since you're feeling good, I'm gonna take a run myself. I'll make my way to the finish line and run the route in the opposite direction. I'll meet you and do a mile or two with you near the end. You need anything before I go?"

"I don't think so," I replied, perhaps overconfident that I would be fine.

"Okay, then. See you on the other side." He turned around and headed back to the car.

I continued alone for a long stretch after he left. I was lost in thought, not trudging through and counting every mile as I had done in Australia. I took time to notice my surroundings. The sky was threatening rain, and I felt an occasional heavy individual droplet on my face, but the ardent April showers were holding off for now. I turned my face up toward the sky and smelled the Northwest: the salt water, the wet soil, the green. These surroundings were so completely different from the Australian wine country. Or maybe it was I that was different. I was celebratory. I'd often heard other runners talk about the adrenaline rush they felt at the beginning of a race, but just like runner's high, I'd never had it before now. My joy could be explained by the fact that I'd had company, and with it a sense of being a part of something, or it could be that I was paying attention to each experience as it arose and not trying to mold it into anything it wasn't. I wasn't having flashbacks or moderating arguments in my head between different parts of me. I was just here. Right now.

Up ahead, I could see the mile-thirteen marker. Halfway! As the road began a very welcome descent, I let gravity have its way with me. I spread my arms and, like a child on a playground, I let go of my controlled posture and flailed a little as I passed one or two other runners on my way down. Near the bottom of the hill, I caught sight of a fellow I'd hoped to encounter somewhere on the circuit. His name was Mel, a seventy-five-year-old runner whom Bill had pointed out before the race began. He was a local legend among runners in our area because of his fanaticism about the marathon (he was, in fact, part of a club called the Marathon Maniacs), and I'd already thought that if I saw him on the course I'd strike up a conversation.

I approached him from behind and took a good look at his gait. He ran with hunched shoulders. His head was tucked down and thrust forward with determination. His pace was slightly slower than my own, and I had to reduce my speed only a little at the bottom of the hill when I reached him.

"Hi there. How's it going?" I adjusted to his pace.

"So far, so good," he answered as we fell in step. I hoped he would be up for talking to me. I was still unsure what the protocol was, but I figured I was savvy enough at knowing when people wanted to talk and when they wanted to be left alone.

I ran beside him for a few moments before asking, "I heard this is your four-hundredth marathon or something."

"Oh, no," he laughed softly. "Only three-hundred and thirty one." *Only!* I thought. To look at his crooked posture, it was almost unbelievable that he could finish a mile, let alone a marathon. He gave me a sideways grin. I imagined he liked to see the way people responded to his announcement of how many races he'd run. He had a mischievous streak, I could tell.

"How long ago did you get started?" I asked.

"I didn't start until I was fifty," he told me. Mel said he had watched his father let life go "downhill" at fifty. That had bothered him and made him want something different for himself, and he'd decided that fifty was the perfect time to start having fun with life. For him, fun meant running. Before today, I couldn't have said I agreed with him.

"Yep," he went on, "the first year I ran one marathon and hurt so bad afterward that I told myself I'd never do it again." I knew the feeling. "But I recovered. And so the next year I ran two, and the year after that four. The year I retired from work, I ran more than twenty." He shook his head a little and then continued, "The first one I did that year I turned fifty, I quit running when I saw the twenty-six-mile marker. I thought the marathon was twenty-six miles, so I just stopped. Some guy came up behind me and said, 'You still have a little ways to go, buddy.' I know better now." He chuckled at his own naiveté.

I looked at him more carefully now. He was my height, and he wasn't stick-thin. He was breathing heavily enough for me to worry about him, but he wasn't slowing down and didn't seem the least bit fazed. The more we talked, in fact, the faster he seemed to run. "Last February," he went on, "I fell out of a tree I was pruning and hurt myself. I chipped my hip bone. Had to take some time off." He had just started running again in the past few months. The weekend before, he'd run a race in Yakima, Washington; this week, it was the Whidbey Island Marathon; and the next weekend, he would do the Wenatchee Marathon, east of the Cascade Mountains. His goal today was to run without walking. That would be his signal that he was back up to speed, despite the pain he had in the hip he'd broken and the pain he had in the other hip from favoring his broken side.

We ran in unison for a while, my breath synchronizing with Mel's short inhalations. Mel told me that his first marathon was an exercise in completion, but how within a few years, something had changed and he couldn't do any fewer than two per month. I regarded him for a moment and wondered why anyone would need this much challenge in his or her existence. Then again, if one marathon last year had changed the structure of my internal life, what would twenty do for me in a year? I wondered how far I could I push myself if I really set my mind to it. Twenty was probably too ambitious, but what about three or four in one year? A marathon every few years when it was feasible to travel to an exotic place wasn't really much of a commitment, especially in comparison with Mel's exuberance, was it? Once the question of whether or not something can be done is answered, what is the next question? How much of it can be done? How fast it can be done? Where it can be done?

Mel hobbled beside me, a little lopsided, smiling, concentrating. Jogging along next to him, I felt happy. He emanated encouragement and determination. He had unfettered merriment in being alive, even with a chipped hip bone, because he could run. I savored the sweetness of being beside him, rolled it around in my heart like one rolls hard candy around the tongue. I was taking in this momentary brightness in my world and letting myself be touched by it. Without analyzing or trying to figure out why running beside this man gave me such a thrill, I simply opened myself and let it be.

After another mile or so, I was ready to pick up my pace. I hated to leave Mel behind, but I knew I couldn't run next to him, siphoning his vivacity, forever. I had the gift he had unknowingly given, so I ran on alone, perhaps a little more quickly than I should have.

WHIDBEY ISLAND HAS THAT classic Northwest landscape, complete with neighborhoods supervised by giant old-growth trees, moss poking up through cracks in the asphalt, and the odor of mold and a bone-freezing humidity. This was all familiar to me because it was what I had grown up in. The infrequent showers that occasionally dribbled on us along the course did not distress me; I'd raced in far worse weather as recently as the preceding month in Birch Bay. All things considered, the environment was cooperating nicely.

The hills were another thing, though, as they came one after another, each one higher than the last, arriving just as my muscles had recovered enough to feel relief. My exuberant state of mind had carried me over several of them through the first half of the race; I almost hadn't noticed how utterly tired I was.

At about mile seventeen, an astonishing, gargantuan hill came into view. Imagine setting your treadmill on the highest incline grade, and then tilt it twice again as much, and you've got the picture. I still felt the glow of my time with Mel, and my energy was tranquil as I mused over how easy my run had been thus far, so, although my muscles were growing sore, I met this hill with emotional placidity. Looking back, I can see that I was, perhaps, a little too serene.

Oh, hello, I thought at the foot of it. I checked my watch and approached it cheerily, as if it were an old friend, rather than the formidable opponent it was. Optimistic that I could handle it, I took a breath, slowed my pace, and leaned forward. Taking minuscule steps, I started a mini-jog. An inch at a time, I progressed up and up. A few feet in, I began to feel the fatigue I'd been ignoring, but still, I congratulated myself for my Zen composure. I glanced at my watch and then looked up to see how far I had to go. Big mistake. The top of this hill was going to gain me quite a bit of elevation. It was a long way up there.

My mood began deflating, but I was unwilling to let go of my happiness. This had been a good run for me so far. I didn't want to lose that. Instead, I thought back to my last few hours with yearning, trying to hold on to the joy—and I kept bouncing, forcing myself to keep smiling as well. At the half-way point, I looked at my watch again. I'd been doing my tiny, bobbing steps for five minutes. My quadriceps began to really ache, but I tried to ignore them. I didn't want to turn my attention from my bliss to my legs. I didn't want to give up my contentment, just to have it replaced by pain. (And I didn't truly understand that the practice of staying in the moment was not about ignoring pain, but rather about noting whatever existed without evaluating it. I was too accustomed to believing that one thing was better than another: happy better than sad, bliss better than pain.)

My legs were unwilling to be ignored, however. My calf muscles, especially my left one, started to seize, threatening to cramp down hard. Then a sharp clenching in my shoulders slipped all the way down to my lower back. This happens sometimes: After holding my neck and shoulders in the same position for several hours, the muscles protest and demand some variety. Furthermore, my thighs burned more by the minute as I continued poking my way up the hill. The final straw was a little pinch in my left hip flexor, a recurring pain I thought I'd solved with new shoes. When it came on, quick and potent, something had to give.

With a very abrupt shift, my peaceful mind, hanging on by a thread at this point anyhow, swiftly disappeared and the Bitch made a brief and sudden appearance, popping in with a very sensible comment: *Oh, for God's sake, you could walk as fast as you're hopping for joy up this stupid hill with half the pain.*

Good point, I acknowledged, humbled but a little relieved to hear the truth of my situation. I stopped jogging and walked, watching the happiness I had been enjoying roll down the hill backward, proving to me that what I'd been reading in my books on mindfulness was true: Every state of mind (sadness, rage, peace, all of it) was about as fickle as yesterday's fashions. Bang! And it was gone.

When I finally saw the zenith of the incline and a hint of the hill's decrescendo that would take us runners back down to sea level, I was enough rested from walking that I thought I could pick up my pace again. But my muscles were despondent. They were like jelly inside my legs, useless.

I was shocked at how suddenly the pain came on, and how my energy and even keel disappeared. The hills had taken their toll. I had been tending to my emotional experience and had remained pretty oblivious to the physical. But the marathon is always—and I mean always, without fail—going to bring a person out of her head and into her body at some point. It won't be the body she wishes she had, either; it will be the flesh and muscle and flab and all of its limits and inadequacies. At mile twenty-two, if it hasn't happened earlier, a marathoner's body will start its noisy dissent. For me, that moment was here. I would have to turn all of my attention to the "work" of the race, pulling my body in the direction of the finish line by force of pure will.

As I tried to pick up a slow running pace again, I saw the road before me. There was an acutely angled decline that led straight down to a waterfront neighborhood road. From the top of the hill, I viewed gorgeous custom-made beach homes on my left, a long flat road beside them, and another hill, huge and right-turning, that disappeared up into the woods. I deflated, but less because of the steep down-and-up my tired muscles were enduring and more because of what I didn't see: I didn't see many other runners. Behind me, there was no one in view. In front of me were a few individuals spread out on the route, with plenty of space in between.

My time of being part of a greater whole, of experiencing myself wrapped in a sense of collective, purposeful, spiritual solidarity with all the other marathoners of the world, was over. I was, once again, just a sole slow woman, alone with her thoughts and her hurting body. Would I ever get used to this together-apart-together thing? Every time I settled comfortably into one state, cozying up to the idea of being a member of something bigger than myself, everyone disappeared and I found myself alone in the shell of my body, searching all the cupboards and closets for even an old skeleton to hang out with.

I didn't know if it was true for everyone, but in my limited experience so far, there was some point during a marathon when the race absolutely, adamantly insisted I dig deeper than I'd ever dug before and push! There was no one else who could take over for me. No one could change the course, and no one could give me the resolve to finish if I didn't already have it. I had that resolve. Not only for this race, but for the ones to come.

I'd resolved to run marathons wearing the hat, so to speak, of a researcher. I was looking for what made a good life, and with every training period and every race, something new was revealing itself. In this race I'd tried to practice staying in the present moment and appreciating the gifts that came my way. This was something I'd pinpointed as important during the training period, when fear had invited me to project tragedy into my future. Staying in the "now" today was easy at first, when I had company, but here, near the end, it was getting harder.

I already knew that if I worried too much about the future, even the future of how I was going to finish this course, I'd lose all the time in the present. Somehow, although I sensed a low point on its way, I was going to try to stay with my feelings and the increasing pain in my body without wishing them away. But it felt tricky. I really just wanted to speed things up and get this race over with.

I started my descent—in more ways than one. I was coming down off my high and heading for flat ground. While *down*hills are usually my favorite kind, this one hurt—badly. My knee and hip joints were in sorry shape. I took the hill slowly, having to walk most of it, which prolonged the race and pissed me off. When I finally reached the bottom and could literally feel the sea in the air on my face and in my hair as I walked beside it, I was drained. I was drained of energy for running. I was drained from the roller-coaster ride that this course had been. I'd had my fill of the present moment, thank you very much. I was ready for the future: me in front of my fireplace, stuffing food into my mouth.

What does someone do when she's done? I wondered. When she's come to the end of herself? When there is no support, no aid station in sight, and her inner well is all dried up? When she's attended to her experience to the point that she can't bear to look anymore? What was I supposed to do? I had six miles left.

I'd burned out so suddenly, I hadn't seen it coming. It was as if the fuel gauge in my body were broken and I'd never had a clue that I was near empty until I ran out of gas. I did the only thing I could think to do: I surrendered. "Accept the things you cannot change" flashed though my mind, recalling family day at my dad's rehab center twenty years before. A little serenity prayer never hurt anyone. I turned my swollen hands toward the sky and said, "Whatever! Okay? Just whatever" in my most sullen voice, also harkening back to adolescence.

I walked the flat road. As I relinquished myself to the exhaustion and the pain, I emptied myself of all expectations. My eyes were down on the street, and I felt my muscles relax as I gave in. The tension in my neck released a tad. *Surrender is nice,* I thought. It gives the mind the gift of possibility, because in surrender there are no more goals, no objectives or judgments, only open space for what is really there. For just a second, I understood that this was really what observing the current moment was actually about. Not the elation or the pain, just the noticing.

Here, in surrender, I didn't need anything. I didn't need to finish the race or to quit the race. I didn't need company or support. I didn't need anyone to rescue me or understand me or see my pain. No fans or encouragement or help were required, because all my expectations were released and only this worn-out body of mine existed.

I walked forward, as it seemed the only idea that presented itself, and I let my body unwind. I forgave it for falling short and forgave myself for my failing energy and attitude. I'd done all I could do. I was willing to consider that maybe I wasn't a runner after all. Maybe my seven-continents vision quest needed to be amended. If that were the case, I'd have to surrender to that truth, too.

Then, coming from somewhere at a distance—heaven, I thought at first—someone was calling my name in a deep voice. "Cami!" I heard someone boom. I couldn't see anyone. Maybe it was my imagination. Or was God a man after all? Was it my time?

"Cami! Cami!" I kept searching the horizon, until I saw Bill. He was at the foot of the right-turning hill I was slowly approaching. I'd almost forgotten he was coming. He was waving. I waved back. It hurt to lift my arm.

"Cami! Run!" he shouted.

"No," I shook my head, but I didn't have the energy to yell loudly enough for him to hear me.

Bill picked up his pace, and in a few minutes he was beside me. "Come on. You can do it," he said as he turned around and walked with me.

"No. I'm too tired."

"Here. Eat this." He handed me an open packet of energy gel. I still hated its slimy texture, but lacking even the energy to resist Bill's insistence, I took it and squeezed it into my mouth. It had a hint of artificial orange flavor that made me gag. Bill handed me his water. My bottle hung empty in my belt. I drank and washed the gel down.

Bill took my hand and we walked that way along the flat road. By the time we reached the foot of the next hill, I felt the caffeine and the sugar in the gel reviving me, just enough to bring back my hope of finishing.

"Okay. Let's run for a couple of minutes," I said.

"You want the Prague Push?" Bill asked, willing to nudge me up the hill if that was what I wanted.

"Not yet. Maybe on top. I'd like to do this myself if I can."

And up we went, running a little, walking a little. I stayed in surrender mode, doing what I could, resting when I needed to. At the top, Bill pressed another gel into my hand. Because one of Bill's children is diabetic, he is especially aware of how a person's body needs exactly the right kind of fuel at precisely the right times. I took it without arguing and chased it down with more water.

Bill stayed with me as we wound our way through some deep woods on a twisting road. He didn't leave me until we finally took a sharp left onto the main drag that led to the Olympic View Elementary School, where the finish line would be in a little more than a mile. Even along this final stretch, the hills kept coming, little rolling hills that looked like Wisconsin's mountains to me now.

Finally, I could see the school's stadium. Bill had run ahead to be there for me at the finish line. I turned onto the school grounds. I'd been out on the course for nearly five and a half hours.

FOR A NONCOMPETITIVE RUNNER like me, the end of a long race is like the last bite of Christmas dinner. You're full. You don't need to eat that last forkful of mashed potatoes and gravy, but you've already cleaned your plate of everything else, so it seems ridiculous to leave one little pile of food for the garbage disposal. It's the same with the finish line. You've proved your point and run your race. You're "full," as it were, of the experience, but that last little stretch remains. So you go for it.

I jogged into the school's driveway, where the buses dropped off their students on the weekdays. It had been transformed for the event into a recovery area for runners. Orange cones indicated the path into the stadium. I caught a stench in the wind and observed, a few yards away, men loading all the port-o-potties onto a truck. Others were disassembling temporary shelters that had housed sponsors and volunteer groups. As I was making my last, tired effort to culminate a beautiful but grueling journey, the marathon I'd committed my entire day to was over. The event was being taken apart before I crossed the finish.

I took a left onto the track inside the stadium. The last few yards of the race stretched along one length of the track. I could see the finish line now.

Bill was there already, shouting encouragements, calling my name. He was the only one. I was surprised at the barrenness of the scene. I had expected at least as many people as had been standing around at the finish line in Mudgee, where there had been only thirty-one runners. But there was almost no one. Even the awards ceremony was over; Dean Karnazes had left for home, and the recovery food was almost gone. Disappointed, I kept my head down and plugged forward. I realized only because of their absence that I had envisioned shouts and cheers. Instead there was just Bill and his camera, yelling all the louder, as if to compensate for the otherwise silent stadium.

As I crossed the finish line, the clock read 5:31. Someone handed me a medal and then walked away. I was nothing but a nuisance to these long-suffering volunteers. I imagined they were irritated by my slowness, by my very presence. I suspected they couldn't understand why anyone as inept at long-distance running as I was would bother to run marathons. I felt, as I had at other times in my life, out of place and unwelcome.

Then Stuart and Mel's faces flashed through my mind. Stuart, who had been running only a little ahead of me, who ran as a way to sort out his moral dilemmas; and Mel, who was still out there on the route, rejoicing in every step he was able to take. They were troublemakers, too. They kept the volunteers late and took up their time, just like I did. They didn't depend on a cheering squad to make their races meaningful. Neither would I.

As Bill was thrusting one of the last of the bananas into my hand, and as I walked toward a small gazebo where I planned to stretch, I realized that I had my own internal locus of celebration. With or without a crowd, I was a part of an exclusive group of people who ran to celebrate each moment in life. No one needed to give me permission to celebrate myself! For that matter, no one needs to give any of us permission to celebrate life: the poems we write, the classes we ace, the songs we sing, the cakes we bake, the work we do, or the races we run. Even Bill, who was for me that day an angel of grace and nourishment, couldn't grant me permission to celebrate myself. I had to reach down into my divine Inner Wisdom and locate my celebration within my own story, in my own internal stadium. And then Bill and my friends and family could bear witness if they wanted to, rather than have the pressure of being the source of my self-love.

Abruptly, I turned around and headed back toward the finish line and the volunteers I'd thought were irritated with me.

"Where are you going?" Bill called.

"I'm waiting for someone," I said over my shoulder. He followed, curious.

We reached the table where the few remaining medals waited for the final stragglers. We hung out until Mel came over the line, and I cheered him through the chute with genuine enthusiasm.

ON THE WAY HOME, I made Bill stop for a large order of french fries. The salt and grease tasted heavenly. I cranked up the heat in the car and tipped my seat back, totally relaxing my tired body. As I licked the salt from my fingers, my mind wandered back to a portion of my conversation with Mel. He said that the year he retired, he'd run twenty marathons. Again, I wondered why.

I don't think anyone can explain entirely why marathon running is so alluring. Actually, where any taxing, limit-testing activity is concerned, it is difficult to say what makes a person compelled to participate, sometimes at her own peril, often repeatedly. Here I was, sitting in the car after being on my feet all day long, exhausted and very, very tender and sore. And what was I thinking about? My next marathon. And where it would be. And how I would change my training. And what my goals would be. *Goals?* I said to myself. I'd never had goals other than finishing. *What sort of goals* could *I have?*

My thoughts were definitely slowed down, due to my physical state. I must have been engaging in some kind of exalted state of self-glorification, feeling like a superhero. I couldn't have walked to the end of the driveway to get the mail, and only a while ago I'd contemplated giving up on my dream to run the continents. I'd nearly decided I wasn't even cut out to be a runner. But now I was imagining myself at the starting line of another marathon. With goals!

So, with my mouth full of fries, I said to Bill, "So where's the next one?"

"You wanna talk about the next one?" he asked, eyebrows raised.

"Mm-hmm."

"Well, for me it's Boston." We were flying out of Seattle in just a couple of days for the Boston Marathon. I was excited to switch roles and be Bill's cheering crew, but I wanted to talk about *my* next race.

"What about for me? What should I run? What's a good one this summer?"

"Really? You really want to talk about this right now? Don't you want to shower first?"

"No. Really. I was thinking I need to step it up a little bit. I've turned a corner. I wanna keep going," I said.

"You didn't look like you'd turned a corner at mile twenty," Bill said.

I stared at him until he turned his eyes from the road momentarily to meet my gaze, and then I opened my mouth wide so he could see my half-eaten fries. I was playful again. I'd regained the giddy feeling I'd lost between miles seventeen and eighteen.

"Gross," he said, turning back to the road. "Okay," he conceded. I watched him as his mind worked. I knew he was thinking about the local and international race schedules for the summer. There were a few websites we frequented with lists of marathons and links to their sites. I'd learned that some runners had the mind to memorize these lists. Bill was one such runner.

"Can we fit in another continent during your vacation this summer?" I asked more specifically.

He was still thinking. Then he smiled. "How about Panama?"

I mulled this over. Panama wasn't really another continent. I couldn't technically count it as one of the seven. Still, it was a place I'd always wanted to visit. And it was tropical; we could get some time on the beach either before or after the race. That sounded wonderful on a chilly day like this. "Why not!" I said.

And with those carefree words, I put myself into a new phase of the quest, one that would fast-track us around the world between August 2008 and March 2010. One that would strengthen the solid foundation for my life I'd been building over the past few years. Within the next few months, Bill and I would sit down and assess our finances, commitments, and vacation time and plan out our around-the-world expedition to conquer the remaining continents.

panama city:
blood, sweat, AND tears
AUGUST 2008

"In and out the tides go, carrying us even while we swim."

—JOAN GOULD, *Spinning Straw into Gold*

"When I first started running, I was so embarrassed I'd walk when cars passed me. I'd pretend I was looking at the flowers."

—JOAN BENOIT SAMUELSON, marathoner

7

That summer, in preparation for the race in Panama (and for all the training and traveling that would come after), I ran with vigor previously unknown. Part of it was that the cold winter was finally over. Winters are always hard for me. The dark cloud cover makes me feel like I live in a small, enclosed box. The advent of summer this time around carried with it more than the usual relief. My body was changing, getting stronger. My muscles longed to be exercised, and my mileage increased. I felt restless if I skipped a day on the trails. I felt myself running straighter, more erect, more confident, faster, and, importantly, with fewer layers of clothing. Something in me had finally clicked into place, and with less clothing weighing me down, it was as if I were stripping off the last remnants of the shame that I'd lived with all my life about being in a female body.

The church's imperative was that women be modest. A woman's body was considered an object that would produce uncontrollable lust in a man. Since lust was a sin, it was a man's job not to look at women's bodies, but it was also a woman's job not to invite them to look. I was taught to hide my curves the best I could (while still dressing in a "feminine" way, because, after all, it was important to remain true to traditional gender roles).

Besides the guidelines from the church, I'd grown up shy about my body for other reasons. There was the obvious obsession, enforced by culture and the media, with women's bodies and pressure to look a certain way, but I was also the only girl among my siblings. What's more, just as I was beginning to develop breasts (early—I needed my first bra in the fourth grade), my mom's new husband moved into our house. When my dad had lived with us, we had walked around in our pajamas and underwear. But when my stepfather moved in, my mother made it clear to me that I was to cover up at all times. I could only intuit that the reason was my growing breasts, and that there was now something embarrassing or shameful about me.

In high school, as puberty completed its process, I gained weight. My breasts became enormous and even more humiliating. Pictures of me from that period suggest a cheerful teenager (voted "friendliest and sunniest smile" by my senior class), generally donning too-tight jeans and oversize sweatshirts that hung unflatteringly over my bosom, covering me from my neck to bottom. The effect was that I looked big and round; I wished to be rail thin and was utterly self-conscious that I wasn't. The smile in those pictures is a disguise, concealing the shame and mortification of a girl working hard to ignore the distinct femaleness of her body and her emerging sexuality.

In the intervening years, I continued to cover myself and be ashamed of my bulges. Even as recently as that first round of training for Mudgee, my Inner Bitch suggested that people were laughing at me as I ran by, all curves and bounce.

But this summer, after my third marathon and in preparation for Panama, I ran around Bellingham in short shorts and a tight-fitting camisole— aware of my cellulite, flabby stomach, and cleavage, yes, but no longer embarrassed by my body's particulars.

Though this newfound freedom manifested that summer, it did not suddenly pop up one day; it had been fermenting for a good many years. The seeds of it started when I began truly absorbing that the rules and norms about gender I'd lived my life by were not fixed—not *real*. I was in grad school at the time, taking classes that were opening my eyes to the fact that gender norms were socially constructed, made of stories we'd heard, examples we'd seen, and judgments we'd endured. Women's bodies were not *really* shameful. Men were not *really* the heads of women. Men's power and women's submission were not the *natural* order of things. They were just stories (albeit very influential stories with *very real* effects).

Learning to think of gender consciously was an onerous process, but a liberating one. My body was one of the final plots in my old story that I had to change. Somewhere along the line, along with my personal embarrassment and the understanding that God would always put a man in charge of me, I'd developed a belief that to be athletic was "unladylike." In my teen years, when I was determined to preserve my virginity, I'd been told that hard exercise could break my hymen, thus technically rendering me a nonvirgin. Messages like this—combined with the fact that not a single female in my family exercised and that many men I knew attributed any lack of athleticism, male or female, to the female gender ("You hit/swing/throw/catch like a girl!")—convinced me that I needn't bother with athletics.

RUNNING WAS A RADICAL change in this point of view. Training for and running the last two marathons took away the stigma of being unladylike. Most assuredly, running was an undignified activity. Between sweat, salt, chafing, the constant need to blow your nose onto the trail, and the stickiness of energy gel and sports drinks, running was gooey, messy business. There was nothing demure about it. Instead, especially this year, as the weather changed and my whole body began to see the light of day, my running seemed to be proof to me that to be a woman was (or at least could be) about being a liberated person, about really letting go and accepting my earthy proclivities, however gelatinous and gummy.

I was finally accepting facts that should be evident to all of us: Female bodies have boobs. I had boobs. Our bodies have fat. I had fat. Bodies come with their own abilities and limitations. And they are each beautiful in varying ways. They are not objects for men to leer at; they are containers for the inhabitants to use as they see fit. I was beginning to understand that my body was a vessel, rather than an object. It was not my responsibility to manipulate how others (men or women, because, let's face it, we feel equally judged by both) saw me. My job was to accept and love and thank this body for all it had given me.

That summer, I started to love my body. I was learning to listen to it. My thighs were saying, *Let me see the sun.* My breasts were saying, *We've been hiding long enough.* And my belly was saying, *Let me jiggle unrestrained.*

It's a good thing, too, that I had the seeds of this new relationship with my body tucked away in my heart as Bill and I made our way to Panama City in August for the Panama City International Marathon. I was about to be tested.

We'd chosen this race as the first of four we'd complete in a year's time. With the vacation time and money we had saved, we could pull off four international trips in one year if we scheduled carefully, ate frugally, and stayed at youth hostels instead of hotels. We were calling it the Year of the Marathon, and Panama was the kickoff race. In preparation for these races, I'd decided to close down my practice in Seattle altogether and move it exclusively to my Bellingham office. I also had an IUD put in. I didn't want to trust that I would remember to take my daily birth control pill with four international trips and four different time zones on the docket that year.

One other thing I did was give myself a time goal for the race. I wanted to complete the Panama City Marathon in fewer than five hours. Based on my training runs, this was a genuine possibility, and though I didn't feel any pressure to pull it off, I was eager to put myself to the test.

WE FLEW INTO PANAMA City a few days before the marathon, to get oriented and adapt to the humidity. You can't see Panama without falling in love. Panama City vibrates with color and activity—on the streets, in the restaurants, everywhere you look. There are cars and pedestrians and old crumbling brick buildings next to new shiny ones. There is honking and the growling of bus engines. The smells of exhaust and delicious seafood dishes being prepared in open-air restaurants mingle together with every inhalation. A few miles out of town, the canal is truly a man-made wonder surrounded by the natural beauty of mountains and lakes and sea. Away from civilization, tropical islands and beaches and forests make you forget urban life even exists.

August is Panama's "green season," and in our first three days there we witnessed several thunderous storms. This was my first time in a tropical country during rainy season. As a western Washingtonian, I was no stranger to rain, for sure, but never had I seen water come down from the sky in streams, rather than drops. As if millions of bathtub faucets in the sky had been turned on all at once, each day, for about an hour in the early afternoon, the heavens drained onto the earth.

Those days, during the storms, Bill and I sat in the breakfast room of our yellow youth hostel and watched the warm rain pour out of the gutters, down a gully, and onto the streets. We watched locals duck into buildings and under awnings and wait patiently for the rain to stop before they stepped out into the large, newly formed pools of water.

By race day—Sunday, August 10—we were under no delusions about what kind of climatic conditions we were likely to be running in. The temperature would be in the eighties, the humidity would be at 80 percent, and we were going to get rained on.

Taking these factors into consideration, the marathon organizers had the race starting at 5:00 AM, the coolest and driest part of the day. On race morning, we took a taxi from our hostel through the eerily quiet city and arrived at the race center at 4:30 AM. A large parking area the size of a football field near Panama City's modern mall had been blocked off for the runners. Temporary tents and lights had been erected, and a small stage was set up in the center of the arena. We wandered among the other runners, wondering where the starting line would be. We couldn't see any markings or chutes. At 4:40, an emcee called everyone to the stage to listen to a live band provide a rendition of the Panamanian national anthem.

I looked around at our fellow runners standing in this large huddle, waiting for the race to start. We were among nearly four hundred participants total (156 in the full marathon). At registration we'd discovered that fewer than twenty of us were from non-Spanish-speaking nations. There were five other Americans somewhere in this crowd. I spotted two of them, a pair of women in their late twenties, standing nearby, waiting patiently for the anthem to finish.

After the band landed its last note, Bill and I introduced ourselves. We made small talk for a while—where we came from, where we were staying, how long we were staying—but what I really wanted to know was what times they were aiming for, so I cut to the chase.

"What are you expecting your time to be?" I asked.

"Four-thirty," one of the women said.

"Or four-forty-five," the other amended. "You?"

"Five," I said with assurance. I was feeling more secure than I had at the start of my other three marathons. It wasn't that the usual doubt was totally absent, but I knew my body better, and I knew a little about how to manage the voices in my head and how to stay in the present moment. I was more sure than not that I could finish the race, and hopeful that I could do it in fewer than five hours, if only barely.

As we continued chatting, mostly about training, an announcement came over the loud speaker, though none of us understood a single word of it. It was followed by a sudden rustling and lots of commotion. The crowd stirred and began moving in unison away from the stage. I caught Bill's eye and noticed the women look at each other with startled expressions. "What's going on?" one of them inquired.

"Is it starting?" I asked. I hadn't heard a gun or a horn. My watch read 4:45. We had fifteen more minutes.

After missing the start of the race in Prague five years ago, Bill and I were both vigilant about start times. We followed the group anxiously around a corner and onto a street that had been blocked to traffic, and realized that the instructions we'd heard but not understood had directed the crowd to the starting line we'd been unable to spot when we first arrived. A banner was stretched across a busy road in front of the local mall. Relieved, we laughed. We'd lost our American compatriots in the rush, so Bill and I stretched for a few minutes together before he bid me farewell and moved toward the front of the group.

Moments later, I heard the gunshot and we all initiated our respective journeys.

Now I was alone among the mass of runners. I closed my eyes and shut out the sounds of nearby voices and distant traffic. I called deep inside to the

Wise part of me. *Here we go again*, I said. *Teach me what I need to learn, and may I have a strong race.* I felt my Inner Wisdom nod her assent. I opened my eyes.

I jogged along and found my pace. Later, the sun would beat down hard on us, but for now it was still dark and I was content to listen to the sound of other runners' breath and footsteps. The collective group was like a pulsing presence reminding me I was a part of something bigger than myself. As we rounded a bend, I saw TV cameras following some of the runners. We'd heard the race would be broadcast on Panamanian national television.

The first many miles took us out toward Old Panama and its graveyard of stone ruins, buildings left decimated by pirates who invaded Panama City in the 1600s. Then we jogged by the shoreline along Avenida Balboa, which runs along the Bay of Panama. As I looked out over the dark space that would show itself to be water when the sun came up, I felt the wind coming off the ocean tickling my bare shoulders. The air was a perfect temperature and I gave way to my newfound sense of love for my body. The moon shone down on my hands, pumping in rhythm in front of my torso. I wanted to close my eyes in the peace of it all and lift my arms to the sky. I was exultant as I quietly asked my body to do something extraordinary for me today and thanked it for cooperating so far.

When you undertake a daunting task, an adventure bigger than you ever thought you'd take on, you don't get to know what challenges the universe will present to you along the way. You can decide where you will go and how much money you'll spend and what your activities will be, but there will always be something unexpected, a hurdle of sorts, that offers you an opportunity to learn something about yourself if you take it in stride. I knew this as I gloried in the first few miles of this run. I'd faced plenty of hurdles in this quest so far: I'd missed starting times; I'd been lost in forests; I'd been in relationship-altering arguments during races. So I knew as I began what I hoped would be my first five-hour marathon that anything could happen. That's why I had asked my Inner Wisdom to be available. Now, all I had to do was watch for the hurdle and figure out how to jump over it when I saw it there in my way.

I realized quickly that losing my way on the course, as we had in Prague and in Mudgee, would not be one of my hurdles this day. The route was lined with volunteers, all in uniforms of various colors. Some were military personnel, complete with badges and guns; others were local police or Boy and Girl Scouts. And there was a whole slew of young men with shaved heads and green T-shirts lined up every few hundred meters, passing out sealed bags of sterilized water to keep the runners hydrated in the heat.

I also realized, however, that there were no mile or kilometer markers on the course. As I contemplated what it would be like to go the whole race with no indication of my distance traveled, I started to worry. Given my goal of five hours, I counted heavily on mile or kilometer markers to help me monitor my progress. It was a psychological crutch I was going to have to do without. I had only a simple stopwatch and estimates in my head about where I needed to be at twenty-one kilometers (halfway), thirty, and finally forty-two. I hoped my pace would remain as consistent as it had been throughout the summer.

Sometime into the first five miles, while it was still dark outside, I hooked up with a guy named Benjamin. Benjamin looked to be about forty-five and was running at almost exactly my pace. I had to push only a little to keep up with him. He was slightly taller than I and carried a spare tire around his middle. He was a genial companion. Between us, we had about a dozen words in common. We pantomimed what we could (while jogging side by side). Benjamin spoke to me in Spanish, and I used English words, focusing on ones that had Latin roots, in an attempt to assimilate Spanish. Somehow we managed. This was his second marathon. His first had been this same race the year before; he'd finished it in five hours and fifty minutes but was hoping to complete it this year in under five hours. I told him this was my goal, too, and since Benjamin knew the course, he was able to tell me when we had reached the halfway mark. "*Media*," he said. I looked at my watch. It read 2:24. We had a shot at our five hours.

Even if I slowed a little in the second half, I could make it! I was surprised at how this knowledge elated me. Having never been competitive when it came to running, not even against myself, I couldn't have anticipated this feeling, this desire, to complete this race within a predetermined period of time. I became even more poised in my running posture now, and increasingly self-assured as we continued along the course. I was thankful to have found Benjamin.

Within another couple of miles (I guessed), just as we were entering Costa del Este, one of Panama City's gorgeous, expensive gated communities, Benjamin left me. He dropped his pace and dropped out of my sight. Benjamin's friend, who had been following him in a car with support, spotted me on the road and shouted, *"Mi amigo?"* I shrugged and pointed behind me, apologetic. I was sorry to have lost him, as much for his loss of time as for my loss of companionship.

By now, the sun was high in the sky and it was hot. I passed Bill at an out-and-back impasse. He had his shirt off and carried it in his hand. I shouted to him, "How are you?" Even from a distance, I could see he was beleaguered.

"It's hot!" he shouted back.

I was warm, too, but the humidity in the air came into my lungs and filled me with energy. I was like a helium balloon floating high. I didn't have it in me to complain about being too warm when I spent so much of my life cold.

The route wound out onto a peninsula called Amador. Here I could see the water on either side of me and observe the ships waiting patiently in line to cross through the locks of the Panama Canal. I estimated by my time that I must be about seventeen miles into the race. I felt tired but strong, which was probably why I didn't see the big hurdle coming at me. In hindsight, I'm grateful I didn't notice what was happening any sooner than I did. Some trials, if they must come, are better as a surprise.

I began to feel distinct drops of something wet on my legs—sweat, I thought. Not rain, I hoped. The rains had been coming later in the days and the sky was still clear, but then again, storms here moved in very suddenly. I perused the panorama. There wasn't a single cloud in the vicinity.

I looked down at my thighs and was horrified to see that the entirety of my upper legs, almost down to my knees, was covered in blood, front and back. Long streaks of coagulated, blotchy blood streamed down from my crotch.

There was a thick, dried red line of it just below where my shorts stopped above my knees. This scabby ring was stopping the blood from flowing farther down my legs.

Omigod, omigod, omigod, I thought. Dread surged up from my stomach to my throat. A brief wave of nausea came and went, and I felt my face go red. I looked around at the volunteers. It was clear people were staring at me and registering what was going on. I was apparently the only one perplexed about the situation. I was having my period—that much I knew, of course. I'd started the day before and was prepared for my cycle as I knew it, which generally involved a tampon change every six hours or so. So what the hell was happening? Was I hemorrhaging? I felt fine, outside of my total mortification. It couldn't be dangerous if there was no discomfort, I hoped.

Then it occurred to me—something the doctor had told me when she had inserted my IUD: "Your flow will be heavier than usual."

Lady, that was the understatement of a lifetime, I thought, as I grabbed a packet of water from a green-shirted young man and dared him with my eyes to look at my legs. This wasn't a heavy period; this was a gush.

I reached around to the running pack on my backside and unzipped the pouch. I had come prepared for a change, but I had only one extra tampon. I pulled it out of the pouch and saw with dismay that the humidity and my own sweat had expanded it. It was wide and wet, already used up, and probably impossible to insert. Anyhow, there was not a port-o-potty, not a phone booth, not a palm tree to hide behind, anywhere within eyeshot. What was I supposed to do?

What the hell *do* you do when the body you've so recently fallen in love with rebels and behaves so badly in public? I had just been high on feeling content—so gratified, finally, at embracing womanhood, so relieved to finally lay down the shame and apology I'd carried around at being born a girl. And now this.

It felt like a slap in the face. It is every girl's deepest secret that she bleeds. It is her nightmare that she will be found out. We know that we are never, never supposed to bleed in front of others, never supposed to subject anyone (especially the men) in our lives to the pungent smells, oscillating moods, and crimson stream of womanhood. It is the focus of a very successful industry to block the blood, to catch it or neutralize the scent of it. Right then, I could do none of these things. In order not to bleed in public that day, I would have to quit the race and go back to my hostel right now. I couldn't bear that possibility. Not now, when the doubts I'd had about myself as a runner were really quieting down. Not now, when I had set my first time goal ever.

Although I had worked hard at stripping off the narratives of femininity that had been laden with embarrassment and awkwardness, in this moment the old stories shouted at me from within my sinews like a bad body memory. I would have done anything to go back in hiding behind my big, baggy, body-covering clothes, but instead I found myself an unwitting rebel against all the cultural rules about keeping the secret of "the period." It was one thing to freely show off one's cleavage or cottage cheese thighs, but not one's monthly *blood*, for crying out loud.

What should I do? I had to think.

I wasn't in any pain. No cramps, no backache—no indication there was anything different in my body other than these red racing stripes. I dumped the contents of the water packet I held in my hand onto my legs, one after the other, and tried to rub off the blood. The only thing this accomplished was spreading it around, getting it all over my hands and washing away the dried ring that was preventing the rivulets from running all the way down to my socks. Now I had streaks spanning vulva to ankle on each leg.

I kept looking around at the leering volunteers on the course and even threw a glance over my shoulder to see how closely other runners were following me and if they could see what was going on. When I saw there was no one within a couple of hundred yards, I slowed to a walk and crossed the road, officially taking myself off the Amador peninsula. A taxi driver honked at me, wanting me to get a move on and out of his way. I saw his expression as he looked me up and down, judging, mocking. He smiled and winked at me suggestively, running his tongue along his lips. As we locked eyes, he honked again. I studied his face, so superior and contemptuous. In the energy of the exchange between us, my faithful protector, the Bitch, spoke up loudly and full of indignant pride.

Screw you, asshole! she said to the taxi driver. *I'm in the middle of a marathon!* To me she said, *Pull yourself together. What are you, afraid of your own body? Move it. Pick up the pace. We have a goal here!*

"Right!" I said out loud. She'd brought me to my senses. What was I thinking? I'd come here for a marathon. Fact: I was a woman. Fact: Women bleed. Fact: I was a bleeding woman running a marathon. Double fact: I needed to get a move on.

Sticky, sweaty, salty, and bloody, I picked up my pace and got back on the course (but not before making the taxi driver wait until I was good and ready). As had happened in Mudgee, I allowed the Bitch to take over for a while. I needed her. I didn't know if, after accepting and loving my body that summer, my current situation was a cruel joke or if God just wanted to be sure that I had fully accepted the body She'd given me. In any case, the Bitch had it under control now.

I stopped a few more times over the next hour to wipe away any trickles that irritated or distracted me, but the Bitch wouldn't let me clean my legs out of embarrassment anymore. When I encountered volunteers or bystanders, the Bitch just smiled at them, as if running with a gush were just as normal as wearing a hat in the cold weather. She insisted I get my wits about me and find my pride. It wasn't easy, but I'd been contemplating the plight of being a woman since I'd first found those verses about submission in the Bible when I was a young teen. Here was my test. I dug deep for Inner Wisdom, and she agreed with the Bitch: *Keep running. Hold your head high.* It was funny how often those two were simpatico nowadays.

At four hours in, I'd made it to the final turnaround point and began heading back into the city's mall district. I was gaining momentum, feeling less self-conscious, when a man in a yellow raincoat rode up next to me on a bicycle. He was a volunteer who had been riding up and down the course, offering support to runners. I'd seen him pass by once before. He came straight up to me and rode alongside me for a moment.

"*Está bien?*" he asked. I wasn't about to answer him in English. I didn't want the Bitch to unleash a tirade on an unsuspecting man (I hoped she didn't speak Spanish), but I also didn't know what he wanted. I expected judgment. I had a prejudice myself: that this man would not honor a woman's cycle. That almost any man would be afraid of my blood and would insist I stop running, instead of letting me decide what my body needed. I thought of the taxi driver. I suspected the race organizers would not want to televise a bleeding woman coming over the finish line. I gave him the cold shoulder.

"*Sí*," I answered, "*bien!*" I was fine, thank you. Go away.

"Really?" he switched to English now and surprised me. "Do you need some support? What can I get you?"

I looked at the man now. His face was kind as he crinkled his concerned brow. I heard the Bitch say, *You take this one. He's safe.*

"A towel would be nice," I finally said, thinking that I would appreciate being able to wipe away the stickiness now and again. He kept his eyes on my face and never let them even sneak a peek at my legs. Through the humid air between us, he communicated respect and concern and not a speck of derision.

"Let me see what I can do." And with a nod, he rode away.

So much for my prejudice. I felt a pang of guilt for my small-mindedness.

I continued for a few more minutes. I was now doubling back on the portion of the course where Bill and I had passed each other earlier. I remembered how, after he had complained that he was hot, he'd shouted at me, saying, "I love you. Be careful." At least there hadn't been any danger on the course, I mused. I was embarrassed, but I was safe and as comfortable as could be expected. Just as I was counting these blessings, there was a sudden flash of light all around me, followed by an angry growl reverberating in the sky overhead, and a waterfall came down from the heavens. Pouring like a bucket dumping directly, specifically, over *my* head, sheets and sheets of water came down. The rain covered my shoulders, my arms, my back, and, of course, my legs. It cooled me down. It washed away my sweat—and my blood.

It was the oddest thing, but I was actually sad to see the red stripes rinsed away. In the last hour and a half, those streams had taken on important meaning. They were my warrior markings. They were visible proof that I had stepped over the hurdle of shame I'd long carried in my female body. I was becoming a whole woman. As the rain bathed my body of the last of its streaks and smudges, it also erased the evidence of my self-love, my ability to fully accept all that I was, no matter how unseemly some of me might be to anyone else.

The other thing the rain did was diminish my vision. The water coming into my eyes caused one of my contacts to dislodge. I had to run now with one eye closed as the heavily potholed streets filled with water in pools that came up to the middle of my shins. With one eye, I tried to negotiate around the deep divots in the road now filled with rainwater. The traffic was thickening now, too, as it was later in the race and the barricades had been removed to allow cars onto the busy Panamanian streets. I was coming into the more urban section of the route and needed to stay alert, lest I be pummeled by a vehicle coming from behind. I had a bad track record with cars while I was running, and Bill wasn't here to yank me out of harm's way. It was a bad time in my life to be half-blind.

The rain came and came and came. My shoes soaked through. For twenty minutes it poured.

I thought the man on the bicycle must have given up on me and taken shelter somewhere. I didn't blame him. You couldn't ride a bicycle in a flash flood. But at the same time, I knew I'd made a connection with him, and trusted my instinct that he and I understood each other. There are times when you meet strangers, and within a few moments you've looked into their soul and seen who they are. I had connected with this man and knew he meant to come back. The only thing I didn't know was if he could ride on these streets.

Just as I was contemplating this, he rode up, drenched, his yellow raincoat dripping. I held up my hands as if to say, *A lot of good a towel will do me now, huh?*

He was not one to take the easy answer, however. He handed me a package wrapped in a plastic bag and stood looking me square in my one good eye, waiting. I opened the bag quickly and saw what he had done. He had gone to a convenience store and purchased me some thick, wide maxi-pads with wings.

I could slip one of these babies into my running shorts without even exposing myself. I breathed out a gasp of relief and felt tears coming to my eyes. I wanted to hug him.

"You can take care of yourself in there," he said, pointing to a building with water coming off its roof, creating solid panes of glassless windows.

I smiled at him. *"Muchas, muchas gracias, señor!"* Who was this yellow-coated man? A stranger, a gift offered to me to challenge my own judgments of others and myself? Was he real, or was he an angel?

He smiled back. "Finish your race. I'll find you at the end," he said. Then he winked at me and rode away. I slipped into the abandoned building he'd indicated, pulled out my old tampon, and slipped a pad into my shorts. The sticky strip wouldn't hold, because of how wet my clothes were, but I figured I'd keep it in place with my hand if I had to.

The thunderstorm finally ceased. All that remained were the puddles in the road and the droplets of water winding their way down my face from my hairline. I'd been running for four hours and twenty minutes. Up ahead of me I saw the two American women who had told me they thought they would be finishing in 4:45. Because of the absence of mile markers, I didn't know how far I had gone, but if these women were on pace, I was doing better than I could have hoped, given all my stopping for washing and dealing with my blood. Could I be that close to the end? Would I make five hours despite my setbacks? I tried to piece together a question in Spanish to ask a volunteer or fan how far I had to go: *"Quantos kilometers à el finish line?"*

I was now on the main drag in Panama City that ran along the waterfront. I asked my question to some fans at the next bend. *"Tres!"* they said, holding up three fingers.

"Really?" I asked, and the fans nodded. Three kilometers? That would be 1.86 miles. It seemed too good to be true. I had scarcely dared to hope for this. After the trials my body and the weather had presented, I was still within reaching my goal. I became completely psyched up by the information. The route was flat at this point. I set my psychological GPS on 1.86 miles and caught a second wind. I was nearly finished! I kept a careful eye on my stopwatch. Even at my slowest pace, I could be coming into the race center in no more than twenty-four minutes. Adrenaline raced through my body as I celebrated. *Almost done! Almost done!* I said to myself.

Ten, twenty, thirty, and thirty-five minutes went by, however, and I still could not see the finish line. A volunteer handing me more water said, "*Solamente tres kilometres!*" I didn't speak Spanish, but I understood this.

"Great," I said, my vigor instantly depleted by the news. Three more? I felt my heart ache, and tears tingled in my eyes for the second time that day. This information, if it was correct (I didn't know what to believe anymore), was my last major hurdle in this race. I had to give over to the fact that I really had no idea how far I had to go. I was tired. My day had been emotionally and physically taxing. My feet were wet. It could be twenty more miles, for all I knew or had energy for. It became clear to me now, four hours and fifty-five minutes into the race, that I would not finish a five-hour marathon. I blinked hard to squeeze my tears away.

I wouldn't make my mark. *Shit,* I heard the Bitch say. *Who decided it was unimportant to mark this course, anyhow?*

I would be close, but there wasn't any way for me to run almost two miles in less than five minutes. My second wind sailed away without me. I'd finish the race, but not well. I might as well walk it in.

Wait just one minute, I heard another voice. Wisdom? I'd thought she had receded to the back of my consciousness once my bleeding episode had been taken care of, but she was right here, ready to remind me of something deeper than I could see in my current state of mind.

You won't come in under five hours. But guess what? There's still a chance for you to do your imperfect best. Give it a try!

Yes. Of course. She was right. We don't always get to meet our marks, sometimes because of choices we make and sometimes because of things beyond our control. Does it have to mean failure? Do things have to line up with all of our original dreams or expectations in order to be celebrated? *Hell no,* I could hear the Bitch chime in. After all I had been through in the past five hours, I could not allow myself to cross that finish line as a failure.

"Okay!" I said aloud. I was exhausted but not injured, discouraged but unrelenting. I would change my expectations to fit my reality and keep running. For a lot of people, running is a competition with others or with themselves, but running had never been about speed for me. Each race had been about living into life's moments fully, learning what the metaphors of "long run" and "holding the course" had to teach me. In these last few years of running, I had always set my goals as internal benchmarks, like patience for my process or taking in beauty or learning to develop an internal locus of celebration when no one was there to cheer for me at the end. Why would I want to rush these learnings?

I resolved to shake off my disappointment and focus my determination on the energy to finish. I had to change my definition of success to include more than meeting an external goal. The external is only one piece of reality; a much bigger and more important reality is how we think of ourselves. I had to finish strong in my heart and be proud of myself.

I refused to look at my watch again. Instead I did what I knew was best to do in tough moments: I thought back to that first thirty-six-minute run around the lake that had started this whole running thing. And I breathed. *In. In. Out. Out. That's it.* I breathed and ran and tried to look ahead for that first moment when the finish line would come into view. And when it did, so did Bill (who had finished more than an hour earlier). He sat waiting with the camera and a tired smile.

Behind Bill was the finish banner and the time clock. There were a few remaining onlookers applauding as I approached. I could see tents set up to provide shade. I could hear celebratory music coming from behind the finish line. I pushed through the finish chute, crossing the line at 5:11:55 (still my personal record, up to that point). I celebrated with a hoot and a final exhalation, slowing to a walk and letting my shoulders, legs, and heart finally relax. I let someone place a medal around my neck and hand me a bottle of cold water. As Bill caught up to me and praised my accomplishment, I was grateful to be done and proud of all my parts for pushing me through. He said I looked strong and steady.

I was.

I looked down at my hands. There was still blood under my fingernails. In one hand I held the bottle of water, and in the other I held the little plastic bag with the remaining maxi-pads.

"What's that?" Bill asked.

"Sanitary napkins," I said. "Given to me by an angel. Someone I need to try to find. Walk with me?"

"Sure," he said. He had a quizzical look on his face, but he'd be patient until I could tell him the whole story.

I paced slowly around the parking lot that had been commandeered as the recovery area. At first I couldn't find him, but then there he was: my yellow-jacketed man. He was real! Bill watched in wonder as I limped up to this stranger, threw my arms around him, and planted a kiss on his cheek.

The man in the yellow jacket embraced me and said in my ear, "You finished!"

I nodded as he held me at arm's length and looked at me in that same way he'd held my gaze out on the course. He winked at me, squeezed my arms, and walked away.

ON THE TAXI RIDE back to the hostel, I told Bill about my race and he told me about his. He'd had a tough go, too. The heat had taken its toll on him early and slowed him down by at least a half an hour. When he'd been caught in the rain, he'd had to slow to a walk just to see where he should put his feet, so as not to turn an ankle in a pothole. He'd come in at 4:08, spent and ready to collapse (and possibly sick—within three days, he would be bed-bound with a fever and nausea that would last most of the rest of our stay in Panama).

I've never given birth, but I've heard that some women feel powerful after their babies are born, after they have engaged every physical and mental resource beyond what they think they are capable of, until they have pushed out a crying, wet, messy, blessed infant. Well, there was no literal baby at the end of my push here in Panama. And though I know I will never experience childbirth, there were new truths being birthed for me with every race I ran. And they were not always delivered easily.

What was alive for me at the end of this race was a great respect for my body. For all the self-love I'd been nurturing in the past few years, I'd held on to some of the shame I'd grown up with. I didn't know before the race that I was pregnant with pride and acceptance for even the basest of my bodily functions, until I had to jump over the hurdles Panama City set in front of me. With a little help from my own cycle, a man on a bike, and a rainstorm, I got more than a medal that day. I threw off all apologies for being born female and received my reward: success as defined by me alone. And I did it all while running like a girl.

asia:
THE tateyama triumph

JANUARY 2009

"Be at least as interested in what goes on inside you as what
happens outside. If you get the inside right, the outside will fall
into place."

—ECKHART TOLLE, *The Power of Now*

"Running is a big question mark that's there each and every day.
It asks you, 'Are you going to be a wimp or are you going to be
strong today?'"

—PETER MAHER, Canadian marathon runner

8

We never questioned where we would run our Asian marathon. While we'd toyed with the idea of going to Thailand because some of our friends were taking a trip to Bangkok, fantasized about the Great Wall Marathon, and even looked at a race in Mongolia, we always knew we would end up running in Japan. It had to be Japan. Bill and I had met in the language program he still worked for, which catered to Japanese exchange students. We had both kept many personal relationships with Japanese friends we'd made over the years, and we had honeymooned in Japan, where we'd climbed Mount Fuji (and then named our dog after her so we would always have the majestic mountain with us).

As we got ready for our 2009 trip to Japan, I reflected back on our honeymoon in 2005. That climb to the top of Fuji had solidified the bond between Bill and me. It was among the first of many intense, overwhelming physical challenges we would do together, and yet, like our running, we experienced it in deeply personal and separate ways. In retrospect, I often think of it as the unconscious beginning of my need for a vision quest.

There is a concept in the Buddhist-Shinto tradition called the *nyubu*. It bears some resemblance to the Native American vision quest in that it is a solo pilgrimage into the wilderness. In the case of the *nyubu*, the pilgrim treks into the mountains specifically for the purpose of renewing or refashioning her relationship with the gods. Some who take this journey stop at sacred sites to worship at various shrines and experience spiritual insights as they wander into the hills. For many Japanese, climbing Mount

Fuji is just such a sacred pilgrimage, one that almost every Japanese person believes she should make once in her life.

When Bill and I and one other friend of ours (Bill's colleague Eric, who was in Japan for work-related meetings) embarked on that climb, I experienced the mystical quality of the mountain, but not right away. We arrived at the foot of the trail at midnight with headlamps and backpacks full of additional clothing to put on as we gained elevation. There was apparently a tradition that hikers would try to reach the top by sunrise, but I wasn't convinced this was necessary. From the trailhead, we looked up and saw thousands of little flashlights and headlamps creating squiggling lines along the switchbacks that led to the top of the mountain.

This was the official beginning of my life with Bill, and I hadn't learned yet about the value of owning my own equipment, so I didn't have my own headlamp. As we began our long ascent, it quickly became obvious that Bill's lamp was too weak to light my way. I would have to rely on light from Eric's newer and stronger headlamp. It was a tough night. I was going to have to keep up instead of moving at my own slow pace, which I later came to understand was essential to my peace of mind and sense of autonomy. The trails were steep and twisty, and though Eric took great care to make sure his lamp illuminated my way, there were times when it was scarcely enough for me to pick my way over the big boulders and get up the ledges we encountered.

The night passed very, very slowly. It was grueling physical work for a sleepy body. And in the dark, with my growing misery, a now-familiar question arose: *What the hell am I doing this for?* It certainly wasn't my idea; I'd never liked hiking, much less this hands-and-knees-scrambling type of thing. And anyway, why were we climbing this famous, stately mountain in the dark? I'd seen plenty of sunrises in my lifetime, and I couldn't help thinking about how much better the climb would be if we could actually see our surroundings.

The interminable hours passed, one careful, blind step after another. As I dwelled on why I was doing this un-fun thing on my honeymoon, some glimmers of understanding began to rise from somewhere inside of me. At first I was only observing the facts. For example, I was relying on senses besides my sight. I was listening for the voices of my hiking companions saying things like, "Watch out here" or, "Can you shine your lamp here?" I was feeling for rocks with my hands and shuffling my feet around to find sure footing. This was not my usual mode for moving about the world, and it got me wondering if there was meaning in it somehow beyond the literal events. Could it be that there was a message here for me? That I was going to need to learn to "see" in new ways, especially in this new partnership with Bill? To learn to feel around and be okay with stumbling a little? I'd never found my balance in my first marriage. Could it be that I was at the beginning of a journey where I would finally get better at scrambling in the dark without knowing where I was going, keeping the faith that it would be worth it?

The symbolism started coming fast as we neared the top of the climb and the air got thinner. I couldn't keep up with my thoughts. Could it be that if I kept at this life and my relationship with Bill long enough, if I grew in consciousness, rising higher and higher, sometimes depending on others to shine a light or lend a hand for the steep inclines, little by little I'd get somewhere and eventually the sun would come up? Would my life get clearer?

When we were almost at the top, my thoughts racing, making loose spiritual connections left and right, the decrease in oxygen in the air began to make me light-headed and my stomach started to cramp. Not more than two hundred meters from the summit, the pre-glow of sunrise winked over the horizon and the world around me began to take shape. There was the ragged trail I'd been walking on all night, its reddish-brown soil littered with blond stones of all sizes. There were my climbing buddies with sweat dripping down from the straps of their headlamps. There were my feet under me, just as they were supposed to be. As it became lighter and we continued our climb, I could take only a few steps, and then I would lose my breath and get a sharp ache in my middle area. Every three or four yards, I needed to rest and the others stopped with me. The sun was now poking a few rays above the earth in the distance.

"I won't make it to the top before sunrise," I said, disappointed and sorry I'd slowed Bill and Eric down. Bill especially was unwilling to leave me there and race to the top without me.

"Let's sit right here and watch the sun come up," he said.

We three sat down on a ridge that was chiseled into the mountainside a few feet above the trail near where we were standing. Hundreds of other pilgrims were lined up on the trail ahead of us and behind us. In totally sacred, awe-filled silence, every human being on the mountain faced east and waited. And then, slow but confident, she came into view: the Orange Goddess that gives everything life, our mother and father, the protectress and destroyer. She arose like the drama queen who sweeps into the room to make sure everyone notices her. She rose, I imagined, unsurprised that everyone had stopped to admire her.

And as I sat there holding what little breath I could get in, I thought to myself, *Here is where you find God and Self together, in the enigmatic combination of hard climbing and sitting still.*

I had just gotten myself up a mountain that only a sliver of the population on the planet will ever climb. I was amazing. And when the sun rose, she didn't eclipse my joy; she shined her smile on it and nodded with approval.

NOW, MORE THAN THREE years later, we were on our way back to Japan to take part in another big challenge—a marathon on our fourth continent. I could hardly contain my sense of excitement. I was going to see Fuji-san again, the first place I'd experienced the divine as particularly feminine and personal.

Bill and I drove to Sea-Tac Airport on January 20, 2009—inauguration day for Barack Obama. We listened to our new president's address on the radio. He spoke of recent hardships in our country and highlighted how the United States had a lot of work to do to repair our image in the world. I nodded as I listened. This would be our first international trip since the election.

I'd never been one of those American travelers who'd sewn a Canadian flag onto her backpack to avoid being identified, but I had most definitely wearied of conversations in which people we met in our travels explained how disappointed they were in our government.

As we went through security and then settled into our seats on the plane, I realized that I hoped to experience on this trip the kind of "repair" the president spoke of. In fact, by going to Japan, Bill and I were working on our commitment to continually build bridges between two cultures, Japanese and American, which seemingly have very little in common.

For years we had both separately (and more recently together) invited Japanese friends and students into our homes and shared American culture with them. For me, however, this sharing was always on my terms: my language, my culture, my home, my hospitality. I'd thought of myself as sort of magnanimous, to tell the truth, hosting travelers and sharing my culture with them. But I'd learned a lot already on this little marathon *nyubu* of mine. I'd learned to listen to lost parts of myself, to face fear by staying in the moment, to run at my own pace and to celebrate myself. And I'd learned, perhaps above all else, that the best bits of Inner Wisdom presented themselves when I stopped insisting on my own way and kept my eyes (or even one eye, in the case of the Panama deluge) open for and worked with whatever terms the course actually provided for me.

Right from the beginning on this trip, I wanted to let go of my own expectations and let Japan teach me on her own terms, as she had when we'd climbed Fuji. We'd chosen a race in a Japanese town called Tateyama, located on the southern tip of the Boso Peninsula in Chiba Prefecture, about three hours outside of Tokyo and on the coast of the Tokyo Bay. We discovered this marathon through Bellingham's Sister Cities Association, which we had recently joined. Bellingham had a fifty-year-long sister-city relationship with Tateyama, and Tateyama had a marathon. I loved the idea of building on a relationship that already existed between our towns, moving the concentric circles of influence ever inward toward the center to the most intimate: person to person.

We contacted the Sister Cities Association representative at Tateyama's city hall directly and let him know we were coming. We said we would love to do a "home-stay" for a couple of our days in Tateyama, if possible; it would give us the chance to meet and connect person to person with a Japanese family and to stay in their home, eating together and communicating about our lives and theirs. Neither Bill nor I spoke Japanese, so we would be forced out of our comfort zone and would have to rely on other means of communication besides language, something I'd practiced up on Fuji. I knew I wanted this challenge, wanted to push myself, not only for the sake of my own growth but in service to the idea of breaking down preconceptions and being a positive representative of my country and my town. If there was a family in Tateyama interested in having us, I wanted to stay in their home and experience a genuine swap of perspectives.

From the very beginning stages of planning our trip to Tateyama, we encountered the rich differences between American and Japanese hospitality. The people of Tateyama overwhelmed us with attention once they heard that two Bellingham residents wanted to come for their marathon. They paid for our entry to the marathon, scheduled a meeting with their mayor, and insisted on picking us up at the airport. And they arranged a three-day homestay. When we finally arrived at Narita Airport after many long hours of traveling, there were two men waiting for us with our names on a sign.

I must say that if you've never experienced Japanese hospitality, you've lived only half a life. In fact, anyone who wants to open herself up to the possibility that her culture is merely a collection of agreements, rather than a natural, self-evident outgrowth of "common sense," should travel to Japan and put herself in the capable hands of the Japanese. In Japan, many of the things you know to be true about the world will be turned upside down. You will experience an entire society where everyone knows the social rules for each and every situation, where harmony and consensus are more valued than individualism, and where an intricate pattern of gift giving and receiving guides people's interactions with others throughout life.

When we arrived at the hotel our Tateyama liaison had booked for us, it was nine o'clock in the evening. A team of eight people (including us) gathered around a table in the lobby and commenced a meeting about our itinerary for the next week. The hotel owner prepared demitasses of espresso for our group and welcomed us to his establishment with a low bow. He indicated we should sit around several small tables that had been pulled together for us. As Bill and I collapsed into our chairs, exhausted, our liaison translated for us what the members of the group (representatives of the mayor's office, the home-stay family, the hotel, and the Sister Cities Association) were planning for us.

I tried to follow all the details but found I was distracted by the way our eager hosts checked with one another to carefully establish agreement before giving us their final conclusions. I'd observed this consensus-building process among Japanese students before. It bore little resemblance to the American way of decision making, which usually involves someone's taking the lead. Here, rather than one person assuming leadership (whether by appointment or by personality), everyone waited for each person to make his or her contribution in a deliberate fashion. There were many long silences between speakers. All would eventually nod in simultaneous agreement before they'd move on to the next topic. In my jet-lagged stupor, I found the silences a little too soothing, and I caught my head drooping once or twice. I finally dug out my pen and paper and took notes as our translator reported the results of each negotiation, both as a way of keeping alert and so I would have a record of our agenda when I awoke in the morning.

As I jotted down the details of the itinerary, I threw glances at Bill. I could see he was struggling to stay awake, too. I knew he'd taken at least a hundred meetings with Japanese colleagues over the years and was probably not nearly as astounded as I was that six people had stopped their lives at nine o'clock on a Wednesday evening to finalize our itinerary so that we would not worry or expend any effort during our stay. It looked like we would not have to lift a finger over the next five days in Tateyama to take care of ourselves.

All this attention made me feel grateful but also a little embarrassed. When I had contacted the Sister Cities Association, I'd never imagined or intended for us to be taken care of from arrival to departure; I'd just hoped for a little help with the marathon application, since it was available on the website only in Japanese, and for an introduction to the home-stay family (which I assumed we would pay for, since that was how I had always known it to be done in the States). But one lesson I would learn in Tateyama was that I was not in charge of how much attention would be paid to me or how many gifts I would be given. Graciously receiving and remaining open to all that the following days would bring was my first priority. It was what I wanted: to enact my belief that authentic exchange was about letting people and their gifts into my heart, as well as offering what I had in return. I just had no idea how abundant Tateyama's gifts would be, or how extremely indebted I would feel before we even got started on the week's adventures.

This humbled me more than I could say, and I got to wondering: Had I ever taken my relationship with foreign visitors, or anyone else, for that matter, so seriously? Had I ever stretched my finances, inconvenienced myself, or even given much time to planning an agenda for someone visiting my home? Or had I rested on my American laurels with the "make yourself at home" mentality and left my guests to rummage for what they needed in my refrigerator and get around town on the bus? I was quite sure that even when I had made special efforts or arrangements for people staying with me in my home, I had never really set my mind to giving anyone the experience of a lifetime, or even a rich experience of my own home, life, and community. I was beginning to see that I didn't really know the first thing about "giving," but I was learning.

The following morning was a Thursday, three days before the marathon. During these three days, we would be under the care of our home-stay family, Kinuyo and Kenji Kawasaki, a couple in their fifties. They were a good-looking pair with one grown daughter, who lived away from home. They had hosted many Bellingham-sters over the years. Kinuyo had visited our town and was on the Sister Cities Board in Tateyama. She and another sister-city member, Kuniko Kitami, picked us up at the hotel that morning around ten o'clock and spent the day introducing us to Tateyama and the surrounding areas.

Word was that Tateyama had one of the best views of Mount Fuji in Japan. I was anxious to see her again, but we couldn't find her on the horizon as we drove the marathon course along the shore and then visited an ancient red shrine built high into a mountainside above a crowded graveyard. There was just too much fog.

On the second day, the fog was quite thick as well. Our hostesses, both spritely, energetic women who chatted intimately to each other in Japanese as they drove us about, occasionally tried to point out where Fuji should be, but the fog continued to obstruct our view. It was winter, after all, and Tateyama, a beach resort town in the summer, was sleepy and a bit soggy and chilly this time of year—much like Bellingham was back home. We were warmed throughout those first two days with cups of tea and plenty of hot noodle dishes. The second day we had lunch at a brilliant noodle house where I was properly introduced to soba (finely ground buckwheat used to make the flour for thick, moist noodles), and a dinner of shabu-shabu (among many other things) at the home of Kuniko and her husband, Yoshitsugu, given in our honor.

By the time Friday evening rolled around, I was drunk with love for Japan in general and Tateyama in particular, but I still hadn't seen Mount Fuji.

SATURDAY AT NOON, WE left Kinuyo and Kenji and returned to the hotel. We hadn't managed to rest much, given that by day we'd been sightseeing with a vengeance (touring flower gardens, receiving international friendship certificates in a special meeting with the mayor, touching the feet of a giant female Daibutsu) and by night we were being entertained like royalty.

It was late Saturday afternoon when the rain finally cleaned the air and the wind blew the clouds and fog away so that Mount Fuji was able to make her first appearance to us. Sure enough, she emerged huge and white and powerful. I saw her first from the window of our hotel room. We'd been given the biggest room in the establishment, with the best view of the water. Fuji loomed perfectly clear across the bay.

"Hello," I said quietly. It had been a long time since we'd seen each other, and I wanted a private moment before I called Bill over to greet our old friend. I sat for a few minutes with my face against the cool window, my breath creating a little round puff of steam on the glass. Finally I called out, "Here she is, Bill."

He came to the window with his camera. "We were right up there at the very top a few years ago," he said, pointing. "Can you believe it?"

I shook my head. No, I really couldn't see myself there at the snowcapped peak of the giant I was looking at now. She didn't even seem real, but she did look every bit as magical as she ever had. "I hope we'll still be able to see her tomorrow when the gun goes off," I said. "I could really use her help."

"You'll be fine," Bill said. "You've got the hang of the marathon now."

I hoped so. I wasn't nearly as apprehensive as I had been before my other races, but there was still the smallest question at the back of my mind about whether or not I could really do it.

We couldn't linger long with Fuji-san. It was time to change our clothes in preparation for the pre-marathon ceremony that evening. Japan seemed able to make a ceremony for almost any event. This was the last of our pre-marathon activities as sister-city representatives. I was anxious to see what it would be like.

Kinuyo came to greet us in the hotel lobby and took us around the corner to a huge auditorium with an elevated stage facing hundreds of folding chairs extending all the way to the back wall. I was still basking in the glow of my short visit with Fuji as Tateyama's mayor, Kenjichi Kanamaru, greeted us briefly in the auditorium and asked us to sit up front. He would be calling us up to the stage, along with a few other special marathoners, to receive a commemorative plaque for participating in the next day's event. Along with a man from Hokkaido who would be honored for coming the farthest within Japan, a baseball player whose last name was Tateyama, and a now-famous comedian who was originally from Tateyama, Bill and I would stand in front of nearly a thousand attendees, receive yet another gift, and give our awkward, unpracticed bows of thanks to the mayor.

Receiving the plaques was a treat, but it paled in comparison with what followed at the end of the ceremony, when a group of eight women from a nearby town presented themselves onstage to perform *taiko* drumming. *Taiko* are wooden drums of various sizes with tightly pulled leather on both the top and the bottom, played with large sticks as the performers stand and dance around them. The drums in this performance ranged in diameter from the size of a large serving platter to that of a semi-truck tire. Each bore *kanji* symbols in black down its side, burned into the shiny dark bark of the barrel.

There was one huge drum at the back of the stage called an *odaiko,* which lay sideways on a large wooden stand. This was to be played from the front end.

I knew about *taiko* because some of my former students had given reports on it in class, but I'd never seen a performance. The women stepped forward. One woman gave a shout and they began to beat their drums in unison. Their combined sound was deep and haunting. With their first motions, my heart caught in my throat. My memory ushered me back to a thunderstorm I'd witnessed while standing at the lip of the Grand Canyon. There was the pounding of the thunder, but then the echoes made the rumble linger like a warning, as if to say, *Remember who you are in the grand scheme of things.* I'd stood there on the bank of the world and watched the lightning flashes illuminate the already wondrous reds and golds and wondered at the immensity of the natural world. I felt the same now.

All eight performers suddenly paused in the same moment to let out a battle cry. They shifted in concert to the left, and then to the right, of their instruments. They marched and swayed together to the beat and shouted what sounded like war cries from their diaphragms—powerful, bellowing hollers that seemed to be a combination of protest and agony and victory all at once. My reaction to the women onstage was unexpected and severe. I was caught off guard. The passion and power these women relayed with their drumming touched something very subterranean in me. I felt they were heralding a rallying call, enticing the warrior inside, the fighter, the one who had scrapped her way through a difficult childhood, who'd settled for less than she'd wanted in her life, and who'd then risen up in adamant protest to declare war on inauthenticity and oppressive internal regimes.

I felt the protest in these women's cries and the beating of their drums— *Bom. Bom. Bom. BOOM*—and it sounded to me like the proclamation I'd been making in my life these last years: *I. Am. My. OWN!* And, *I. Live. Out. LOUD!*

But it was not only the protest I recognized. It was also the victory in the beating of the women's drums. I could hear *I. Win. I. WIN!* as they pounded. Back in my church days, we had often talked about how the "deep calls to deep," meaning that God tried to speak to the hidden parts of our souls. I'd not often felt like there was a profound two-way communication going on between God and me, but now something was definitely calling to a deep part of me.

These women drummers with their instruments, voices, and marching called to the Wild Warrior Woman inside me, angry sometimes, but strong. A little worse from the battle, but also now full of a kind of joy I didn't have words for. They made me want to shout with them, to bang on the empty chair beside me and stomp my feet to the sound of their percussion. I wanted to rise when they yelled one of their incomprehensible (to me) victory cries. And when the woman playing the low, bellowing *odaiko* at the back of the stage had her solo, I wanted to stand on my chair and hoot and cheer her on. "Yes! Hell yes!" I wanted to scream. "You go, girl!"

And yet, as overwhelmed and enthused as I felt, there was still just enough good girl in me to keep me sitting on my hands like a polite audience member. I glanced around the now-dark auditorium. I wondered if others felt as taken in as I did. I noticed a few people chatting with their neighbors or even checking the time on their watches. The *taiko* performance was apparently old news to the people around me and not speaking to the locked-up Warrior Woman inside the entire audience, but it was speaking to mine.

Too soon, the finale of beats and stomps and cries of passion was at last punctuated with a final, powerful blow to the big drum at the back, and the audience began to applaud. I let the air out of my lungs (I hadn't known I was holding it in) and let the tears come.

"Oh my God," I said to Bill, grabbing his arm beside me. "I've never seen anything like that."

When he turned toward me and saw my face, he reached over and put his arm around my shoulders. "Keep that rhythm in your footsteps tomorrow during the race," he said. "You'll beat five hours yet."

AS WE GOT READY for bed that night, I sat by the window again, looking in the direction of Mount Fuji. I couldn't see anything outside other than the lights of Tateyama reflected on the water, but I knew she was out there. I thought about how, without speaking a single word I could understand, the *taiko* women had gifted me with an articulation of what the marathon meant to me.

The beating of their instruments had told me something I needed to hear: that I'd turned myself into someone I wanted to be. I was a whole person (sure, with plenty of scars and a lot of room left to grow), and I was a runner (sure, a slow one who wouldn't win any prizes anytime soon, but still . . .). In the morning, I planned to run infused with the vigor of the *taiko* drummers. While Bill was in the bathroom getting ready for bed, I had a little talk with the invisible Mount Fuji.

"Hey," I said. "How about you show up and celebrate with me in the morning?" And after a minute I added, "Oh, and if you do, I'll dedicate the day to you and run a sub-five-hour race. What do you say?"

I listened to see if she would respond, but she was more of the strong, silent type. I'd have to wait until the morning to see if we had a deal.

WHEN WE AWOKE, THE sun was shining. A breeze was blowing through the trees out on the street and Mount Fuji was there, faithful and solid, ready to cheer me on. I was glad she had agreed to show up. As we dressed, ate, and sipped on some green tea, I announced to Bill, "Today will be my first sub-five-hour race."

"Oh yeah?" he said. "How do you know?"

"I made a deal with Mount Fuji."

Bill didn't bat an eye at my announcement—he knew my penchant for conversations with inanimate objects, animals, and even people who didn't talk back. "Great," he said. "I'll be waiting with the camera when you finish."

The start of the race was only a couple of blocks away, so we took our time and made our way over when we were ready.

All Japanese runners are organized into clubs. These clubs don't much resemble the running club we belonged to in Bellingham. They do meet for and support one another on training runs like we do, but they're more a highly structured troop or team than a club. For example, they tend to have about sixty members, all active, who all register for races together based on their identity as a club. They meet before races and stake out a spot near the starting line, situating themselves as a unit on a tarp or in a tent where they store their postrace changes of clothes and meet after the race to celebrate and eat. And they have matching sweat suits. We'd often seen the question on many applications for marathons around the world that read: "Which running club do you belong to?" We'd always filled in: "Greater Bellingham Running Club," knowing that this wasn't exactly the answer to the question.

When we arrived at the starting area, we saw that some of the clubs had even set up camp stoves and portable picnic tables. There were large groups in green, chartreuse, black, and purple milling around everywhere. Because we didn't have a recognized club to congregate with, Kinuyo and Kenji introduced us to a couple of runners, who invited us to join them on their tarp. We stood around with our new friends for about half an hour, until one by one they began their warm-up routines. Up near the starting point was a soccer field where runners were doing laps. To the north side of the field, a big time-clock counted down the minutes to the start of the race. It had been erected so that everyone could plan out their prerace exercises accordingly. Hundreds of people jogged around in circles, stopping from time to time to stretch. We jumped into the circle with the rest of our temporary club and warmed up.

One of the women from the club, Masako, took me under her wing. True Japanese hospitality would not abandon me even in the moments before the gun went off. I would be hosted all the way to the starting line. Masako was an avid marathoner with a slight injury, so, as we chatted, she assured me she would be running this race at a slow pace. I knew from experience that when most runners said "slow," it never meant slow like *my* slow. Her usual times were just under four hours. She was a good runner, and even an injury wouldn't slow her to my pace. I told her that I expected to run this race in five hours and that she should not try to stay with me. I wasn't certain how far she planned to extend her hospitality, but I couldn't imagine a serious runner, even in Japan, sacrificing her time to keep another racer company. For her sake, I hoped Masako and I were on the same page about this.

Just minutes before the gun, Masako tapped me on the arm and said,

"Let's go. It is time." Together we headed to the starting line. I was surprised to see everyone lining up by number. There were signs telling us where we should stand (bib numbers 1100–1700, for example). I lined up behind the sign that indicated my bib number and stood beside my new friend, who wriggled into the line next to mine, a little out of order, so she could stay near me. The runners were also divided by sex: the men on the right side of the chute, and the women on the left. Bill and I lost each other in the crowd of five thousand runners and never had the chance to wish each other luck or to give our customary goodbye kiss.

Before we knew it, the gun went off. A zillion little beeps chimed as we crossed the starting line. The first few kilometers wound along the bay. To our right, Mount Fuji supervised our progress. I smiled at her and whispered my thanks once again.

As I'd hoped, once I settled into my pace toward the back of the pack, Masako felt free to blaze ahead. She left me with a promise to see me at the end and plowed on into the cheers of the thousands of fans along the course.

Several months earlier, I had traveled with Bill to the Boston Marathon and camped myself among the multitudes at mile seventeen to wait for him to pass by. The noise on the sidelines was like that of a crowd in a football stadium. Many of the runners in Boston had their names written on their jerseys or down their arms so they could be called out by name. I stood for two hours in one spot waiting for Bill, screamed myself hoarse, and watched thousands of other runners beam past me. The vibration of the fans banding together to create one deafening voice seemed to function like a tailwind for the racers. They smiled and waved and virtually skipped in response to the support. I thought at the time, *It would be so great to have a crowd on the course when I run; I wonder if I'll ever get to experience this.* Today, in Tateyama, Japan, I was getting that experience.

Bill and I were the only foreigners in the race, as far as we could figure, and most certainly were the only Caucasians. Before and behind me, dark-haired runners bounced along while I, even at only five-foot-six, seemed to tower above many, which made me conspicuous to the bystanders and fans.

As we turned away from the water on the first bend of the route, I picked Yoshitsugu and Kuniko out of the crowd. They waved and cheered me on. I smiled and raised both arms in greeting. Another two kilometers in, I saw some of our other sister-city friends from the potluck dinner on Thursday night. I yelled, "Hello! *Arigato!* Thank you! Thank you for coming!" At around the same time, shoulder to shoulder with hundreds of runners, a woman shuffled her way in next to me and settled in at my pace to say hello. She struggled in English to ask me where I was from and if this was my first time in Japan. I answered her slowly, simplifying my language, as I had learned to do when I'd taught English as a second language, years earlier. Then she asked me a perplexing question. "Are you high school?" she said.

"High school?" I repeated.

She ran quietly beside me for a moment. I figured she was trying to piece together a way to rephrase her question (while I wished for the millionth time in my life that I'd studied Japanese in college). Perhaps she thought I was a high school teacher, an exchange teacher, maybe. "Or you go to university?" she finally asked.

I laughed. "Me?" I smiled at her. "I am forty-one years old." I said. I held up four fingers on one hand and one on the other.

"*Oh!*" She laughed now as well. "Me too. I born 1968."

"1967 for me," I said.

We continued our simple conversation for several minutes. She explained that she thought I looked very young for my age. I was flattered, but I assured her she would feel differently if she saw me at the end of the race.

My obvious conspicuity was working in my favor, I realized. I represented a good chance for other back-of-the-packers to practice their English. This would mean I'd have periodic company. After a while my conversation partner said, "Do your best," and jogged on ahead of me, leaving me free for someone else to approach.

"Do your best" is a common motto in sporting activities in Japan. I noted, in fact, that everyone on the sidelines was shouting it as runners passed by: "*Gambate*" (pronounced *gom-baa-tey*). As we ran through tangled, twisting narrow neighborhoods and alongside dozens of small family businesses, the streets were packed with families, children, and the elderly, who had filed out of their respective dwellings and planted themselves for the better part of the day on the sidewalk to watch the spectacle. They yelled, "*Gambate!*" as we ran passed them. The attention was exhilarating. No wonder every runner I knew wanted to run Boston, where the crowds were as legendary as the race. I would have to tell those who were not likely to ever qualify (like me) about Tateyama.

As I continued, I studied the faces of the fans. I especially enjoyed meeting the gazes of some of the small children and the very old people who seemed to be eyeing me suspiciously, as if I were an oddity of some kind. Most looked away quickly when they noticed I was looking back. Sometimes, if they kept eye contact, I waved and said, "*Konichiwa,*" which often summoned a giggle.

Some fans along the route had set up their own unofficial aid stations. I'd never seen such a thing. One crew of women served their treats on ceramic dishes. They offered *onigiri* triangles wrapped in seaweed, miso soup, hot green tea, hard candies, and salty treats. As I ran by, runners gathered around their table, partaking of the savory snacks and then gently placing the porcelain bowls and cups back on the table before getting a move on.

I dared not stop at these tempting spreads. I was watching my time carefully. Before we had left Bellingham, Bill had printed out several sets of splits for me. I was still useless at calculating kilometers in my head, so I'd asked for a cheat sheet. I had the page with splits for a 4:59 finish time tucked into my running belt so I could access and reference it often. The course, which traveled along the waterfront, with a view of Fuji at both the start and the end of the race, circled through the innards of Tateyama during the middle miles.

Every two kilometers were marked on the course. At ten kilometers, I was running a few minutes faster than Bill's splits said I should be. At sixteen, I was nine minutes faster.

Around the halfway point, I found myself on a beautiful stretch of roadway. Tateyama is in a flower-producing region, and the course ran along one of the most well-known streets, the Flower Line. Millions of gorgeous rape flower blooms filled either side of the street. If it was this plush in January, I had to wonder what it would be like in March or April. As I ran on this portion of the course, no one talked to me, so I had a little time for reflection. I turned the music in my ears off and tried to tune in to the sounds around me. *Bom. Bom. Bom. BOOM.* I heard the sound of my own shoes hitting the pavement. *I. Win. I. WIN!* They seemed to be chanting in honor of the previous night's *taiko* performance.

What a funny mantra my feet had taken up. This whole race, in fact, was surreal to me—different in every way from my usual running experience. For example, not once that morning, as I stood at the starting line, had I wondered if I had it in me to complete the race. All traces of self-doubt from the night before were erased, totally absent. And now Mount Fuji, the fans, and even the mantra of my own footsteps seemed to agree that there wasn't any reason to worry. I could do this race. I'd won. I'd turned myself into a marathoner. It's true I'd done it backward, but that was sort of a trademark of mine (get married young and *then* get to know myself and my dreams; get divorced and *then* get a job to support myself; commit to running a marathon on every continent and *then* learn how to be a runner).

The fans called me back into the moment. One old woman was studying me. I was coming toward her, and though I caught her eye and held her gaze, she didn't turn away. Instead, she smiled back at me and kept staring quite brazenly. When I was a little closer, I smiled too and waved. Immediately, she waved back and shouted in English, "Yes, you can!" It was President Obama's campaign slogan. Incredible. And I could see that, yes, it was true. I could do it—I just might run a sub-five-hour marathon. Only a few weeks earlier, I had run a thirty-kilometer race in Arizona in 3:13. Why couldn't I run at that pace now? The conditions were amazing, the course was easy enough, and my feet were chanting victory.

When I hit thirty kilometers a while later, I was at 3:18. Not bad. At thirty-five kilometers, even after the only challenging hills on the course, I'd been running for three hours and fifty-three minutes. I was slowing down for sure, but I could *almost* walk the last seven kilometers (4.35 miles) and still come in under my five-hour goal. This gave me a sense of relief, so I relaxed a little and stopped looking at my splits. I thought about taking it easy, maybe walking for a half mile. I was running so slowly, I was almost walking anyway.

Then I thought back to the summer and to Panama. There was no blood running down my legs in this race, no horrific rainstorm, and no inhumane humidity. If I'd ever had an excuse to give up, it would have been in that race last August, but I hadn't. I'd kept going. And I certainly had no reason to give up now. I had to keep running. I hadn't needed help from my Inner Bitch this time, and Wisdom hadn't made any profound appearances. With less than five miles to go, I realized that the Warrior Woman had been unleashed and that I was indeed running an unfettered victory race. All I had to do was continue to move my legs forward in agreement with the work that I had already done.

As I came down the final, small decline and saw the water, pain finally registered in my quads and hamstrings. It was arriving late this time. And for another short moment, I was tempted again to walk. But when the mountain came into my line of vision and smiled at me (I'm quite sure I saw her do this), I remembered how she had lifted me up and introduced me to myself in a new way on my honeymoon, and had given me a glimpse into my future quest. I owed her a lot and I wouldn't fail her now. Pain be damned, I wouldn't walk for even one meter. I'd finish strong. I continued toward the water and even reached my hands toward Fuji, but as I veered onto the road that ran along the beachfront, the mountain moved behind me to the left. I wanted to be able to see her when I finished, so I strained my aching neck to keep an eye on her snowcap. Eventually, however, I lost sight of her. But I was okay. I was infused with the fortitude and determination of my Inner Warrior Woman. A flash of triumph flooded through me. I shouted, "Woooohoooo! Yes! I win!" Some runners behind me tittered and whispered something to one another. There wasn't much shouting among the athletes here—all was serious concentration at this point—but I figured I was already badly out of place so a little hoot wouldn't hurt anyone.

When I hit the long, straight stretch I recognized as the beginning (and therefore the end) of the race, I saw a man standing on the sidelines, holding a large sign reading: 2 KILOMETERS REMAINING. At least, I assume that's what it said, as there was a number 2 with some Japanese writing beneath it. I was so close, and the race had been so good to me. Then the oddest thought came to my mind: *Why not finish with a push?*

I'd never done that before, never sprinted at the end of a race, not even at the end of a 5K. But it was an inspired idea, so I gathered my wits, dug down deep to drum up a little more Warrior energy, and pressed my heels into the pavement, shoving off strong with the fore of each foot. A scene of my "race" in Prague flashed through my mind: me crying, Bill pushing on my back, me nearly getting killed by a passing car, Bill yanking me off the road. I had to laugh even as I picked up the tiniest bit of speed. What a contrast this was with almost everything that had come before.

A few moments after starting my final push, I saw Bill up ahead, camera in hand. He had finished his race more than an hour before (3:41, he told me later) and had had time to recover while waiting for me. Now he was here to see me come in.

I WAVED WITH BOTH hands to catch his attention, though surely he wouldn't have missed me with my blond hair coming loose from my ponytail and flying wild in the wind. He waited for me to come up parallel with him and then jogged beside me.

"Hey, look at your time!" he said, grinning.

"I know. I did it. I'm coming in under five! Right?" Adrenaline was pumping into my tired muscles. "Am I close to the line?"

He looked at his watch. "You're coming in *way* under five!" he said. "It's around the bend. Go for it!" He dropped back and let me move into the finishing chute before swerving a bit to the left and running ahead behind the spectators to get a photo of me finishing.

Sure enough, as usual, the crowds had thinned out, but since we'd started with so many, there were still a few hundred runners and fans along the edges of the chute. There was Kinuyo and Kenji and their daughter, Hiromi. There were some of our other new friends. And there was the mayor! Then I saw the finish line. The sounds of encouraging applause washed over me. This was such a welcome difference from the lonely finishes in Mudgee and Whidbey Island.

There it was. FINISH was written in English. There was no mistaking it. And the clock below it read 4:52! I raised my hands in the air as I heard my microchip beep, and I screamed, "*I win! I win!*" Exultation and satisfaction made my skin prickle as I pushed "stop" on my watch and slowed to a walk. I'd beaten five hours! I'd run with all my might at the end! I'd made my mountain proud! One point for the Warrior Woman!

My exuberance was short-lived, however. Once I stopped moving, I felt nausea settle into my stomach. I'd pushed myself pretty hard, and now my body was shutting down. Bill was there, flighty with the excitement he thought I should be feeling. He was snapping pictures of my every move, weaving around me like a pestering fly. He was recording every ugly facial expression as cramps threatened to seize my entire left leg. I kept batting him away, half laughing and half dying to collapse and be left alone. There was no way to collapse, though, no time to indulge my physical discomfort; people were fussing over me, congratulating me. Our host family was there on the spot, ready to escort us to the recovery-food area. There would be green tea and miso soup awaiting us. And crab leg bisque. (I have to admit, I would have preferred pizza.) I hobbled along behind everyone as best I could, barely having time to notice that club members had recongregated around their tarps and were partaking in elaborate barbeques and potlucks. Kinuyo and Kenji whisked us through the grounds to a table and finally to a chair.

In one dramatic *whoosh,* I flung myself down. Here I sat and stretched, unwilling to move until my muscles relaxed and gave me the go-ahead.

LATER THAT NIGHT, I was sore. What I mean to say is that I was raw, tortured, paralyzed with pain. We'd been delivered back to our hotel room and had taken our showers. Now I sat wrapped in a blanket, watching out the window as the colors in the sky acted as backup singers to Fuji-san's finale. She was fading from view fast. The television was on behind me with the sound turned down low. We couldn't understand what the announcer was saying anyhow, but we wanted to find out who would be the sumo grand champion. We knew Kenji would be watching across town.

Bill went out to get himself some food at a nearby mall, and I asked him to turn the lights off as he left so I could watch the mountain as long as possible. I felt a powerful combination of pure, grateful love and unspeakable sadness at having to say goodbye. In the morning, we would be driven out of town to Yokohama, where Bill would visit some colleagues; then we'd make our way to Tokyo. Bill would fly home and I would stay with friends in the city for one more week.

Something about Japan seemed to give me eyes to see my own reality, my own self, in ways that didn't occur to me at home. It could be the way all responsibilities of normal life were replaced with a sense of being cherished and nurtured, as if I myself were a precious gift meant to be treated with delicacy and care. Or it could be that when I was there I was on an entirely different plane. Food, time, and hospitality were all handled differently, but so were truth and patience and strength. As the last of the light faded outside, I said farewell to Fuji. Akinori Asashoryu won the title of sumo grand champion, and I put my tired Warrior self to bed. It had been a successful *nyubu*.

africa:
THE langebaan
long haul MARCH 2009

"People get into a heavy-duty sin and guilt trip, feeling that if things
are going wrong, that means they did something bad and they are
being punished. That's not the idea at all. The idea of karma is that you
continually get the teachings you need to open your heart. To the degree
that you didn't understand in the past how to stop protecting your soft
spot, how to stop armoring your heart, you're given this gift of teachings in
the form of your life, to give you everything you need to open further."

—PEMA CHÖDRÖN

"You're running on guts. On fumes. Your muscles twitch. You throw up.
You're delirious. But you keep running because there's no way out of this
hell you're in, because there's no way you're not crossing the finish line.
It's a misery that non-runners don't understand."

—MARTINE COSTELLO, about the New York Marathon

9

I was tired out by the time I got home from Japan, and yet, Warrior Woman that I was, I was right back into my training two days after settling back in. With our Africa marathon only six weeks away, the week I took off in Tokyo without Bill was my time off from running—and I walked at least thirty miles that week. Race day in Tateyama turned out to be the last time I saw Mount Fuji again. The weather turned cloudy and rainy and remained that way until the moment I boarded the plane to come home.

The weather was just as cloudy, if a little colder, back in Bellingham. I woke up each morning, drank a mug of coffee to warm myself up, and then got busy with work, training outside in the chilly air and finalizing details for our Africa trip. We had decided to do our Africa marathon in March at a small race that ran through a national park north of Cape Town, South Africa. After that, we would fly to South America in June to complete Brazil's Rio de Janeiro Marathon.

I hoped my vision quest would culminate in our final continent, Antarctica, the following March. We were on the waiting list for one of only two organized marathons I could find on that continent, and it turned out that March 2010 was the soonest we could expect to be confirmed. I could imagine myself raising a glass of champagne and celebrating being one of approximately a hundred women worldwide to have completed a marathon on every continent on Earth. It was an exciting accomplishment, and one that had much more significant meaning to me now than it had when we'd first dreamed up the scheme.

At the moment, however, there wasn't much time to revel in my anticipated glory. I had to focus on the next few, very busy weeks. We were one-third of the way through our Year of the Marathon, and we needed to pin down a plethora of details. I would expend my immediate energy on finding lodgings and making an itinerary for South Africa.

I HAD ACTUALLY TRAVELED to the African continent once before. I'd even passed through South Africa on my way to Mozambique. I was in my late twenties and had just taken a job teaching high school English. As the school year came to an end, I was certain I'd made the wrong career decision. My students were a pleasure, and I was interested in my subject matter, but the work hours were inhumane. I left my house by six thirty each morning and returned home twelve hours later (I ran the after-school drama club), only to face several more hours of class preparation and paper correcting.

By the time summer came around, I was a zombie, barely scraping my way through each day. I didn't possess the type-A liveliness that the job required. By chance one afternoon in May, another teacher stopped by my room to introduce me to a guest speaker she'd invited in for a geography lesson that day, a missionary to Africa who had brought slides of his most recent trip.

I asked the missionary if I could see his pictures, and as we turned down the lights and settled into a couple of student desks, the images on the pull-down white screen in my classroom mesmerized me instantly. The blue of the sub-Saharan sky was like neon; the leaves on unfamiliar trees glistened in the sun against a backdrop of red earth. Children ran barefoot on hard-packed dirt roads, hands above their heads in a wave, smiling into the camera. I was drawn in further with every click of the slide projector. It was an utterly foreign world a million miles away from my exhaustion and disillusionment.

When the slide show was over, noticing my interest and enchantment, the missionary dropped the bomb I didn't even know I was hoping for. "We're going to Mozambique this summer. Why don't you come with us?" he asked.

And so I did. That summer, at twenty-eight, burned out, misdirected in my career, already fearing that my young marriage was not going to be what

I needed, I decided to go to Africa for six weeks as a short-term missionary. What could make more sense at the end of a school year that had sucked me dry than to travel to one of the poorest regions on Earth and preach about God's love and justice?

Well, the decision carried some kind of distorted logic at the time. After all, Jesus had said that his "yoke is easy" and his "burden is light." I'd internalized this to mean that if I kept doing God's work, harder and longer, and sacrificed more of myself, I would eventually feel some kind of connection with God that would lighten the heaviness I carried around in my heart.

Looking back, I saw that even then I had been on a search for meaning. But instead of exploring and questioning with an open mind, I believed I was supposed to already have the answers the rest of the world was presumably seeking. This, as it turned out, was a burden too heavy for me, a yoke that sat on my shoulders like a gigantic boulder. I came home from the six weeks more fatigued and depressed than I'd been when I had left. I made it through one more year of grueling, long days as a public school teacher and then filed my teaching certificate under "E" for "expired," which I knew I would let it become.

This time around, I planned to go to Africa, and to Brazil after that, as a plain old member of the human race, rather than as a messenger for anyone or any doctrine. If I'd learned nothing else in Japan, I had at least learned how to be a good guest, how to soak in the offerings of a particular place, and put aside, as much as was humanly possible, my preconceived expectations.

BILL AND I FLEW directly into Cape Town from Amsterdam. We were as prepared as we could be, in spite of our crunch for time. We packed the best we could for layering, including some sweaters for the cool evenings and short sleeves for the warmest days. March was the beginning of fall in the southern hemisphere, and Cape Town's average temperature was supposed to be around sixty-eight degrees.

We were looking forward to getting out of the rain at home and investigating the southern tip of the African continent, but we were starting tired.

This trip, coming so quickly on the heels of our return from Japan, meant that I'd had time to formulate only the sketchiest of itineraries. We knew we would be in the Cape Town area for about five days before the marathon, during which time we wanted to explore the port on Table Bay, see Table Mountain, and hopefully get down to the cape itself. Then we'd make our way north to Weskus National Park and to the town of Langebaan, where the marathon would take place. After the marathon, we wanted to go inland to do some serious wine tasting. The specifics of our day-to-day, however, were very much up in the air. We would be winging it, which wasn't our strong suit as a couple.

We landed in Cape Town after dark on a Sunday and managed, bleary-eyed as we were, to find the taxi I had arranged to meet us there. Our driver was to transport us to the area of town known as the Pinelands, where Colette's Bed and Breakfast was. We'd chosen this guesthouse because of its proximity to the airport, but it was still a thirty-minute drive along a very busy stretch of highway.

The freeway we traveled was clean and well maintained with newly painted reflective white lines, but I was surprised by how many pedestrians were walking alongside the steady stream of traffic. Every so often, like a quick-moving shadow, someone would chance it and dart in front of several cars clipping along at sixty miles an hour to cross to the other side of the street. I noticed right away that our driver hardly flinched and none of the other cars slowed to acknowledge a person making a run for it. *What are so many people doing on the highway?* I wondered. I couldn't think what would require them to walk along a dangerous high-speed freeway in the dark. I'd seen chaotic traffic in Mexico and Panama, but there seemed to be some kind of tacit agreement between drivers and pedestrians in both of those countries. People watched for cars, and cars for people. Here, this was the vehicle's domain, clearly, and the cars were in charge. I didn't want to engage our driver, who was already making me nervous with his descriptions of various Cape Town points of interest while nearly swerving off the road. Besides, I was *so* groggy and weary, I could barely string two words together.

Grateful and barely functional, we landed on Colette's doorstep. Colette, a woman with a kind smile and graying hair, greeted us warmly, gave us a tour of her establishment, and then left us to ourselves. Once we were finally settled in under clean white sheets in one of her beautiful attic rooms, not even the sound of heavy wind blowing noisily through an open skylight could keep us from drifting off into a sound sleep.

We didn't awake until very late the next morning. Colette made us breakfast and drove us into the city. All we had time for that day was a walk on the reclaimed waterfront and a short boat ride into the bay to watch the sunset. The air was fresh and warm, and I only had to put on a thin sweater that evening. It felt good to be outside without being bundled in the bulky coat I would be wearing at home this time of year.

The day after that, we opted for a history lesson and bought tickets to sail out to Robben Island, where Nelson Mandela had been an inmate for eighteen of his twenty-seven years spent in prison.

Anyone who thinks Alcatraz is creepy should take an afternoon to visit Robben Island. It is infinitely more ghostlike and sad because the former inmates themselves (in the flesh) are employed to conduct the portions of the tour that take visitors through the prison buildings where they used to be incarcerated.

Before we met the prisoner who would show us his old living quarters, we climbed aboard a bus that shuttled us around the island. It was here that I first felt the pangs of racial tension and dissonance, which I suspect everyone who visits South Africa must feel. Thirty-five white tourists listened as Valerie, our young black guide, stood at the front of the bus and pointed out the rock pits where Mandela and his fellow political prisoners (those who had protested against apartheid) moved rocks from one pile to another all day for no constructive reason whatsoever other than that it was the task they were told to do.

Valerie wore a bright purple broomstick skirt and a yellow tank top and projected her voice toward the back of the bus like a pro. She explained how the blacks in South Africa were considered noncitizens in their own land and how they were required to carry something called a "dompas," "dumb pass," to identify themselves if they worked in a white area. She explained how the rest of the world had done little to pressure the old South African government to change its unjust laws.

None of this was necessarily new information to me. I'd read Afrikaner authors and watched films depicting the political scene in South Africa over the years. What was new to me was Valerie. What was she, twenty-seven at most? That would put her at about eight years old when Nelson Mandela had declared the end of apartheid, in 1990. I had a sudden vision of a young Valerie being faced with restroom signs that read WHITES ONLY, and the impact of history was suddenly personal and poignant.

Back in the days when I had a magical connection with God, I used to know what to do with sympathy for others and the dissonance I experienced regarding my own position of privilege in the world as a white American. I felt then that I had a special kind of influence on the planet. In my old paradigm, I had something to give that others did not have. I had my understanding of God, my belief that He was ultimately responsible for sorting everything out according to His own will. This meant that it wasn't really my responsibility to challenge the status quo, only to pray.

At the same time, I believed I knew The Truth, which would save people's souls if they were open to letting it in. Even when people were unjustly locked in prisons, starving, or dying of disease, if they believed in God, at least they'd be in heaven when it was all over. When I traveled as a short-term missionary, my goal was to go to a foreign land and to proselytize or build a building or teach a skill to someone poorer and needier than I, and then I could feel I'd done my part. But my old version of empathy did not acknowledge power differentials, nor did it give credit to people for their own innate strength and wisdom. From my vantage point now, that old approach to the world was not only not good enough, it was barely even tolerable to me anymore.

Sitting on that warm bus with Valerie at the front, I felt a spiritual emptiness. I closed my eyes and tried to reach deep for the divine Inner Wisdom that had been present for me these past few years. I admit I wanted some new, easy way to manage my disquieting thoughts, but Wisdom was silent. I was just going to have to live with my feelings and growing number of questions, rather than try to alleviate or answer them in a trite or formulaic way.

My legs were sticking to the vinyl seat by now. The bus was warming up with the passengers' stale air. We turned onto a looping road that circled the barren land of the island. The soil was unarable, dry, and sandy; the foliage was sparse and the ground flat. The few buildings we passed were functional, square, and cement.

When we finally pulled to a stop, Valerie asked if we had any questions, but the only questions I had I knew would be inappropriate to ask: *What is it like for you to give tours to white tourists?* I wanted to know. *Do you feel contempt for us?* I wondered. And then there were my questions about myself, like *How do I find a meaningful new way to be a respectful citizen of the world?*

Of course, Valerie was employed to tell a story, not to make a moral judgment about Americans' complicity in tolerating apartheid or to offer to make sense of anything for me or anyone else. She did not exude even the slightest bit of hatred, fear, or derision, but the separation between this young guide and her charges was almost tangible. It was like a thick smoke between us. At the end of the day, my questions were my problem, not hers.

AFTER THE TOUR, WE went straight back to Colette's, where I fell asleep feeling the weight of the day we'd just had. In the morning, we "hired" our car and got ready to try driving on the left side of the road—something we'd gotten some practice doing in Australia. It felt good to have a lighter day on the agenda—no museums or tours. Our only plan was to make our way down the False Bay coast along the east edge of Cape Peninsula National Park, a must-do route, according to everyone we'd talked to about our trip.

On the way out of town I was relaxed, happy to be in the warmth of the southern hemisphere. I enjoyed watching the green trees along the sides of the road pass us by, and relished the sun coming through the passenger window. We took our time, puttering along the coast, passing one seaside resort town after another, one sandy beach after the next, stopping whenever we felt the urge.

The experience at Robben Island lingered with me on the drive as we passed numerous vacation homes and cute little shops sprinkled on the hillsides. A steady stream of tourists like us stopped here and there to meander through the well-kept streets, and I kept reminding myself that we were seeing only part of a picture. It was hard to tell we were in Africa. We encountered very few people of color, besides an occasional store clerk or parking attendant.

By early afternoon, we stood with a dozen other foreigners at the light-house on Cape Point and watched the raging ocean below the cliff smash against the rocks onshore. Here we were, in the realm where two oceans meet and collide. Bill and I lingered at the lighthouse and looked below us at the foaming waves and the stone cliff beaten smooth by eons of tides coming and going. The wind was relentless, warm but intense, as we directed our gazes due south toward the bottom of Planet Earth, toward Antarctica. We snapped several pictures: Bill with his hair standing on end, overlooking the cliff, me with my dress flying up and the ocean behind me.

We changed into our running clothes in the restroom and took a short jog on an uneven trail over to the Cape of Good Hope and watched as a heavy fog rolled in, obstructing our view of the water and the yonder point from which we'd just run. Like an ominous messenger, the fog came suddenly and without any prelude. It overtook the light of day and our vision of just about everything. Disappointed at losing our panoramic view, we sat on a ledge with our legs dangling and tried to wait it out. But the fog didn't seem to want to clear away, and eventually we decided we needed to head back north to Cape Town.

I was glad we'd made it to the cape before the fog had rolled in, but with it came a new, troubled feeling. I didn't think of myself as particularly superstitious, but I was inarguably intuitive. As the fog had overshadowed our view of the water, I'd felt a little wave of uneasiness come over me.

Once we were off the tip of the peninsula, however, the sun was shining again and I temporarily forgot my vague premonition. We ate a gourmet dinner at an upscale restaurant on a pier for just under $10. Then, after dusk, we drove back up to Cape Town via the same seaside road that had brought us down that morning. We took a wrong turn, however, and inadvertently wound up on the highway that passed straight through the center of the city, the same highway we'd taken in from the airport.

The uneasiness I'd felt back at the lighthouse returned as Bill slowed the car to make way for a pedestrian shooting across the freeway. I followed the jaywalker's movements and watched as he scrambled up the side of a fence and flipped himself over the top. Where was he headed? I focused my eyes as best I could in the darkening of the day and concentrated my gaze beyond the wall. And that's when I finally saw it: The Cape Flats. It was Cape Town's gigantic series of crowded townships just southeast of the city's business district. I realized that I'd missed it on our way into the city three days earlier because I hadn't been looking for it.

Stretching for miles, silent and dim, a tall, shabby enclosure wrapped around it, as if to keep it from spilling over. It looked to me like a gigantic sea of shadows, like what you see when you gaze down at night from an airplane at a black lake sitting in the center of a city full of lights. Looking to one side of the highway, I saw a beautiful, sparkling town with manicured landscaping, welcoming and wealthy, thriving—and white. Turning my head to the other side, I saw the Flats, a vast city unto itself filled with more than a million people living in structures that could not really be called houses.

Even from my seat in the car, I could see boards and scrap metal and mismatched pieces of wood roped or nailed or taped together to give shelter. The dividing line between those who worked hard to meet their basic human needs and those who had the option of fiddling around at the top of Maslow's hierarchy was suddenly starkly clear. The separation was blatant and unapologetic. Apartheid might be over, but apartness clearly wasn't.

THE FOLLOWING DAY WAS Thursday, and it was time to load up the car for our drive to Langebaan. I wasn't ready to leave Cape Town, and I could have used a quiet day without any traveling or sightseeing, but we had to go.

The drive to Langebaan took only a couple of hours, even with a stop at a winery and a detour into a little town called Darling. We ate a lunch of egg sandwiches at a café there and then got back in the hot car and finished our trip up the coast. We arrived at Weskus National Park, the site of the marathon, at about two o'clock on Thursday afternoon. Before we arrived in Langebaan proper, we diverted into the park through a southern entrance and obtained a map so we could drive the marathon route.

As we approached the site of the race, it occurred to me how very little I'd thought about the marathon over the past week. We were tapering and intentionally not running much. Plus, Cape Town had been a lot to take in. I'd developed a dull headache that I hadn't been able to shake.

The race came to the forefront of my thoughts now as we looked at the map, and I started to feel excited about the chance to repeat the triumph I'd experienced in Japan. I also felt some apprehension, however. I'd never run two races so close together, after all, and I worried that my muscles hadn't had enough time to recover.

Weskus National Park lies along an inlet that forms a lagoon. If you hold up the thumb and forefinger of your right hand as if you have a quarter between them, you'll see the general shape of the inlet in the space there. The race would go from Tsaarsabank, a spot on the far west (your thumbnail) where the Atlantic Ocean was visible. The route would follow along your thumb to the crease between your two digits. At the crease, there would be a short out-and-back, after which you would take a right and follow up to the tip of your forefinger, ending in the city of Langebaan.

As we drove, I noticed the way the road rolled through the desert terrain and curved between large fields of low-lying vegetation. South Africa is renowned as one of the most biologically diverse places on the planet, but to my untrained eyes it was all dry, waist-high, brownish-green brush. I was happy to discover that the park looked a little humdrum, just a gradual incline here or there, followed by some nice flat roadway for long stretches. There didn't appear to be any major grunts to haul myself up. As marathons went, in my experience so far, it didn't look terribly challenging.

Just as I was reflecting on the probable ease of the course, Bill slammed on the brakes, jolting me forward in the passenger seat. I looked up to see that he had just barely avoided a gigantic ostrich. Neither of us had seen her sneak out of the overgrown tumbleweeds that edged the road. She was an ugly thing with bugged-out eyes and a warty nose, easily eight feet tall and close to three hundred pounds, and she towered over us, glaring with a malevolent expression. I shuddered as she stared at me through the windshield. She held my gaze for a very long, frightening minute, trying to communicate a warning of some sort, I thought, and then sauntered across the road, swinging her big rump behind her. I slumped down in my seat and put my hands over my eyes.

"Ick. You don't suppose I'll run into one of those things while I'm running, do you?" I asked Bill.

"Nah," he reassured me. "They'll get scared off the course by the first runners out. Don't worry about it." He put the car back in gear and drove on.

We reached the far side of the park and exited directly into the vacation town of Langebaan. In the late afternoon, it was sleepy. It sits on a hillside right on the water, and its beach is miles long and full of people sunbathing or kite surfing. I hadn't gotten as far as Thursday in Langebaan in my planning, so Bill and I still needed to locate a place to stay the night. We found a motel with a kitchenette and a full view of the lagoon and then took a ride to the grocery store to purchase the makings for a spaghetti dinner.

As the sun went down, I prepared our meal of noodles and tomato sauce, and we ate it with some of the chenin blanc we'd bought at the winery outside of Darling. Then we watched a little TV and went to bed early. I was glad to lay my head down, glad to be a little drunk, glad to zone out in front of a mindless comedy.

I drifted off and slept peacefully until, at three in the morning, I woke up shivering. On every quest or journey, there has to be some sort of major physical test. I thought getting my period in Panama had been mine. I'd already decided that the themes I was grappling with on this trip were meant to be less personal and more about larger cultural and social issues. I'd temporarily forgotten that it wasn't my job to decide what hurdles life threw in my way.

I had that dry feeling behind the eyes that comes with a fever. My abdomen began cramping sharply, and the dull headache I'd been nursing turned into something powerful and throbbing. The longer I lay there, the worse my intestinal cramps became. I wondered if I had come down with appendicitis and was scared by this thought. What if I needed to go to the hospital so far away from home?

I tumbled out of bed and felt my way in the dark to the bathroom. I had a violent case of diarrhea. It seemed to come and come and come. Bill was asleep as I sat there on the toilet. I hated to wake him, but I felt afraid of being alone. I'd traveled all around the world and had never had anything like this happen to me. What had I eaten? Spaghetti with no meat. An egg sandwich.

I did feel a slight relief of the cramps after emptying my bowels, until the next wave came. As I sat there, doubled over and perspiring, I concluded that I must have gotten food poisoning somehow. Bill would have it, too, I guessed.

Eventually, I climbed back in bed and patted him on the shoulder. "Hey," I whispered. "Do you feel sick?"

"Huh?" he said and rolled over to face me. He opened his eyes a sliver to look at my face. "What's wrong?"

"I'm sick. Diarrhea, headache. I think I have a fever. Feel me and see if I'm hot."

Bill raised himself onto one elbow and put the other hand on my forehead. "Yep. You're hot," he said.

He rolled out of bed and rummaged through his luggage. When he came back, he offered me a pain reliever. I took it, but I couldn't get back to sleep. Until the sun rose, I vacillated between freezing, sweating, worrying, and running to the toilet.

I got up Friday, the day before the race, not feeling any better. My fever was still present and the diarrhea kept coming. Now I was in a serious quandary. I knew without a doubt that I was not healthy enough to run a marathon the next day. Even if I recovered before the morning, I would probably be weak. I drank water one small sip at a time all day to stay hydrated, and I stayed in bed. I couldn't bring myself to eat anything besides a few crackers.

The usual voices in my head were oddly removed throughout the day as Bill kept a watchful eye on me. He made sure I was covered with a blanket and tipped tiny sips of sports drink into my mouth from time to time, like I was a premature kitten. At 8:00 PM on Friday, he sat beside me on the bed, gave me a very stern, parental look and said, "The race is in eleven hours, you know. You may not be able to run it, Cami."

I looked away from him and up at the ceiling. The ceiling fan in our room twirled and wobbled, slightly crooked on its base. I'd heard what he'd said, but I hated his tone, hated feeling like a child who didn't have her own authority to make a decision. The Bitch showed up in full force in that moment, despite how crappy I felt. I snapped at him, "You don't get to tell me what I'm doing tomorrow, Bill. I'm an adult and I'll make that choice for myself." Even I was taken aback by the ferocity of my response. I knew in my heart that Bill was only extending me some permission he thought I might need to let some pressure off, but the Bitch didn't want anyone's permission *not* to run this race. She didn't like to be disempowered, and it was her job to object and complain when she felt patronized.

I saw surprise in Bill's face at hearing my angry tone, and I tried to soften the Bitch's approach a little, adding, "I came to Africa to run a marathon, and I'm going to do it regardless of how I feel." I wasn't as sure as I hoped I sounded.

Bill had the good sense to understand that he had inadvertently engaged me in a power struggle, and he changed his tack. He stood up and walked away from me, nonchalant. "Okay, well, if you change your mind, there's another race next weekend we might be able to get you into. You'd have a second chance to run Africa."

This was a good move, and it calmed me. I was able to open my heart briefly to the possibility that I wouldn't be able to run in the morning. But as I drifted off into a sleep that would be interrupted by countless forays to the bathroom, my resolve to be at the starting line hardened into determination. The Inner Warrior I had gotten in touch with in Tateyama began to beat her drum, very softly but with increasing fervor, reminding me that the marathon was my wilderness on an important quest. It was the mountain of my *nyubu,* the best way I knew to be my best self, helping me rebuild my life from a pile of religious and emotional ashes into a structure I could inhabit. I had to do that run tomorrow! I owed it to myself.

Saturday morning, March 14, I awoke, tumbled out of bed, and emptied my bowels. What was left in there, I couldn't imagine. Then I popped a handful of acetaminophen to keep my fever down and got dressed in my running clothes.

Bill eyed me silently. Only once did he try to speak to me. "You sure about this?" he asked.

I only nodded and continued dressing. I knew I had to do it.

There comes a time in every quest when you look past your genuine constraints, your disempowered state, whatever the cause, and you do what your core self is screaming at you to do. I'm glad this test came five continents into my journey, after I had already experienced giving up on training runs out of sheer laziness, after I'd bled into my socks in Panama, and after I'd triumphed by beating five hours in Tateyama. Those were all things that contributed to my knowing that I could and would run through this illness. If it had come any earlier, I doubt I would have been able to discern whether my choice was self-abuse or self-determination. This choice was built on belief in my body, mental strength, and faith that I would know what to do in the face of a crisis. I'd learned that these three things could take a person a long way, and I hoped they would take me forty-two kilometers.

By six o'clock, we arrived at a waiting row of buses and made our way to the first one. As Bill and I climbed aboard and reached the top step, I stopped dead in my tracks. My eyes adjusted to the dim light inside the bus, and I saw something I had not anticipated: people of all colors sitting side by side! There were white people and black people and brownish people and people of Asian origin, all chatting excitedly about the adventure we were about to embark upon together. For the first time on our trip, I saw a rainbow of faces all together—all in one place. All of the apartheid categories (Afrikaans, English, black, colored, etc.) were loaded together on that bus.

I leaned over to whisper to Bill, "Will you look at this?"

He took a moment to figure out what I was talking about, and then I saw his face register understanding. He said, "Well, what do you know?" We walked down the aisle toward an empty seat at the back of the bus. "They say athletics are an even playing field."

"I never played sports as a kid. I guess I missed that," I said over my shoulder. But, at least on this morning, every athlete seemed to have the same status: marathon runner.

The bus took us the same route Bill and I had driven two days ago, only in the opposite direction. Bill made small talk with the runners who sat around us, while I tried to ignore the occasional cramp or wave of nausea. When the bus finally deposited us at Tsaarsabank, I made my way to the starting line with new trepidation. I thought I knew what to expect of the course: rolling hills, dry, sandy terrain with low shrubs, sweeping views of the Atlantic Ocean and the Langebaan Lagoon, and, of course, ostriches. I felt determined about my decision, but determination didn't mitigate the fear and apprehension I also felt.

The morning was beautiful, and I tried to take my mind off my intestines by taking in the scents of the flora all around us and breathing in the southern air. The temperature at that point was comfortable, approximately seventy degrees Fahrenheit. There was a slight breeze and an air of excitement from the chattering runners. The sound of the ocean lapping onto the bank nearby was rhythmic and calming.

South Africans, much like the Japanese runners we had encountered a few weeks earlier, ran as clubs. Each club member had a permanent running license sewn onto the back of his or her shirt, which gave identifying information and permission to take part in organized events. Bill and I had been given temporary licenses to safety pin to our backs. As we stood waiting at the line, these paper licenses tagged us as either foreigners or new runners. We noticed other runners glancing at us. Some said hello or nodded. I smiled weakly and waved back. I hated that my lethargy was preventing me from reaching out, but at the moment I had to conserve all my energy.

Now it was 7:00 AM and I had a moment—with the adrenaline of 560 marathoners talking and stretching all around me and the sun poking her nose above the water to the east—when I felt almost well. For just a second before the race began, I had a respite from the cramps and the ache in my head. It was then that I heard the Warrior Woman giving me a little pep talk: *You ran under five hours in Japan just a few weeks ago! You're in good shape. You can do anything for five hours. Just put one foot in front of the other, girl.*

Bill, who was still at my side, stared at me until I turned to look at him. In the dawn, his skin looked smooth and his blue eyes were almost periwinkle. I had a little wave of compassion for him. This whole trip, he had either been processing complex social questions with me or taking my temperature. I smiled at him. But his mouth wasn't smiling back. It was twisted over to one side, and I knew him well enough to know that he was debating whether or not to wish me good luck, or to make an attempt at forbidding me to go through with running this race.

"You sure you want to do this?" he asked, one last time.

"You know," I said, "I want to try. If I weren't in Africa, I might have stayed in bed today, but I came a long way from home to do this. If it gets really bad, I'll ask for the aid car. I promise." Then I kissed him goodbye and pushed him toward the front of the pack, to where he was supposed to be standing, hoping to give him permission to run his own race, rather than worry about me. A moment later, the horn blew and we all began running.

Within the first few steps, I felt a hot gurgle in my colon. What was I getting myself into? But soon enough, my body seemed to adjust to the tempo of my movement, and for a few miles it behaved itself. I wasn't particularly energetic, but I was solid. I was no longer a novice at this, after all.

I'd reached that point in my practice where something that had once taken so much effort and conscious concentration finally becomes second nature. Something that at one time had felt foreign and unnatural was now a part of what my body knew how to do. There seemed to be some truth that "practice makes perfect." My limbs, my mind, my cardiovascular system knew how to do this. *It's going to be okay,* I thought.

But then the sun rose up above our heads. By 9:00 AM, before I reached the halfway point, the temperature in the air, which had been very pleasant and mild at 7:00 AM, had reached one hundred degrees Fahrenheit. I hadn't been expecting this. In Cape Town, not a couple hundred miles away, I'd been wearing a sweater for part of every day. Here on the course, there were no trees, and consequently no shade.

Worse yet, the aid stations ran out of water! Never in any race I had run, however long, had the volunteers run out of water. I'd been at the back of packs five thousand runners strong, and still the stations had had water when I came through. I wondered how much water the front-of-the-packers had to be sucking down. Bill told me after the race that he estimated he'd consumed nearly three gallons' worth of the little sealed plastic packets of water they were passing out. Also, I learned later that the event had drawn nearly twice the runners it had served the year before and the organizers had been surprised. This left those of us at the back without water. And so we were offered Coke to replenish the liquids we were losing, but I didn't dare take anything as acidic as cola into my system right now. People were panicking. I heard one woman shouting at a volunteer, "You've got to do something. We could die in this heat, you know! This is irresponsible."

I hadn't descended into freakout mode with the others, because I always carried one bottle of water in my belt, but I knew I would be in trouble when my personal stash ran out. In my condition, I needed not only to stay hydrated, but also to keep my core temperature down. Fortunately, some of the aid stations had some remaining bits of ice in their coolers. I took my chances with its water quality and swallowed some whenever it was available.

At kilometer eighteen, a volunteer in a truck came by, throwing packets of cold water to runners in my vicinity. I took some, as much as I could. I refilled my own bottle and I guzzled the rest. It tasted pure, like a tonic from the gods. It was also a big mistake. The water flushed quickly through my system and my cramps returned, almost as intensely as they'd been the night they'd shown up. I knew the only way to relieve them was to empty my bowels. But where? There weren't even any trees to hide behind, much less portable toilets, and I didn't have any toilet paper. I fought off the urge to go as long as I could. I looked around. Yes, there were plenty of runners behind me. I wasn't going to get any privacy, it seemed. I'd have to find a bush to squat under and let the world watch.

I had thought bleeding in the Panama marathon was as indelicate as I'd ever have to be, and now this. My need was becoming urgent. There wasn't much time to bemoan my situation. I found a shrub, pulled down my running shorts, and did my business. I closed my eyes so as not to have to see if I had witnesses. I felt immediate relief and the cramps let up.

As I ran on, I felt almost amused at the indignities I'd endured for the sake of the marathon. When I had started running, I had never imagined it could get worse than a little sweat and snot—but we never know all that any commitment entails before we hit the hard parts, I suppose. And there were more hard parts ahead for me in this one.

The hills that had looked rolling and easy in the car two days earlier were endless and numerous on foot. The road just seemed to keep going up, with little dips in between to fool us into thinking we were getting a break now and again, but we really weren't. The humdrum course I had hoped would feel fast instead felt monotonous and never-ending, like running on a hamster wheel, looking at the same picture for hours.

Who the hell decided this would be a good place to run a marathon? I heard the Bitch ask. Then a very bedraggled voice chimed in: *Why not stop and ask to be taken to some shade and given some ice?* I considered these questions. I'd come too far to dismiss outright any voice that spoke up in my consciousness. I had to consider whether I was risking permanent damage by continuing. Was I really so compulsive that I had to finish what I started, no matter how dangerous or unpleasant? Certainly not. I was a known quitter in lots of areas of my life. I had no problem quitting in the middle of a board game or a household project. I'd quit plenty of jobs and even a whole marriage. So why was I still going in this particular race?

But I knew why. Although I was miserable and although I watched my time slow with every kilometer, until I knew it was unlikely I would make it to the finish for the cutoff time (5.5 hours), I knew I had what I needed to finish. I knew that finishing would make me feel rich and true to myself.

I knew that not everything was worth pushing through. Lots of things in life deserve to be quit and left behind, but those things (activities, commitments, projects) that enrich us and reward us deserve a better effort. They deserve for us to empty ourselves into them, trusting that we will be refilled and revived when all is said and done. The key is to know which things are which. This was one of those things for me that called for my extra effort. This line of thought quieted my voices. I carried on slowly, one step and then the next.

INTERESTINGLY, ALTHOUGH THE RACE had fewer than six hundred participants, I was never alone at the back of this pack. I'd seen many of my current companions on the bus that morning, and some were still with me now. A few of my fellow dawdlers, seeing that I didn't have a permanent license, asked me where I was from. One woman chatted with me for a while and told me about her favorite races around the country. A couple from Cape Town commiserated with me over the heat. I was encouraged by these brief conversations. Although I didn't have much strength to spend on talking, I borrowed the strength of the others around me, as we often do in crises.

The kilometers passed slowly. More hills came and went; I walked most of them. The vegetation never varied from the low, odiferous shrubs I had squatted behind a couple of hours earlier, but peeks of the water surprised me from out of nowhere at times and promised a refreshing, cool splash when this was all over.

Finally, when I was nearly depleted, drained of all I had to give this race, I saw the little resort town of Langebaan in the distance, sparkling in the sunlight. As I jogged (slowly) toward town, I also saw something I hadn't noticed when Bill and I had driven the course, or on the bus that morning: the biggest, longest, windiest freaking hill I'd ever seen in my life! I'm not sure how I'd missed it both times, but I had. It was at least a kilometer long, or maybe I should say "tall."

I was still half a kilometer away from its base, but the moment I realized

I'd have to brave it, I burst into tears. I'd traveled a long way in this race and remained resolute, if weary, but when I saw that hill, I felt a combination of rage and terror. I was so spent, so ready to be done, so needing to lie down and let my body begin to repair and restore itself.

"Damn it!" I sobbed. Only one runner was close enough to hear me losing it, but I didn't care and I didn't think he'd blame me. I just couldn't imagine from where I would mine the energy to make it up that hill. I even looked around to see if there was a volunteer or an aid station, momentarily considering quitting. But there wasn't an official within earshot, only that one other tired runner. I wanted so badly to see Bill and to stop moving and to find some shade. The only way to get these things, it appeared, was to go up and over that hill. So, with tears streaking down my salty, sunburned face, I started to climb, slowly, walking one labored step at a time.

I really didn't know where the strength for each of my strides was coming from, unless I was absorbing it from the guy grunting along behind me. He was shadowing me by about ten yards, climbing shirtless, baring his dark, broad chest and round belly. He held his jersey in his hand and occasionally caught up to me, waved it at me, and smiled. He spoke a language I didn't recognize, but I could tell he was trying to communicate something very emphatic, as he ended each sentence with exclamation points. I imagined he was saying something inspirational, like, "Come on! We can do it!" Or he might have been cursing, too. In any case, his presence was comforting, and I offered him a faint smile to concur with whatever he was saying.

After what seemed like two years, we made it to the top of the hill. My friend and I congratulated each other. I wiped my tears away and saw that the fates were finally smiling on me (or at least smirking). Everything from here on out was downhill for the final two kilometers into the town. I waved goodbye to my companion, leaned forward, and let the welcome sea breeze carry me down toward the water. I am nothing as a runner if not opportunistic. I had good knees, empty bowels for the moment, and no reason not to take advantage of gravity's pull, so away I went. One more bend, and there was the finish line. As soon as I saw it, I renewed my crying. Bill and a few dozen other finishers stood along the sidelines, cheering for me.

As I crossed, I repeated, "Oh god, oh jeez, that was hard. That was so hard."

Bill rushed around to the other side of the finish line and pulled me into a hug that held me up for a moment. "I was so worried about you," he said.

I looked at my watch and guesstimated my finish time (5:35). I had missed the cutoff by five minutes. No medal for me. A wave of disappointment crashed over me, but it was not as salient as my immediate need for shade and liquids.

"I've got to sit," I panted.

I wanted to feel exultant, as I had after other marathons. I'd run arguably the most difficult race of my life; I'd earned the right to feel triumphant, even defiant toward the most significant limitation I had faced to date: illness. But I did not feel either. I felt done. I'd given all that I had and it was finished.

As quickly as I could, I found a tent and sat down on a patch of dry grass. My body went limp. I wanted to curl into a ball and close my eyes.

Bill stood over me, assessing my physical state. I looked up at him pleadingly. Could he get me something cold? Anything?

Bill fetched the only thing he could find for me, a cold cola, and sat down on the grass beside me.

"How are you?" he asked.

"Not well. But I did it."

"Just sit here for a while and stretch." He had that annoying authoritarian tone in his voice again, but I only had the energy to obey this time. I drank my Coke and gingerly stretched out my legs, back, and shoulders. I closed my eyes and squeezed the tears from them. And I rested.

"Hello," I heard a familiar masculine voice behind me, disturbing my moment of self-pity. The greeting was followed by a strand of foreign words.

I knew who it was right away and looked up into the face of my friend from the hill. He put out his hand to me, and when I took it he pulled me to a standing position and threw his arms around me. He continued uttering incomprehensible words.

As spent as I was, I had to laugh at our dysfunctional communication. "Congratulations to you, too," I said. "Good job. You doing okay?"

He replied. I suppose he said he was tired and that he was glad to be done.

With a final pat on my back and a raised fist in the air, he left me. A woman in the tent had observed our embrace and our mishmash of languages. She approached me and asked where I was from.

"From the U.S.—Washington State," I said.

"My name is Jean," she said. "Welcome. And congratulations on finishing. What was your time?"

"5:35," I said. "I just missed the cutoff."

"Oh, no. Then you didn't get a medal," Jean shook her head. "That won't do. You'll have mine, then. You can't come all this way and go home without a medal. I can run this again next year if I'm desperate for the medal." Then she took her medal from out of the sports bag she held on her lap and handed it to me.

I tried to refuse it, but Jean insisted, thrusting it at me. I thanked her and nearly resumed my tears in the face of her generosity. But just then, Bill and I heard someone on the microphone talking about the Americans who had just finished the race. Someone else had apparently overheard my interaction with Jean as she offered me her medal, and now a man with a microphone was introducing us to the crowd. Before I knew what was happening, we'd been identified as "Americans from Washington." We were offered beers and congratulations and pats on the back. We both waved at the dwindling group of tired runners and received their greetings. I wondered how long I could hold myself up. But I was also very aware that we were among an extraordinary mix of South Africans we would never meet again, so I leaned against Bill and shook as many hands as were shoved in my direction.

This was a different kind of South African experience than we'd had in Cape Town. Here there was a gentle respect, one runner for another, and a quiet celebration of each other's accomplishments, like I experienced back home. I was proud to see the marathon pull this off.

I was also ready to go back to bed.

I LAY LOW THE next day, picking up my illness where I'd left off but managing to enjoy the lagoon a little. The fresh air, warm sand, and cool blue water were healing.

Two days after the race, on Monday, we took our rental car and a map Colette had sketched out for us and headed east. Our plan was to go to the wine country. I still wasn't well and was drinking large quantities of water to restore what I'd lost in the race. The liquids went through me quickly. My fever dissipated, but cramps still came and went. I wanted to try to taste some wine, but I'd have to take it easy.

I thought the hardest part of the trip was behind me, but I was about to have to dig for deeper strength than I had in a long time. As Bill and I drove into the wine country, we were much worse for wear. Bill was drained from bearing the brunt of the responsibility for taking care of me and for getting us from point to point. I was little help with navigation or anything else, really. We bickered as we drove, finding ourselves peeved by the smallest offenses and unable to enjoy the views of the rolling green hills and jagged rocky gulches we passed.

I had to ask Bill to find me restrooms so many times throughout the day that when we finally made it to Tulbagh, the first wine town that had been recommended to us, we were too late to taste wine. It was getting dark, and we realized we needed to find a place to stay for the evening.

We stopped at several of the quaint, colonial guesthouses along the wine route and discovered that they were greatly overpriced for the area. According to the guidebooks, we should have been paying half or a third of what they were asking. It was getting darker by the moment, but we decided we would drive farther down the highway to the next town anyhow.

Bill was dragging. He had been doing almost nothing but driving and catering to my need to find toilets all day. He'd stopped at the grocery store and a pharmacy along the way, too, to get me food I could stomach and antacids. I had been terribly boring company at best—and cranky and difficult to manage at worst. Now he was driving around in the dark on the wrong side of the road, attempting to find a reasonable place to stay—someplace clean, safe, and affordable—so we could both rest.

Twice, Bill pulled the car over onto the right side of the street and faced bright headlights coming straight toward us, as I stuttered out a terrified, "W . . . wa . . . *watch out!*" We had to find someplace to stay soon, before he caused an accident.

When we saw the BED AND BREAKFAST sign about ten miles out of Tulbagh, we were both relieved. It was a big, welcoming white house with a high, imposing fence around it, promising safety. We parked the car and got out. As we walked toward the gate, we both noticed the painted sign on the side of the house, which read HOUSE OF BREAD.

"Oh, it's a bakery, too," Bill said.

I knew it wasn't a bakery. I was aware of a faint foreboding feeling about what was about to happen, but I was sick and it all happened so quickly. Bill rang the bell and a man's voice answered.

Bill said, "Hi, you have two travelers out here looking for a place to stay. Do you have space?"

"I'll be right there," the voice said.

In a few moments, a white man of about forty-five with a pleasant smile came to the gate and opened it just enough to get a good look at us. He stood a step above us and gave us a suspicious once-over. Then he said, "Listen, before I let you in, I have a question. I hate to ask you this, but you see this house doesn't belong to me. It belongs to the Lord, so I can't just let anyone in. Are you married?"

Right away, my heart fell into my already sour stomach. I wanted to turn on my heel and walk away. But where would I go? I was silent as I tried to think of a satisfactory way to address this man's question. All the religious dogma I'd worked so hard to separate myself from came flooding into my consciousness. My legs felt rubbery as thoughts flipped through my mind at high speed. I put a hand on Bill's shoulder to steady myself. I'd been judged (and judged myself and others) too many times based on someone else's perspective of what "the Lord" wanted. I'd worked hard to sort my way out of that black-and-white world where "married" people were in the right but divorced people (or gay, cohabiting, or single people) were bad, wrong, or insufficient somehow. I didn't want to go back there, even for one night.

I saw this man as asking me to agree that he had the right to decide my worthiness in God's eyes. I wanted to respond to his question wisely. I tried to access my Wisdom, but she was sluggish, as she had been on this whole journey.

Meanwhile, Bill had no idea about the tornado of thoughts this man's question had sparked in me. While I struggled to come up with an answer that would satisfactorily let this man know that he had offended me, Bill simply answered, "Yeah, sure. We're married."

These were the words Mr. Bread needed to hear, and he deemed us acceptable to pass through the doors. "Oh, well, then, welcome to the House of Bread," the man said, "where Jesus is the bread of life. Come on in. Let me show you around. It's eighty rand for the night." Bill smiled at me. Forty dollars. What a find! I could see the gratitude on his face. For forty bucks, he would soon have a place to lay his head. He was about to get a reprieve from the stress of driving, the heat, and the responsibility of taking care of me. Bill was ready to crash.

For me, my symptoms became more acute. The base of my head throbbed. I watched Mr. Bread as he showed us around. He seemed like a nice enough fellow on the surface, yet I couldn't reconcile his kind demeanor with the idea that the only couples he could have in his guesthouse were married ones. I followed him around the grounds. He spoke with pride about the beautiful garden he kept. He told us he'd come from Namibia and loved South Africa and was glad to be here. He'd purchased this place and nurtured it and wanted to share it. He and his wife were very pleased to be offering respite to tired people, he said. They hoped to be a blessing along the wine route.

I listened, but I wasn't in my body. Instead I was back home, sitting with my friend Stephanie, who, at age thirty-five, had finally come out to her family. I was with her in her apartment while she wondered if God would love her if she admitted to herself and others that she was a lesbian. I was wondering how she would feel that I, the one cheerleader she'd had during that time, the person who had promised that God wasn't stingy and homophobic, had acquiesced to sleep in a place where she wouldn't have been welcome.

I followed the two men into the courtyard as Mr. Bread showed us how each of the rooms in the guesthouse had one of God's names nailed above it. There was El Shaddai, "God is sufficient." Next was Adonai, "Master," and Elohim, "Creator." Our room was Jehovah-Salom, "Peace." *Humph,* I thought. Finally, the man left us in our room and said goodnight. We closed the door and Bill sat down with a heavy, relieved sigh. As for me, I began to cry.

"What is it? What happened?" he said with wide eyes.

"I can't stay here," I said, shaking my head. "I will have to betray everything I believe in if I stay here."

His eyes opened even wider. I could see his expression shift between anger, confusion, and compassion for my tears and helplessness.

"What do you mean?" he asked.

"How can I face everyone at home if I use my privilege of being married to stay in a place some of them would be excluded from? It's like being a prostitute, like selling your soul for a good night's sleep."

The truth is, at some point, we all sell our souls for something convenient or easy. We don't always have the moral strength or skill to stand up for what we believe. In the old days, I called this sin. And that was the way it felt now. I remembered Prague, and for the first time I understood how Bill must have felt when we had cheated our way into that race, knowing we would cross the finish line under false pretenses, without having really earned the right. I felt we'd just stolen our way to a set of clean sheets without having earned the privilege that let us in the door. It was a shame.

In the space of a very few minutes under Mr. Bread's roof, I had reverted to being a binary thinker who could arrange reality into only two categories: right or wrong. Being here under these conditions was wrong. Period.

Bill sat staring at me for a long, long time as I wept. Finally, after rising to get me some tissue from the bathroom, he pulled his chair forward and leaned toward me, taking my hands in his. He said to me, "Cami, do we need to leave?"

The question quieted me. He was actually willing to leave with me if I needed him to. I wiped my eyes and really looked at him now. His skin appeared gray, not the beautiful tan I was used to. His hair looked more salt than pepper, his wrinkles more deep-set; his eyes were sunken, his strong, square jaw seemed less sturdy than usual. He looked like I had felt at the end of the marathon.

Suddenly I saw how self-centered my wallowing had become, how caught up in my own head I was. Bill sat before me at least as overwhelmed and worn as I had any right to be. The person I loved and who loved me best in the world just might not make it to the next town. We were already here. I'd already transgressed my principles. And frankly, my crying had taken the last bit of strength out of me anyhow. Again, as with the decision to run sick or skip the marathon, I had to choose between two not-so-great choices: leave to relieve my conscience or stay to let my loved one rest. *You see, the answers are never as simple as we might wish,* Wisdom chimed in, speaking to me at long last.

"No," I said, relaxing my shoulders into a slump. "No, what's done is done; let's go ahead and stay here."

We got ready for bed and climbed in. I was resigned to stay, but the guilt of my transgression still pressed down heavily on my chest cavity. What was one supposed to do when she sinned? What inner force was she supposed to call up when she had already betrayed her default, the thing she was supposed to be able to fall back on—her values? I used to know what to do: I would pray. I would confess my sin and ask forgiveness. I hadn't done either of those things in the usual sense for a long time. But I was willing in the moment, for the sake of peace of mind, to build a bridge between my old habits and my new developing paradigm.

After all, this guilt I felt now was very similar to the old religious guilt I'd felt much of my life. It was the kind of guilt that floods in whenever a mistake threatens to separate you from your ability to believe you're a good person. For me, it was insidious because it insisted I could not trust myself to follow through on my own convictions. Maybe my old ways (with a new twist, of course) were exactly what I needed for this guilt. Maybe confession could set things right somehow (or, if not "right," then at least better), even now.

At the moment, I didn't have any of the people I felt I had wronged handy to confess to, so I would have to use my imagination. In my mind, I would sit down with everyone I could think of who wouldn't have been allowed to stay at the House of Bread for one reason or another and confess what I had done. At the kitchen table of my mind, I made tea and explained the situation and said I was sorry for not being stronger. I needed them to bear witness to my shame and see my greater intentions. In my imagination—and later, in reality, when I actually told people the story—my friends were more gracious than I had been to myself. Each said, "Well, you were tired. I probably would have said anything just to get to bed at that point."

Finally, I realized there was one more person I needed to apologize to. It was the Lord himself. Yes, Jesus. I'd never wanted to believe that Jesus was so close-minded, so priggish, such a fundamentalist as some people believed. I suspected he would have been annoyed at the way he was represented by many who claimed to model themselves after him. He must have sympathized with the very dilemma Mr. Bread was putting people in: Jesus's own parents had been shut out of several guesthouses the night he was born, probably for not being properly married. Oh sure, there was a census being taken, and Bethlehem was overcrowded. Everyone said, "There's no room here." But I'll bet Mary and Joseph were smarter than to believe that. She was a teenager, he her older fiancé. She claimed to be a virgin, although she obviously had a well-baked bun in the oven, and they had no place to go to deliver that baby. Nobody wanted the mess of childbirth on their motel floor. The couple finally ended up in a barn, where Joseph had to deliver the baby onto a floor of hay. With this as the start of his life, recorded for the world to read over and over every December, Jesus would have been irritated by Mr. Bread's question, I was sure, and not at all pleased with my inability to stand up to him.

I invited Jesus to have some tea with me, ready to speak to him for the first time in a long while. As he sat across from me, I remembered all the Bible stories I'd read about his standing up for the rights of others, pushing back against those who wanted to stone or shun people for their sexual habits or "improper" behavior. He'd set a good example for me that I hadn't followed that night.

"I'm really sorry," I finally said. "I should have stuck up for you."

Clear as a bell, I heard him say, *Don't worry about it. You'll get another chance.* And I knew it was true. The world was full of prejudice and intolerance. There would be a host of chances in my lifetime to be true to myself and to the people and principles I cared about. Next time I'd be better prepared.

By the morning, I'd miraculously developed compassion for Mr. Bread. What I realized with a little rest was that I had been where he was only a few years earlier, compulsively trying to follow laws and rules that I thought were God's laws and rules. When I went into the lobby to say goodbye to him, I saw a sincere person who believed that certain other people would be excluded from the arms of his God's love. He had no idea how damaging his question was, nor how, ironically, it had helped me build a bridge between my history and my present. I knew from his apologies the night before that he wished God was a better, nicer person than he believed God to be, but he just wasn't there yet.

I was sad for Mr. Bread because I used to think God was a jerk, too, and I offered, in another of the quasi-neo-prayers I'd been saying all night, that someday he might be able to open up his gates to anyone who came by. I believed (or projected) that Mr. Bread wanted to offer real, Christ-like hospitality. I just hoped like hell that no tired gay couple (or unwed mother with her fiancé) happened upon the House of Bread, only to be rejected before he changed his perspective.

BILL AND I CONTINUED along the wine route for several days before returning to Cape Town to catch our plane back to the States. By this point in our relationship, we had known each other nearly twenty years. We'd traveled to eight countries and all over the United States together. We'd run hundreds of training miles together. Bill understood my penchant for overthinking existential questions, and I understood his occasional moodiness. Not much fazed our partnership, but this trip had taken its toll. We were tired of each other, of the heat, and even of traveling.

It was time to go home. Bill was ready to drive on the right side of the road again and to feel the cool Northwest spring air on his skin. I was ready to return to my dogs, my community, and my own bed, where I could finish my slow recovery from whatever illness had besieged me in Langebaan. Still, I was bringing home some hard-won souvenirs I would cherish for the rest of my life: a new set of questions about my responsibility as a citizen in an imperfect world, a precarious new bridge between my history and my present spirituality, and one kindly given marathon medal.

cobwebs
AND casseroles
APRIL–JUNE 2009

"Your problem is how you are going to spend this one and precious life you have been issued. Whether you're going to spend it trying to look good and creating the illusion that you have power over circumstances, or whether you are going to taste it, enjoy it, and find out the truth about who you are."

—ANNE LAMOTT, from her 2007 commencement address at University of California, Berkeley

"To get to the finish line, you'll have to try lots of different paths."

—AMBY BURFOOT, marathoner

10

I came home from South Africa burned out, frankly. Once home and in our respective routines, Bill and I treaded lightly around each other and stuck to our own pursuits. We'd had more than our share of face-to-face time in the past months, jammed into coach, shoved together in small hostel beds, with little time alone to process all that we'd experienced on our last trips. It was April now, and we had ten weeks until our next excursion, to Brazil. We already had the tickets, and, though I hated to admit it, a part of me (my body, for one) needed more than a ten-week respite from international travel.

Within a week of coming home from South Africa, I received a frantic phone call from my cousin saying that her mother, my aunt Sue, my dad's younger sister, was in the hospital. She had become short of breath one evening and had been taken to the emergency room, where they had put her in a drug-induced coma so they could stabilize her vitals with machines and prevent her from pulling tubes out of her throat. She was carrying almost fifty pounds of excess water weight in her system, had congestive heart failure, and was about to be diagnosed with something akin to emphysema, though she had quit smoking more than a decade earlier, after my grandfather had died of lung cancer.

I went to visit Aunt Sue in the hospital once she was stable enough to be taken off the sedatives. Sitting beside her bed, holding her rough, dry, puffy hand, and looking at the tubes shoved into her mouth and up her nose, I was overwhelmed by life's fragility. If Sue didn't get better, I would lose one of those precious few people in my life by whom I didn't feel judged. Sue had always treated me as an equal, even when I was a child. It was in her character to embrace everyone in her life, no matter what his or her flaws, with open-minded acceptance.

I knew my aunt had been hard on her body. At fifty-six, she was obese and underexercised and had overindulged in vices throughout her life. Still, she was vital, funny, and sexy in her own particular way. With a toss of her long blond hair and her deep, hoarse laugh, she could lighten a heavy moment and bring perspective to any situation.

As I sat next to Sue's immobile body, I realized for the first time that I could easily have ended up in the hospital myself the month before. The doctor I had seen once I was back in the States didn't know what I had caught in Africa, and my symptoms added up to any number of diagnoses. She did say she wished I hadn't run the race in such a compromised condition. She didn't understand that I'd had to—that not running wasn't a serious option. The doctor warned me that I now needed to rest and let myself recover. I promised her I would try, but opted not to tell her that we had another international race on the horizon shortly.

My cousin and I chatted in my aunt's hospital room in quiet tones. Occasionally, Sue asked for pen and paper so she could communicate an idea, but most of our thoughts remained unspoken. In those long moments, I reflected on the ways in which I'd always worked to avoid my family's plight of poor health by being vigilant with my intakes and outputs. But having very recently had my own brush with illness, I knew firsthand that there were many ways to be hard on the body. Anyway, everyone dies, and we don't usually get to know when the time is imminent.

Rather than causing me to feel more cautious about my one fragile life, these reflections invited me to feel grateful for all of the risk-taking I'd engaged in these last years. In one of those rare clear moments, like the one I'd experienced when I stood at the top of Fuji-san and saw my own connection to all that existed in the world, I now looked over at my aunt and saw that as burned out as I felt right now, I needed to renew my vow to suck every drop of living out of this life I had, to sieve out every grain of happiness, grief, excitement, stillness, or anger that a fully lived life could offer me.

On my drive home from the hospital, my contemplations ran fast. The last months had been a whirlwind, and I needed to take some time before flying overseas again to collect myself—all the parts and voices—to heal my body and then refocus for the last couple of laps on this marathon quest. I needed to consult my Inner Wisdom and ask her to distill what she had taught me. I wanted time to record things I did not want to forget.

The next Friday evening, Bill and I sat at the kitchen table for dinner. Our condo, small and cozy, was warm. The glass chandelier that hung above our tiny round table shone its light on our simple dinner of Caesar salad and French bread. We ate quietly, each following our separate trains of thought.

I broke our silence. "I need to regroup," I said. "We've taken in a lot, and I need to go someplace where I can just sit with it and clear some cobwebs out of my head before we move on to the next race and the next set of revelations."

Bill looked at me and nodded. He could certainly relate. "What do you have in mind?" he asked.

"I'm thinking about going to visit Wendy at the beginning of June, before we fly to Brazil."

He nodded again. Wendy was one of my oldest friends. She owned a bustling used bookstore in Big Stone Gap, Virginia, called Tales of the Lone-some Pine, but she also had a secluded cabin in the hills of Tennessee that I hoped to retreat to so I could think and write and breathe before taking on one more time zone, one more language, and one more marathon. Exactly my age, Wendy is round-faced, straight-talking, and maternal, with a no-nonsense expectation that everything will turn out fine if you can sit still and wait for ten minutes. "Good idea," Bill said.

I called Wendy the next day and asked, "If I pay for a plane ticket to come see you, will you take me to your cabin and feed me?"

"Absolutely!" she said. "I'll start the casseroles now."

TWO HOURS OUTSIDE OF Knoxville, Wendy's cabin is idyllic. It cuddles up against a hillside and faces a small valley with a shallow pond in its gulch. Back at home, the end of spring was chilly and rainy, as usual, but in the Tennessee hills it was warm. The mosquitoes were just beginning to emerge and the trees were filled in with plush leaves. Each morning for two days, Wendy and I drank coffee on the porch that overlooked the pond and watched two humongous trout swim circles, popping their noses up to the surface on occasion to indulge in an insect floating on the water. I worried about getting a tick and catching Rocky Mountain spotted fever, while Wendy laughed at how easily my anxiety about getting an exotic illness was activated. She urged me to relax.

After coffee those first mornings, we retreated to separate rooms in the cabin. Wendy worked on a novel she was writing, and I closed my eyes and listened. When a person has met as many new aspects of herself as I had in the last years, she needs to honor them with some unobstructed quiet time. Quiet wasn't my natural state, but it felt good. I opened my eyes frequently and wrote down what I was hearing—from Wisdom, from the Bitch, from the Warrior. I was happy we were all together without a racecourse to navigate.

By the third morning, I'd had enough of sitting still. I needed a run. Wendy dropped me at the corner of a long country road she thought would be safe for me to traverse on foot. I jogged up and then down the rolling hills alongside farmhouses and log cabins, catching the scent of honeysuckle in the air. I let my thoughts fly free in a stream of consciousness.

I noticed the way my muscles felt happy. My body was fully recovered by now, though I still tired easily. I wondered how the dogs and Bill were doing back home. I thought ahead to the Rio Marathon in just a couple of weeks and hoped I'd be ready. I sent silent wishes to my aunt for her continued recovery, which was happening slowly but surely, much to my relief. And I opened up a container of worry I had kept the lid on during my retreat these past few days, about Antarctica. I was fretting about this critical leg of the journey, the final race that would allow me to close the chapter on this particular quest.

The problem with closing the Seven Marathons on Seven Continents challenge was logistical. Just before I left for Tennessee, I had received an email from Marathon Tours, the company that ran the marathon in Antarctica we were signed up for, saying I wasn't confirmed for the March 2010 trip. Maybe, they'd said, I'd get a place on the 2011 boat to Antarctica.

They'd placed me on that waiting list. If I didn't get confirmed for 2011, they'd bump me to 2012.

I got the news on Monday, June 1, 2009. The message read: "We have been restricted to one ship for 2010. Thus, many people who were confirmed for 2010 are now confirmed for 2011."

After reading this note, I'd sat with my hands on my keyboard, too stunned to think of a reply. It didn't take me long to recognize my anger anymore, and it roared up as I sat in complete stillness, staring at the screen.

There were not many options for running the marathon distance on the continent of Antarctica. One was inland at the South Pole, and although it looked like the kind of once-in-a-lifetime experience I would give my right arm for, it cost almost that much. Bill and I had dwindled our savings down to a nub to live out this quest. My own money market account had shrunk down to zero. We had funds enough for the Marathon Tours race, the one in question, which took runners on a cruise through the Drake Passage and spit them out on land for a few hours for the race. It was expensive, too, but less than a third of the South Pole race.

Getting booted to the 2011 waiting list wasn't what made me angry. It was true that I hoped to complete my seven-continent marathon quest before 2010 came to an end, but I'd grown up unaccustomed to getting what I wanted just by asking; I was a blue-collar kid who rolled well with the punches, adapted quickly, and readjusted my expectations when required to do so. What made me angry was being dismissed. I'd never been good with that.

Several months earlier, I had written a check for $600 to put Bill and me on that 2010 waiting list. The tour company had told me that I was likely to be moved up to the confirmed list because the rate of cancellation was always high, and because the economy was bad and many people were forgoing expensive trips.

In the weeks leading up to my visit with Wendy, I'd started to feel disquieted by the lack of communication from the tour group. They were sitting on our money, but they weren't sending me updates about our status. After I'd made calls and sent emails to inquire whether or not we'd gotten confirmed yet, the brief note I received from them implied to me that it was immaterial to them whether or not I ever got on the boat. Perhaps my own sense of expectation about running this marathon in 2010 intensified my need for genuine human connection and empathy on the matter. There seemed to be dead air on the other end of what I thought should be a two-way conversation. Was there no one to whom I could explain how important this was to me? No one to hear me out and offer a solution? I felt dismissed and alone, up against a huge dilemma.

With my fingers still hovering at the keyboard, I'd stared up at the wall in front of my desk, thinking about how to respond. The Japanese watercolor painting of bamboo shoots that hung on my office wall seemed to invite me to take a breath and think before writing something like, "Well, thanks for telling me, butthead. How about you send me my money back and I'll go with the other company?" But Wisdom prevailed for the moment. My quest to run the continents was important to me. I didn't want to shoot myself in the foot; I knew I couldn't afford the other company. I would have to keep trying with this one. I believed it was my only chance to run on the last continent.

I closed my eyes, quieted my Bitchy voice, and, as sweetly as I could, wrote a polite but direct response explaining that the race was important to me and that I'd do whatever it took to get on the boat, even if I had to sleep on the floor, I joked. The next day, I received a response that repeated the information I'd already received. The gist of the email was that the people running this race were those who had deposited in 2007, and so I would have to wait. In my mind, this statement translated to *Wait your turn and get over it.*

Okay. Yes, the folks whose money had been earning interest for the tour company since 2007 certainly deserved priority—I could go that far. But still, why hadn't I been notified that there were people who'd been waiting to run this thing for more than two years? I read the email again and then took my Bitchy, angry self down to Starbucks for a coffee. I ordered my double short soy latte and sat down in one of the soft worn chairs tucked in the corner by a window. Then I sipped my coffee slowly and seethed. We were committed to investing a hell of a lot of money to live out a dream here.

Didn't I deserve some cordiality? A little "We look forward to serving you in the future" would sure go a long way.

What to do now? I could put off Antarctica for a year or two, but I was also in the home stretch. I didn't want to wait one or two more years to finish my quest. Plus, it would mean paying my substantial amount of money to a company that was rude and that I was annoyed with. What had I learned about life through all this running and traveling? I'd learned that I wasn't the person I used to be.

Once upon a time I had been a very good girl. I'd waited my turn in lines, held my tongue, and cried all alone in my room when others ignored me. But now my body and mind felt strong, and the more I ran, the less I cared if people liked me or if I was demure or nice enough for their tastes. I'd lost my appetite for falling in line. All of this made me happier, but it also made my life complex.

These thoughts came back to me now, as I ran on a Tennessee country road, and at this moment, with the perfect sunshine on my shoulders and the sweetness in the air and Wendy's cooking waiting for me back at the cabin, I suddenly knew that, as the complex woman I'd become, I couldn't let someone else decide where and when I got to travel or how many miles I was allowed to run when I landed. I couldn't bear the thought that someone else, especially an impersonal company—which to me felt rule-imposing and authoritarian—would have the power to sanction or deny the final leg of my vision quest.

I continued jogging next to hayfields, bypassing barking dogs and roaring lawn mowers. As my feet hit the ground, I heard a refrain begin to echo, very faintly at first, in the recesses of my memory: *Bom. Bom. Bom. BOOM!* I thought I heard something else; I listened more intently. *I. Win. I. WIN!* came louder. It was the Warrior Woman rising inside me. She was telling me something important. I tuned in and heard: *Find. Your. Own. WAY!*

"Find my own way?" I echoed aloud. But how? I hadn't ever faced this particular kind of conundrum (how to get to the ends of the earth), but I knew I was up for the challenge, especially after a couple of days in reflective appreciation for my own growth.

Eventually, I reached my turnaround point, at the top of the highest hill in the vicinity. I pulled out my cell phone to confirm that I had reception, and then I rang Bill back in Bellingham.

"Hi," he answered. "What are you doing?"

"I'm running. It's beautiful here. How are you and the pups?"

"Doing great," he said. "Nothing to worry about," he added. "Are you regrouped yet?"

"I think so," I said. "I've been thinking about Antarctica."

"Me too," he replied. "I have some ideas." Here was something I loved about Bill: Though we each ran our races solo for sanity's sake, he was the best team player I'd ever known.

Apparently, on separate sides of the country, Bill and I had been coming to the same conclusion. Why not find our own way to Antarctica and run 26.2 miles? We now had a GPS tracking device that we could use to measure the distance for ourselves. It certainly wouldn't be a Boston qualifying race, but did I need anyone to say that my miles qualified for anything? I didn't. I needed only to be satisfied that I had done my best and gone the distance. I'd come a long way from the days of looking to an external set of dicta for validation and guidance. And Bill had come a long way from needing a marathon course to be "regulation" in order to feel it had integrity.

Neither Bill nor I had done any research yet about how difficult it would be to get to Antarctica. As we briefly pooled our knowledge, all we knew was that the continent was not owned by any particular country, that tourists did go there somehow, that it hosted several international research and scientific bases, and that most, if not all, of Antarctica was a "protected environment," whatever that meant.

Standing at the top of a Tennessee hill, I understood we had a lot of work to do if we wanted to make our own way to the bottom of the planet.

"Well, you'd better get on the computer and start our research," I told Bill.

"Will do," he said. "Have a good rest of your visit with Wendy, and come home safe."

"Will do," I repeated back to him, and hung up my phone.

I started a slow jog down the hill, tuned in to the Warrior beat of my pace, and let my imagination run away with me. How could I get to that final landmass? Boat? Helicopter? Superpowers? In my mind's eye, I saw Bill and myself bundled in Gore-Tex, trudging over snow-covered hills in a blistering windstorm. Though it was nearly eighty degrees at the moment, I shivered at the visual of us in those conditions. Still, as I had said a thousand years ago in Prague, when I had first thrown perfection under the bus, it would make a good story.

Before I realized it, I had run all the way back to the corner where Wendy had dropped me off. I saw her long red hair streaming in the wind and her upraised hand waving to catch my attention.

"Heya," she said to me in her Southern drawl, with just a hint of the Scottish burr she'd picked up from her husband.

"Hi," I said. "Guess what? I'm going to Antarctica."

"Cool," she said, pun intended. "Tell me all about it over casserole. Let's go."

We drove back to the cabin, ate lunch, and resumed our previous schedule for the next couple of days until it was time for me to return to Bellingham. Once I got home from Tennessee, we had only a few days before we flew to Brazil. I was ready now. I had renewed my commitment. The cobwebs were cleared from my tired mind. My body was healthy again. And I was hatching a plan to get to Antarctica.

south america:
THE rio resolve
JUNE 2009

"Use anything you can think of to understand and be understood,
and you'll discover the creativity that connects you with others."

—MARTHA BECK

"If you feel like eating, eat. Let your body tell you what it wants."

—JOAN BENOIT SAMUELSON

11

As soon as we arrived at Sea-Tac Airport once again, I had to put my plotting about Antarctica on hold. I settled into the immediate bustle of ticketing and security checks and last-minute calls to say goodbye to family and friends before turning off my cell phone for two weeks.

The flights (from Seattle to Atlanta and Atlanta to São Paulo) went smoothly, except that I got bumped to business class for our first leg, while Bill was abandoned to the lifestyle to which he had become accustomed in the rear of the plane. I smuggled him a warm sandwich and a bag of chips to atone for my good luck, but, alas, there was nothing I could do to deliver him my bottomless glass of chardonnay.

As we flew into São Paolo (with me back in coach), I leaned against the window and gaped at one of the largest cities in the world from the air. Even from our elevated position, there was no end to it on the horizon. The highrises and sparkling lights and zooming highways crowded in against one another, reminding me that I was nothing but a drop in a massive population bucket. How many people lived here? I tried to call up what I'd read in the travel guide.

As if he were clairvoyant, Bill said, "Around twenty million people down there," shaking his head.

"Incredible," I said. It truly seemed a credit to humanity that so many people could live crammed together in that tight, concrete environment without utter anarchy breaking out. "It's like a sci-fi movie. Can't wait to see it close up."

Once we were on the ground at the São Paulo airport, Bill's friend Dimas and Dimas's son, Lucas, would meet us. In 1967, Bill had come to Brazil as an exchange student and lived with Dimas's family for six months. Because of this connection, I was considerably less concerned about the organization of this trip than I had been about any of the others to date. From what I understood, Dimas had the first ten days of our trip scheduled and our lodgings situated. Only after leaving the greater São Paulo area for Rio, and, by extension, for the marathon, would we have to take over our own course plotting and direction finding.

We wandered around the São Paulo airport for a few minutes after getting through immigration, trying to spot Dimas and Lucas. I, of course, knew only that I was looking for a man about Bill's age and another man around thirty. Bill was searching for someone he hadn't seen in decades. We gazed into many faces that returned our questioning looks with blank stares. After about a half hour, we began to fear we'd somehow missed our connection, and started to discuss alternative plans for getting into the city for the night, thinking we might phone Dimas in the morning to try to hook up again.

Just then, however, I watched as a good-looking, sharply dressed fellow, accompanied by a handsome younger man, walked gingerly up to Bill and studied his face before uttering a very tentative "Bill?"

Bill returned Dimas's scrutiny, void for a moment, and then I saw recognition dawn on both men's faces.

"Dimas!" Bill acknowledged, and there were hugs and kisses and introductions all around before we were whisked out of the airport to Dimas's car for our short journey "home." I was relieved to have found them and to be attached to competent guides, especially once I saw the horror that is Brazilian city traffic, which whooshed and zinged past us at frightening speeds as we merged onto the highway.

Lucas, a beautiful young man with dark hair and large, kind eyes, drove us through the chaotic streets to his condominium. He lived on the sixth floor of a secured building in the center of the shopping district. We would have only the afternoon with Dimas before he needed to catch the bus back to his own home, in Ribeirão Preto, a couple of hours away, which was where Bill had lived during his high school exchange. We would follow him there in a few days, after we had explored the giant city. Dimas took us to dinner, asked Lucas to take good care of us and to orient us to São Paolo, and then kissed us goodbye. During the short hours we had with him that day, Dimas told Bill repeatedly that he was glad to have his lost brother back.

Dimas's effusive affection toward Bill made me believe that Bill's absence had been felt here in Brazil every single day for the past forty years. Tired as I was, I felt happy and warm inside. Based on Dimas's emotional reception, we weren't really tourists here at all—we were family.

By about seven o'clock that evening, I was ready to get to sleep and try to adjust to my new time zone. As I showered and freshened up before bed, I couldn't help musing about how instrumental this "other" family had been in Bill's life. He had recounted stories to me about them for years and described how his exchange in Brazil had changed him, opened up his eyes to culture, politics, and family customs beyond his own. Their contributions had never left his consciousness; he'd continued to build on them for the rest of his life. Even Bill's mother testified to (actually, complained about) a dramatic change in Bill after he returned from Brazil.

My observations of Bill now that we'd returned to Brazil made me consider my own "other families," the people who had taken me into their homes and changed my life. For me, because of the serial transitions in my nuclear family while I was growing up, I craved attention from adults to help me feel stable and attended to. My grandparents were the loves of my life, always pitching in where they were needed, but there were also others who'd extended their helping hands along the way. A couple of those people came to mind now. When I was in high school, I'd formed a special bond with my French/drama teacher, Joan. She gave me emotional support all through my lonely adolescent years. Later, when I needed to move away from home after I graduated, but before it occurred to me to get a college degree and before I knew how I would make a living to support myself, Joan cleared space for me in her house.

Meanwhile, Linda, a neighbor woman who often told me she thought of me as one of her own children (she'd made my eighth-grade-dance dress for me, taught me to drive, and coached me through my first job interview) loaned me her old red Volkswagen Beetle so I could have transportation during my time living at Joan's. (I eventually even put a big dent in Linda's car, just like a real daughter might have done.) These two women opened up the world to me with their inclusion and kindness. And I genuinely believed I was as important to them as they were to me.

In a similar way, Dimas's family had given Bill a more expansive world-view than he would have known had he stayed in his upper-crust Chicago suburb his junior year of high school. At a critical juncture in his life, they taught him that the world was made up of people different from him and his family, and that he was part of a larger whole. And now I was witnessing the fact that the changing of lives ran both ways. Over the next week, I would come to understand that in fact Bill's presence in this large, extended Brazilian family had sparked a commitment to international exchange that almost every member shared. Dimas's siblings, children, and nieces and nephews created opportunities for themselves to live and study abroad so they could learn to be citizens not just of Brazil, but of the world. I admired that and felt myself falling in love with the whole clan before I even met them.

We stayed our first several days with Lucas in his apartment. The first day, he showed us how to navigate São Paolo on foot and by train before he attended to his own obligations. We wandered out onto a main drag a few blocks from the apartment and stood with our necks craned up toward the sky. Brick and cement and marble and glass stared back at us, seeming to reiterate that we were very small beings in a very large world full of billions of other small beings. The bland hues and abrupt straight lines of the buildings communicated an ambience of efficiency and institutionalized money making. *No nonsense here,* the city seemed to say.

As always, once Bill and I had our bearings, we ventured out, visiting museums, parks, and monuments until we were ready to collapse. Bill wore our GPS on his wrist as we wove our way through alleyways and city parks and between buzzing, erratic motor vehicles. On foot, we clocked over forty miles during the four days we were in São Paolo, far more than we should have during a taper, with only a week and a half before our marathon. In the evenings, we picked up food from the grocery store down the street from Lucas's place and made light, simple dinners and sampled Chilean wines. When Lucas was home, we watched *futbol* matches together on television until we had to retire out of sheer burnout. *So much for all the rest I've indulged in in the past couple of months,* I thought.

But rest, in a manner of speaking, was exactly what was on the agenda for the following week. Our plans were to take the two-hour bus ride to Ribeirão Preto and spend five days with our entire extended Brazilian family before taking a twelve-hour "sleeping bus" from Ribeirão to Rio de Janeiro for the race.

Since his junior year of high school, Bill had been back to Ribeirão Preto only one other time, in 1973, for a six-week visit. The town of one hundred thousand people had since grown fivefold. Dimas collected us again, this time from the bus station, and took us to the home he shared with his wife, Ana Rosa, in a large downtown condominium.

I sat back as two of Dimas's siblings, Carlos and Jussara, his mother, his brother-in-law, his niece, his best friends, and even an ex–cousin-in-law welcomed Bill back into the fold. They kissed and questioned him, muddling through bits of two languages to tell long-overdue life stories. Bill had come full circle.

I, on the other hand, was about to make a beeline into the tastiest week, and worst marathon preparation, I'd ever engaged in. The moment we arrived in Ana Rosa's home was the moment any good sense I'd gained over the past few years about getting ready for a race left me. Ana Rosa, who had Lucas's eyes and a mischievous smile, indicated that we should sit in their informal living area, which was wedged between a sliding door leading to an outdoor deck and a large formal dining area. She disappeared briefly and returned with a pot of the strongest, sweetest coffee I'd ever laid my taste buds on. A few minutes later we heard a *ding,* and Ana Rosa disappeared again. When she came back this time, she carried a basket of warm "cheese bread": soft, creamy biscuit morsels that melted as they approached our lips. And that was only the beginning—we were in for almost a week of celebrating, eating, drinking, and repeating.

Over the next few days, there would be a welcome-home dinner for Bill, a Sunday family supper, and a birthday party, to name only the highlights. Just when I thought we had eaten an early meal and would all get to bed before midnight, another dinner would materialize (sometimes as late as eleven o'clock), and more eating would ensue. I knew all this eating could lead to nothing good for my body, but it was impossible to resist. So I indulged—out of politeness, I told myself.

Besides eating, I became the silent observer at the table. I watched the body language of all present and the volley of words passing between them. Occasionally, as I stuffed more *feijoada*, seafood curry, into my mouth, I heard a phrase or a syllable that resembled French or English and I could guess at the topic of conversation. Sometimes someone translated the gist for me. And then there were short stretches when everyone switched to English, however unconfident they may have been with the language, purely for my benefit. I was embarrassed by but grateful for this gift when it happened. The rest of the time I tried to glean what was happening through my intuition and my knowledge of family systems. As a trained family therapist, I was accustomed to attending to the way people leaned toward or away from one another, the way eye contact functioned in a given family, and the manner in which family members bridged gaps in conversation with, say, a hand gesture or facial expression. But usually my perceptions were contextualized with language I recognized. Here they weren't, mostly. Purely through observation, I picked up on tensions or old debates, favorite topics or private jokes.

I wondered why every family therapist training program didn't require trainees to sit a few hours with people who don't speak their language, as a way to hone other kinds of understanding besides just that which comes from words. For that matter, why didn't every couple engage in such an exercise before committing their lives to one another and to a lifetime of living with someone who came from a different family culture from their own?

In between meals, there were quiet hours when the household retreated to *sesta*. I have never been a napper, so I spent these hours out on the porch. June is the beginning of a very mild winter in Brazil. I had to cover my arms with a light sweater before taking my book and journal outside and planting myself on the lawn furniture, with a northern view of Ribeirão.

Though the streets were bustling with pedestrians and traffic, as they were in São Paulo, this was no gray cement jungle. Looking at life from several floors up, I took in the complex swirl of color and movement that made this city vibrate with life and joy. The building across the street, a salon, was painted with bright pinks and purples. I spied on friends bumping into one another on the sidewalk below, gesticulating dramatically as they conversed before moving on. Ribeirão was also carefully augmented with well-cared-for trees and parks. Here on my balcony, like a princess appreciating her spoils, I recovered from each previous night's meals. I could feel myself gaining weight by the minute. And I was becoming constipated beyond belief.

One afternoon during *sesta* time, two days before we departed for Rio, my constipation became acute. I finally decided I needed to get some help— traveling can really work over your digestive system. In South Africa, mine had worked overtime; here in Brazil, it decided to be on vacation, along with my good sense about how to eat before a marathon.

I tracked down Ana Rosa in the house and tried to explain my predicament.

"Ana Rosa?" I called when I spotted her at work in the kitchen, preparing our next meal. "I have a problem."

"Okay. What is happen?" she replied. Ana Rosa's English was better than my Portuguese, for sure, but it was still rudimentary. I would try English before embarrassing myself with pantomime.

"I'm constipated," I said, then waited. She repeated the word slowly and gave herself a moment to decide if she understood, then shook her head in the negative. Now I tried to put a Portuguese ending on the English word. I'd tried the technique of simply changing the pronunciation for "constipation" in Spanish-, German-, and Japanese-speaking countries. It had never worked. But it was worth a try. "*Con-sti-pa-cao,*" I guessed.

"No," Ana Rosa shook her head right away. She definitely did not know this word. Next she took me by the hand and we were off to find Dimas, who was a doctor with a strong grasp of English medical terms. I was grateful not to have to resort to drawing or charades to get my point across.

Dimas squared us away swiftly, and soon I was back on my porch with a cup of strong senna tea.

With the antidote to my problem in my hands, I now turned my thoughts to the marathon coming up the following weekend. I'd almost forgotten why I'd come to Brazil, I'd been so busy channeling my chubby Inner Princess and reveling in the new relationships I was creating.

Now I took a sip of my tea and contemplated my situation. This was my second-to-last race on a long journey. Even with the extra pounds and my current extreme bloating, I hadn't the slightest doubt I could complete the run. My training had been sufficient, if slow, as I'd rested my body and recovered from my illness in South Africa. And I'd really reposed my anxiety while in Tennessee with Wendy. In fact, I was still in complete relaxation and celebration mode. I had nearly accomplished my goal of running on every continent. Not only that, but it had changed my life.

I thought back to the beginning of my marriage with Bill and the fear I'd had that I would slide into a nuptial numbness and forget the commitment I'd made to personal examination and authenticity. As I had hoped, the marathon had prevented lethargy. Even as I perched on the balcony, fatter and happier than I'd been before arriving in Brazil, I knew that running had become my route to self-knowledge and self-acceptance.

I suppose I had been afraid, sitting on my psychotherapy couch that day long ago, before I'd chosen to embrace this unusual vision quest, that lethargy and self-acceptance were the same thing—that if I loved myself, I would have no motivation to change. That premise had turned out to be false.

Here again I sat, this time completely content in spite of my abdominal discomfort, without a shred of the emotional paralysis, apathy, and anxiety that had woven through my life in my twenties and thirties, completely happy for the moment—and still totally committed to growing and learning.

It was possible to love myself *and* still carry out my pledge to continual self-improvement. How many clients had I sat with over the years who believed that self-criticism, guilt, and anxiety were their friends, their only path to change and growth? Well, I knew firsthand and for certain now that it wasn't true. All you really needed was something hard, like the marathon (or life), to kick your ass from time to time. And you would grow. It wasn't optional.

A few hours elapsed for me in this state, exalted on my perch, passing time in aimless appreciation, when Ana Rosa interrupted my thoughts with the announcement that it was time, once again, for coffee and cheese bread.

IN ORDER TO GET from Ribeirão Preto to Rio de Janeiro for the race, we took an overnight "sleeping bus" on Tuesday night. Unfortunately, Bill and I could not both get sleeping berths. At my insistence, Bill took the bed and I took the upright seat in the upper deck. When Bill does not sleep, he barely functions the next day, and I needed him alert to help negotiate our way through the streets of Rio. Besides, I'd taken a first-class airplane seat without him and felt it was only fair to even things out.

After saying a teary and tired goodbye to our family, Bill snuggled into his cushioned pullout easy chair in an enclosed, heated area, with a fluffy blanket and pillow the bus company had provided, while I, freezing, shifted stiffly in a vinyl seat on the upper deck.

It was a miserable night for me. I was ragged and achy by the time we got to the bus station in Rio the next morning. A stationary restroom and a cup of thick Brazilian coffee went a long way toward refreshing me (and finally taking care of the days of cheese bread stored in my intestines) before we had to find our way to the hostel we'd reserved. It was Wednesday. We had four days to get our bearings.

Two important things happened those first days in Rio before the race. First, Bill and I discovered that Rio de Janeiro is, without compare, the most naturally beautiful city on the planet. Even from the busy avenue that ran perpendicular to the little side road our hostel was on, we could see the Christ the Redeemer statue atop Corcovado in one direction and Sugarloaf Mountain in the other. If we walked a few blocks, we were at the beach. Miles of sand dotted with scarcely-clad darkened bodies stretched in all directions, while both historic and modern buildings of many architectural styles looked on from across a dangerously busy street. This would be our view along the marathon course.

The other important happening in the days prior to the marathon was that we met two other runners who were staying in our hostel: Kevin and Omar. Right away, I felt especially connected to both men for different reasons. For Kevin, running the Rio race would mark the completion of a marathon on his seventh continent. He'd participated in (and enjoyed) the Antarctica Marathon with Marathon Tours the year before and had saved South America for last.

Kevin had a vociferous appetite for adventure and for all of his diverse athletic pursuits; his eyes shone bright with accomplishment and determination. He was a spitfire who grabbed life by the ear and made it come along with him where he wanted it to go. I admired his energy and the force with which he'd followed his trajectory. Through him, although my path to Antarctica would be different by necessity, I could see that running seven continents could be done. I'd read about others, but I'd never met another seven-continent racer face-to-face in my travels. We were going to get to celebrate together after the marathon, and I would hold that prospect in my heart over the next months as I drafted my unusual route to my own final run.

Omar was in a wholly dissimilar position with regard to the marathon. A gentle twenty-seven-year-old from Mexico whose primary life goal was to further his education through a study-abroad program he was preparing for, he would be running his first forty-two-kilometer race. I could see a familiar timidity and doubt in him as he told us how he expected to finish only about thirty kilometers of Sunday's race. He felt he was not strong enough to complete the whole thing.

"I will use this as a training run only. Then I will run my real marathon in Mexico City in September," he told me on that first afternoon, as we sipped beer in the courtyard of the hostel.

"Why not try to complete this one, Omar?" I asked. I'd been quizzing him about his training, and it seemed clear to me that he'd put in enough long runs over many weeks to be ready now for a full marathon.

"I don't believe I can do it" was all he could say.

It wasn't only my own urgent *carpe diem* mentality that insisted Omar was ready; Bill and Kevin agreed with me that Omar *could* do it if he wanted to. We became his cheering section, promising him that he could complete the Rio Marathon and that it would boost his overall self-confidence.

Saturday, we each made our way to the marathon expo to pick up our race packets, and when we reconvened at the hostel in the evening, Omar announced that he'd given our exhortations some thought and was going to go the distance the next day.

Together, we made up Team Rio. Never a team-sport participant, I joyfully embraced the idea of having a team to launch me at the start of the course in the morning.

SUNDAY MORNING, RACE DAY, seemed to arrive in the middle of the night. We'd barely fallen asleep at 2:00 AM, as the hostel was just quieting down, when our alarm sounded at four thirty. At five fifteen, Team Rio jammed itself into a taxi and we made our way from our little purple hostel to the finish line at the Flamengo Beach. We couldn't see the ocean water in the dark. Nor could we hear the waves of the tide over the engines of the buses that waited to take us to the starting line, 26.2 miles out of Rio's hectic hub to the relatively sleepy town of Recreio.

This was a point-to-point marathon, my favorite kind because it made me feel like I'd gone somewhere. Once the buses dropped us off at the starting line, we milled around and watched the sun rise over the Atlantic Ocean. I wondered how many bodies of water I had raced beside now: rivers, bays, lagoons, and now my second time to begin a race with the Atlantic looking on. Before this year, I had never even seen the Atlantic Ocean. Now I had dipped my toes in her waters standing on two continents: Africa and South America. As we stretched and munched on granola bars, local fishermen pushed their boats over the waves into the sea, and people in wetsuits with large, colorfully illustrated boards paddled into the surf.

My three men and I snapped pictures of the sky and the rocky coastline as the colors shifted over the water from blue-gray to green to red and orange and finally back to a deeper blue. I wasn't used to seeing the sun rise over an ocean. At home I could see Puget Sound from my west-facing front yard. In the evenings I often stepped out at sunset to watch the big yellow ball disappear beyond the horizon and to observe the shifting colors in the sky over the water. I was a little disoriented to see the events happen in reverse this morning.

There were clouds, but not many, and there was a perfect, gentle, warm breeze coming from the south. I was warm, my digestive system was clear, I was more than well nourished, and I had companions to start the run with.

Without much fanfare, we were herded toward the starting area. No one seemed to be seeding him- or herself by pace, so Omar, Kevin, Bill, and I all stood together as we waited for the horn. I kissed Bill and gave the others high-fives.

"Have a great race, guys. See you at the end for a celebration!"

Once the horn rang out at eight thirty, I bid goodbye to the rest of Team Rio as they ran ahead, and concentrated on finding my pace.

My body was heavy. I counted my breath to help me steady my energy. *In, two, three. Out, two, three.* I wanted to center myself, call up my voices, and find out who my inner companions would be today. What was my mood? I certainly was not Bitchy. In fact, I felt no angst whatsoever and looked forward to whatever the day brought. I was not feeling especially introspective either, so my Inner Wisdom would probably not be whispering nuggets of truth and revelation to me. All the Brazilian food and family I had encountered had lulled me into a very content, relaxed state. That ruled out the Warrior, too. I wouldn't be waging any battles today.

I'd hit the start button on my stopwatch when the horn went off, and I soon saw that I was puttering along pretty slowly. At this rate, it could be tomorrow before I finished. Ah, well. This would be a Princess run, then, a hedonistic, take-in-the-world-with-your-senses-as-if-it-all-belongs-to-you race. An epicurean run, if you will. One thing this marathon was not going to be about was a personal record. And that was just fine by me.

I looked out to the east, where the sun was still low and where the ocean splashed and sputtered onto the shore. The water was cobalt, foamy, wild, speckled in light, violent, and lonely, I thought, despite her majesty. She proclaimed herself the container of life, overwhelming, demanding, and complicated. She was filling a hole in the heart of the world, vast and powerful, but seemed to be doing it all on her own without any companions that could equal her. Today, I would be her friend, tiny and insignificant, but faithful.

The Atlantic Ocean commanded my attention as I ran next to her. Sometimes in front of me, sometimes behind, always to my right, she wrapped herself around the coast of Brazil and around my consciousness. She spoke to me, saying that she belonged to me for now. And I belonged to her. Though I was a stranger here, she reminded me that I was a citizen of a world connected by her beautiful body. I'd seen her in Africa. And if I made the effort, I could see her from the east shore of my own country and the west shore of Europe. This seemed like a good thing to do someday. I put it on my list of adventures to pursue, as I jogged alongside her.

I began to ponder the impending end of my current adventure. In five or so hours, I would be done with my South American continental run, and I would have only one more continent to touch down on. Suddenly, with the lonely, beautiful ocean as my only companion, I felt sad. Soon my self-spun vision quest would be over. I was not afraid, because, as I said, I knew life would not let me become complacent. And I knew the marathon would continue to be a significant part of my life. In fact, I was already concocting other marathon goals, such as trying to qualify for the Marathon Maniacs club, so I was not concerned that my days would become boring or that I would lack objectives related to my running. I simply felt a bittersweet sadness that the quest, which had taught me to listen to and know myself, was winding down.

It was no wonder my Inner Princess had emerged on this trip and insisted I take it easy, let people feed me, and experience feeling full of life.

She wanted me to taste, see, and take ownership of my experience. And today she wanted me to run very unhurriedly beside the ocean, with all my senses heightened and my soul open.

The course was flat as it wound its way along the coastline. I watched almost the way one watches a film as the terrain at the water's edge became rocks and cliffs, then sand and palm trees. Beach after beach glided by at my slow pace. From Recreio to the Barra da Tijuca shoreline to the Quebra Mar, São Conrado, and Leblon beaches, the sun shone on the rose-, blond-, and peach-colored sand.

My legs were strong, if elephantine, in their performance. I knew all I needed to do was move forward and that at some point I would see the finish line. The day warmed quickly. Every few blocks during the early and later stretches of the course, refreshment stands sold fresh coconut milk and cold beers. More than once I was tempted to stop for a drink, but I kept moving.

As the hours progressed, each beach I passed was more crowded with patrons than the last. Eventually, I began to see signs of urban life. Then, around mile nineteen, I got my first glimpse of Sugarloaf Mountain. Sugarloaf, or Pão d'Açúcar in Portuguese, watches over the Rio coastline from the top of its 1,299 feet of granite and quartz. It beamed in the sunlight, smiled at me, and reassured me that the end was not so far away.

Now I was running along Ipanema. The roads were closed to vehicle traffic for the weekend, and the beach, even in the winter, was a mecca for both ill-fitting thong bikinis and perfect, smooth, golden flesh. Circles of young people kept soccer balls in the air. I saw that the ocean was not so lonely here, as I continued to follow the orange cones that indicated the course, grateful for the aid stations placed faithfully every three or four kilometers along the route.

By this time, late in the race, I could feel the predictable ache in my legs, back, and shoulders, but I still felt the Princess, sure she was the owner of my fate and that my happiness was secure. There would be no crying here in Rio, as there had been in South Africa; nonetheless, my pain was intensifying as I approached Copacabana Beach. I don't know if the onlookers along the pedestrian trail that paralleled the beach had more enthusiasm for runners at the front of the pack, but at more than four hours into the race, I was left to myself. Obviously, no one realized there was royalty passing through. Patrons of the beach and families out for a Sunday walk were totally indifferent to me and to the other stragglers.

Once or twice, someone did applaud as I passed through, but for the most part, the folks in Rio seemed fairly unimpressed by my efforts. I wasn't bothered by this; my need for the acknowledgment of others had diminished increasingly as I'd tuned in to my own internal chorus of voices, and also as I'd learned to listen to trees and wind, mountains and oceans.

Finally, I reached Flamengo Beach, where I had caught the bus about eight hours earlier. There was the finish line, a speck in the distance. A large park at the edge of the beach was serving as a recovery center for the race and was peppered with temporary tents and port-o-potties. Here, fans and runners lined the fence and cheered as I approached. I looked for Bill's face in the crowd and couldn't see him, but I was half a kilometer from the actual finish line yet. As I drew closer to the finish banner and still couldn't find him, I wondered what to do. I was a self-sufficient runner, but I'd never come over a marathon finish line without Bill there to greet me, and for a brief moment I thought maybe I should pull over and let other runners pass until I could spot him. But then I heard him calling my name and followed the sound of his voice until I saw him.

Bill was balancing on a stone fencepost to elevate himself above the crowd, and, as usual, he had his camera in hand. I gave my best elbow-to-wrist queenly wave and smiled, but I felt a sharp pain in my shoulder and neck with the movement. I'd been on the course for five hours, thirty minutes, and twenty-three seconds. All the muscles in my body were stiff and spent. But I'd seized the day. There could be no doubt about that.

I crossed the line and heard the beep of the chip registry under my feet as I slowed to a walk. Closing my eyes, I gave silent thanks to my body for doing what I'd asked it to do, and to the ocean for her love and support. Unfortunately, closing my eyes caused me to lose my balance for a moment. I snapped my eyes open to find my equilibrium, and as I did I saw dear Omar standing directly in front of me. A Mexican flag was tied around his neck and flowed down his back. His arms were open wide to take me in and bring me back into balance. His face was shining with pride. I knew he must have finished his race and felt the power of completing his first marathon.

"Great job!" he said.

"How did you do?" I asked as I held on to him.

"I finished in 3:48," he replied, beaming.

"Oh, Omar, you did it. You must be exhausted. What are you doing here? You should be in the shower."

"I was waiting for you," he said. He'd stood around after his first marathon for almost two hours just to welcome me over the line. Only another marathoner would know that this was no small sacrifice. I knew.

Volunteers were standing on the sidelines with bundles of medals. They were shuffling me through the chute, pushing me forward to get me out of the way of the finish line. To get my reward, all I had to do was get my chip from my shoe and trade it in. I found an open space and bent at my hips to reach down toward my feet, but my body revolted with surges of pain in my lower back. Omar shook his head at me and lifted my shoulders to return me to an upright position. Then he, tired and sore as he must have been, knelt at my feet and unlaced my shoe, removed my timing chip, and retied my shoe before walking me to the edge of the crowd, where I traded the chip in for my medal.

All this while, Bill had been capturing pictures of Omar and me from outside the chute, but now he came around front of the ruckus to meet us. Once I was finally out of the finish area, Omar handed me off to Bill and headed back to the hostel to get cleaned up. Kevin was already there, getting ready for our celebration later that night. We would follow them just as soon as I had stretched and recovered enough to move again.

THAT EVENING, WE SHARED a celebratory *churrasco* (barbecue) buffet with Kevin and Omar that rivaled Bill's welcome-home supper the prior week. Afterward, Bill and I hobbled back through the Rio streets hand in hand. We took our time making our way back to our lodgings and then sank early into a very satisfying sleep.

The next afternoon, we packed and readied ourselves for our long plane ride home. Because we had some extra time before our taxi arrived, we took a stroll down the road from the hostel to a little pub we'd walked by many times that week. Plunking ourselves into a couple of chairs, we ordered two *cervejas*.

While we waited, I let out a deep, long breath I didn't realize I'd been holding in my lungs.

"What's up, Cami?" Bill asked. He reached across and placed his left hand over my right one, which was resting on the tabletop.

"I'm happy," I said. "Fulfilled, maybe. And sorry it's almost over. And worried about figuring out Antarctica. All of those things."

"Me too," he said.

We sat awhile, quietly. I was thinking of how Bill and I had been brought together in challenging ways this last year, how we'd pulled through some hard moments and grown closer—and how sometimes this quest had highlighted our differences and had forced us to go in separate directions (or at least at separate paces). I couldn't quite believe there was only one more trip. And again, I fretted about how we might make that trip happen. What if we couldn't? What would that mean?

My thoughts were interrupted by the waiter coming with our beers. I stared at the bright blue can in front of me. The image of a penguin stared back at me; above his head was the word ANTARCTICA in large, shiny white letters.

Surprised, I took in a quick breath. Who knew there was a beer in Brazil called Antarctica? It was the sign I needed to once again replace my fretting with determination.

I lifted the can to Bill and said, "Here's to figuring it out!"

"Cheers," he said.

getting there

" . . . [M]ake a radical change in your lifestyle and begin to boldly do things
which you may previously never have thought of doing, or been too
hesitant to attempt. So many people live within unhappy circumstances
and yet will not take the initiative to change their situation because they
are conditioned to a life of security, conformity, and conservation, all of
which may appear to give one peace of mind, but in reality nothing is more
damaging to the adventurous spirit within a [wo]man than a secure future.
The very basic core of a [wo]man's living spirit is [her] passion for adventure."

—JON KRAKAUER, *Into the Wild*

"Some people say I have an attitude. Maybe I do. But I think that you have to.
You have to believe in yourself when no one else does—that makes you a
winner right there."

—VENUS WILLIAMS

12

My Inner Princess was elated. She'd been indulged in Brazil and had engaged in an entitled existence. I'd never been big on "entitlement," coming as I did from a belief system that claimed humans deserved nothing if God didn't decide to give out favors. By now, however, I'd changed my mind about the depravity of the human race. Not only were all people entitled to be loved and nurtured, but when someone worked hard, she was indeed entitled to enjoy the results of her work. I'd actually enjoyed gaining some weight and taking a slow (but long) victory lap beside the Atlantic Ocean in Brazil. I considered these experiences my reward for the hundreds of miles I'd logged the first half of the year.

Once I got home, however, life was again a buzz of activity. Straight away, we needed to get started on our research for Antarctica. I bought myself the one and only travel guidebook I could find. Mostly, it described the very few locations on the continent that accommodated visitors. It also gave lists of tour companies qualified to get permits to transport their clients to these areas. Another useful piece of information was the fact that the only decent weather season on the Antarctic Peninsula and its islands was between December and March. It was already July 2009 when we got back from Brazil, so we had nine months (not much time, according to my sources) to plan.

A final, critical fact I discovered was that an international treaty signed by the nearly fifty nations that conduct research or have interests on the great landmass meant that there were copious restrictions placed on visiting Antarctica. The continent is not home to any indigenous populations (such as those who live in the Arctic up north), and no single country claims sovereignty. Instead, this slab of frozen earth, 98 percent of which is covered with ice, is sparsely inhabited by a smattering of representatives from invested nations and governed by peaceful agreement between the participating countries. A portion of this agreement is called the Madrid Protocol; its primary purpose is to protect the Antarctic environment from human impact.

Finding a place to run on the seventh continent was going to be harder than I had thought. There were only a couple of airstrips, very little infrastructure to speak of, and scarcely anything that could be called a civilization—just pockets of lonely scientists and their support crews scattered in obscure areas. Even these brave individuals were rotated out with regularity, probably in order to avoid madness. I decided that the best way to start my research would be to find an Antarctic insider to advise us, so I got on the ball and launched an email campaign to my entire network of friends and acquaintances. Did anyone have a connection to someone who could help us learn about or get to Antarctica? I needed information that wasn't in my book.

Since Antarctica boasts the highest average elevation of any of the earth's landmasses, where on the continent was there enough dry and reasonably flat land for a person to run a long route without special equipment? If I did find a locale suitable for running the marathon distance, what kind of transportation and permission would be required to dock or land there?

During those early days back from Brazil, before I got any real responses to my request for connections in Antarctica, I received a message from a stranger named Marie, a woman who had also participated in the Rio Marathon. Marie had stumbled upon my blog, it turned out. She was an Australian who operated a successful business providing training programs and support for runners. She called it Lazy Runner (just my kind), and she, too, was on a crusade to complete a marathon on every continent and hadn't yet run Antarctica. Like I had, Marie had signed up with Marathon Tours and was on a waiting list a couple of years out. She said she was interested in being kept in the loop as I sought an alternative to the formal race.

Throughout July and August, I followed up on each lead that came my way. I sat for hours in my big chair with my notebook computer on my lap, searching for information and composing inquiry emails to anyone who might be a potential source of knowledge. I wrote to eco-tourist organizations, freight-delivery ship captains, and cooks who had worked on Antarctic bases.

I sat in my living room during the hot days of summer, facing the only window that opened toward the street. As the days passed, I kept notic-ing that my neighbor Julie, formerly a heavy woman, walked her little dog through the neighborhood each morning, looking very much like a different person than she had one year ago at this time. Julie worked nights and got done with her job as a labor-and-delivery nurse just as I sat down to check my emails for the first time each day. Every morning, right before going to bed, she and her pooch traced a circuit past my yard, up the street, and onto the trails and neighborhoods behind our condos. Often I'd see her repeating the process before leaving for work at night.

I was aware that I'd been so preoccupied over the last months that I hadn't made much effort to speak with any of my neighbors, but now that I was sitting regularly in front of my window, it was impossible to miss the change in Julie. She had shrunk by half. By the end of August, my curiosity about how she'd lost all the weight was heightened, but I didn't want to appear the nosy neighbor, so I just kept observing her pass by without ever going out to say hello. I focused instead on my own morning tasks and on planning for a trip that was taking me beyond everything I knew about international travel.

I'd experienced enough of my own transformation in the past few years to know that whatever was going on for Julie was a good thing. She radiated good humor, smiling and even waving at me on occasion as I peeked at her over my computer screen. When our paths finally crossed out in front of my house one day, I could no longer mind my own business.

As I pulled into my parking slot, I went over what I might say in my head. I wanted to avoid giving an insensitive compliment like "Wow. You look great now," which could be interpreted as "You used to look awful." Julie had never looked awful. She'd always been a dynamic blond beauty with sparkling blue eyes and a quick smile.

I climbed out of my car and advanced toward her on the sidewalk. I waved and called, "Hey, Julie!"

"Hi, Cami. How's it going? How are you enjoying the end of the summer?" She smiled widely and ambled in my direction, bridging the gap between us.

"It's great. How about you?" I inquired.

"Doing good," she said and paused for a moment.

I took this opening to jump in with a probing comment, hoping to satiate my inquisitiveness about Julie's weight loss. "I can't help noticing you've made some changes." I waited, holding my breath, hoping my remark was innocuous enough. To my relief, Julie laughed.

"Ya think?" she asked. "Pretty great, huh? And you won't believe what I'm doing now," she prattled on before I could ask anything more prying. "I'm training for a marathon!"

Now my curiosity morphed into an instant feeling of camaraderie. "You're kidding!" I nearly shouted. "Did you know that Bill and I are marathoners, too?" The nomenclature rolled off my tongue with easy confidence.

"No, I didn't. And I wouldn't exactly call myself a marathoner yet," Julie was quick to qualify. "But I've always known there was a runner inside me, and I'm finally trying to free her."

An Inner Runner itching to get out? Now I was even more intrigued. "How far along are you in your training? Which race are you going to do?" I rattled off my questions.

"I've got a fifteen-mile run coming up this weekend. I'm shooting for the Bellingham Bay Marathon at the end of September if I can get ready by then."

We stood in front of my window for another half hour as I quizzed her about all aspects of her running. We discovered that our paces were comparable, and before we parted, I invited myself on her nineteen-mile training run in two weeks. And that was how, after eight years of being a committed but solitary runner, I finally found a running partner.

It was perfect timing, too. My running was transitioning from a travel adventure/spiritual vision quest into something less dramatic but still essential to my well-being and identity. I was less introspective these days, more cheerful and more matter-of-fact in my head as I ran. I was beginning to feel I needed new distractions and challenges to keep myself engaged. A running partner would be a welcome diversion on my usual training routes. And as for the challenge, with several months before our next international trip, I'd made the commitment in my mind to qualify for the Marathon Maniacs club by running a series of local races. Julie turned out to be exactly what I needed to help me get through all that was on the horizon.

Once we were on the trails together, the old routes felt fresh again. Julie was talkative, interesting, and committed to her new venture, and fit my pace perfectly. As I was facing the end of an exciting quest and hadn't quite figured out where my running would take me when it was over, her wide-eyed enthusiasm and newfound appreciation for a body that could run benefited me in ways I couldn't have anticipated. I observed Julie's self-doubt about her upcoming race with compassion, remembering how unsettled I'd been at my first few starting lines.

When the day of her first race arrived, at the end of September, I was enthused by the chance to support someone in her first long-distance-racing enterprise. Throughout that morning, after the gun, I followed Julie by car, parking and stationing myself at intersections to cheer her on. At mile fifteen, as we had planned, I jumped in with her and jogged alongside her for the rest of the race, feeling gratitude for and pride in my new friend. When she said her legs hurt, I assured her it was normal and told her she could make it, just as Bill had told me in Prague.

When we reached the finish line and I caught sight of her family, many of whom were crying over her triumphant achievement, I drifted away to leave her with her victory and felt the same powerful connection to that Something Greater that I'd felt during my own races many times. Little had I known that my nosy interest in Julie's weight loss would turn into something that I wasn't even aware I needed.

MEANWHILE, AMID MY EFFORTS to find a way to get us to Antarctica, Bill discovered a company based in Punta Arenas, Chile, a town at the tip of

South America that advertised small tours to King George Island, situated in the Southern Ocean off the tip of the Antarctic Peninsula, the same location in the Shetland Islands where the official Antarctica marathon was held at the beginning of March. Victory Adventures provided two-day fly-in tours of the island, with a one-night sleepover in the small research community there known as Villa Las Estrellas. Both days, tourists would visit several locations on the island, experiencing the environment and wildlife in an eco-friendly manner. Victory's website said it could create Antarctic vacations with attention to the particular interests of its clients. I wondered if the company could accommodate us and our unusual request to find a running route.

Since King George Island is where Marathon Tours ran its 26.2-mile route, I was certain that there were enough roads or trails to allow us to complete the marathon distance. If Victory could get us access to even part of that course, we would be in good shape. Another positive point for using this company, if it could arrange things for us, was that Punta Arenas, the Chilean town that served as home base for Aerovías DAP, the airline that flew the tourists to Antarctica, was another of Bellingham's sister cities.

I wrote to the tour company's contact, a fellow who called himself Captain Ben, in late July with an inquiry, explaining our situation and asking if Victory could get us to King George Island and provide a place for us to run the marathon distance.

The captain wrote back to us without delay and said he was working on our request. Within a couple of weeks, he proposed a scenario: First, he'd arranged for us to run back and forth between a Chilean scientific base and the Russian base on the island. He couldn't get access to the full course Marathon Tours used, but he had been able to secure permission for our presence at these two research stations and for the two-kilometer path that ran between them. A route that short would mean running back and forth more than twenty times. It wasn't ideal, but if we were game, we could complete our distance on the first day of the excursion and then go sightseeing on the second.

A qualified guide would be present to oversee our run. This was crucial,

Ben explained, because of the international environmental guidelines pertaining specifically to the island. The guide, a man named Alejo, lived on King George Island most of the year and had hosted other runners. All was set if we agreed to the plan. But there was a daunting caveat: Aerovías DAP (DAP is an acronym for the name of the airline's founder) would fly the plane only if the vessel was 75 percent filled to capacity. The little dual-prop aircraft that would take us over the Drake Passage could hold eight people. That meant we needed a minimum of six passengers: Bill, me, and four others.

Captain Ben explained that since we had only one guide, it might be best if all the passengers on our trip intended to run with us. That way, he said, we would not have to find and pay for another qualified guide to take nonrunners touring while we ran, nor would we have to try to find four other tourists willing to stand around tapping their toes for six hours while the two of us finished our forty-two very repetitive kilometers.

I was intimidated by the idea of trying to find four other people who might be interested in trotting back and forth (and back and forth), even if it was with a view of pristine icy waters and the possibility of an occasional penguin posing as a cheerleader. Bill and I discussed where we could find others who, like us, did not care if any official agency or group qualified the "marathon" they ran on Antarctica. Who besides us would prioritize a crazy plan like this over remaining on a list, even for several years, to get confirmed for an organized, well-supported race with champagne waiting for them back onboard a cruise ship?

The day after we got Ben's proposal, I took a run with Julie and explained what we were contemplating.

"So, let me get this straight," she said. "You pay for the trip. You fill up the plane with other runners. And your marathon doesn't count by anyone's standards but your own?"

"Exactly," I said. I could feel the Bitchy voice in my head preparing a rebuttal. It did sound absurd when Julie distilled it down to the basic facts, but I was already growing attached to the idea, and I found myself willing to defend it.

"Well, you go, girl! Who needs someone to tell you what counts in this life? Let me know what I can do to help. I wish I could go, but I can't take off in March."

I breathed a little sigh. That was how I felt, too. I didn't really care about anything "counting," but I did care about the distance, which I planned to measure with the GPS. All I needed to do was find four other people of a similar mind.

The first person I checked in with was Marie, of course. She wanted to touch down in Antarctica as soon as possible, but I wasn't sure how she would feel about everyone measuring her own distance, or about the repetitive nature of the course. Her response to my email explaining the plan was swift and resolute: She was absolutely in, without hesitation. I smiled when I read her reply. Now we needed three more.

Marie had strong connections with the media and the running community in Australia. I wrote a description of what we were up to, which began: "Are you looking for a way to complete your seventh continental marathon? So are we. We've come up with a plan. Check out the details." This was followed by a very clear description of the arrangement we'd made to trace and retrace a two-kilometer trail between two bases. We made it plain that our intent was to find at least three more runners to join us, so that we could fill a small airplane with people who were content to measure their own distance and didn't care if the route was sanctioned by anyone official. Marie posted our ad on her business site. I posted mine on my blog, asked our Bellingham running club to publish a link to my website, sent out emails to every list of runners I could get my hands on, and asked the Marathon Maniacs club to post a link to my site as well.

AS QUICKLY AS PUSHING "enter" on a keyboard, I heard from a young woman named Marina, a Maniac who was keen on our idea. She suggested we also add a forty-two-kilometer route in Punta Arenas so she could complete her South American marathon while we were there. She broke down the Maniacs' fairly simple requirements for a marathon to "count": A race must be advertised, and the results must be posted on a website. The Maniacs also required five starters and three finishers to call it "official."

Bill and I discussed this and, knowing we could find someone through the Bellingham Sister Cities Association who could advise us regarding routes we could use for a spontaneous marathon course, decided we could happily complete forty-two kilometers in Punta Arenas if it meant Marina would join us on the airplane to Antarctica. I counted on Marie's being willing to start the Punta Arenas "race" with us, even if she didn't want to go the full distance before running on King George Island less than a week later. Now all we needed was one more starter in Chile for our Maniac, and two more air passengers for our captain.

The situation was becoming complicated, but I was having fun. I began receiving inquiries from interested parties all around the country. Most balked when they heard that everyone had to measure their own distance with their personal satellite tracking devices. Others decided the dates didn't work, or it wasn't their kind of adventure.

Marie and Marina remained steadfast over the following weeks, working almost as hard as I did to recruit other runners. Eventually, Marina roped one of her Maniac friends into joining us. Now we had five starters for the Punta Arenas run. Almost at the same moment that Marina's friend signed on, I received an email from Captain Ben saying that someone who was interested in coming along simply as a regular tourist, a photographer from Russia, had contacted him; he was content to hang around and wait for us to complete our run, because the March dates we had chosen worked well for his travel schedule.

This got us to six passengers. Good enough. Alleviated from my recruiting duties, I could now turn my attention to finding air tickets to Punta Arenas and communicating with my bank about wiring the deposit to Victory Adventures.

All was arranged. We could stop following up on other leads (such as the suggestion that we take jobs as janitors at one of the research bases to gain access) and plow ahead, create our itinerary, and reserve lodgings in our sister city.

ONE CLOUDY OCTOBER MORNING about three months after beginning my planning process, as I sipped coffee with my computer open on my lap, I saw a message from Marathon Tours in my inbox. I clicked to open it, puzzled at why the company would be contacting me at this point. The author wrote: "I have read that you are trying to organize your own marathon on King George Island this year. Please be aware that running on KGI is a very sensitive issue at the moment. You must submit an IEE [Initial Environmental Evaluation] to the EPA [Environmental Protection Agency] in order to gain permission. You must get prior permission through the proper government agency before performing any activity in Antarctica. I have had major political problems as a result of another group arriving on KGI and trying to run without the proper paperwork and mitigation procedures for not impacting the environment."

Naturally, this alarmed and confused me. I was not working with an American company, so I couldn't understand how the U.S. Environmental Protection Agency needed to be involved. If anything, the Chilean government would be the permission-granting agency in our situation.

I immediately forwarded this email to the captain and asked him again if we had all of our paperwork lined up properly. He reassured me that he had been organizing exactly this same trip for ten years, and that we had permission to be at the two science bases connected by the short footpath we would be running on. The footpath itself was a trail that King George Island residents utilized daily to get from one place to another. There would be virtually no environmental impact from five people trotting to and fro on it. For the particulars of our activities, we had all the paperwork in order, the captain said.

I wrote a quick, mollifying email to Marathon Tours, reassuring them that we had all of our permits in place and that our small venture with five runners should not result in any negative impact on their company. I wondered (but didn't ask) how they had found out about my plans in the first place. I'd been recruiting runners like mad, trying to fill the airplane so I could fulfill the final leg of my vision quest. I guessed that either someone had forwarded them one of my pleas or they got Google alerts on Antarctic marathon plans.

One month later, I received an odd email from Marie in Australia. She reported that someone at the "Australian Antarctica Base" (which, incidentally, is not located on King George Island) had contacted her. The writer said something similar to what Marathon Tours had written to me—that Marie needed to make sure she had completed the proper Australian paperwork and that the organization was going to contact the Chilean government and ask them to investigate Victory Adventures in order to determine if it was a legitimate tour company. Clearly, word of our little adventure was getting out on a broader scale than either of us had intended. For good measure, Marie removed all the information she'd posted. I did the same. And I kicked myself for not being more discreet with my recruitment tactics—but then, I hadn't known it would be necessary.

Now I was quite concerned because it seemed our two-kilometer jogging route had become the focal point of an international investigation. What could be the problem with running on a well-used footpath that was a portion of the tour Victory had been organizing for more than a decade? Essentially, we were regular tourists with no intention of veering off of a singular trail that served as the main road for all other tourists, as well as for the forty to one hundred people who lived and worked on the island at any given time. There was a church there and a small school, according to my research. People walked to those places each day using this path.

Besides that, we were following the rules, hiring a company that had filed and double-checked its paperwork. All the while we'd been working with Victory, Bill and I had done our due diligence. We'd read all available reviews and recommendations about the company. We'd checked the captain's references. Everything was in order. I stayed calm, reassuring myself that whatever had been put in motion here would settle down once (or if) Victory Adventures was investigated.

But within two days, before I had even sent Marie's message to Ben to get his take on the situation, he forwarded me an email that he'd composed and already sent to DAP, stating that our "running expedition" was being "completely canceled."

I was flabbergasted. And devastated. As quickly as I could, I contacted the captain by phone and asked him what had happened. Why had he canceled our trip? What was the matter? He told me that all of our paperwork was indeed in order, but that DAP had been contacted by both the U.S. Department of State and INACH, the branch of the Chilean government that monitored the comings and goings on Antarctica. The CEO of the airline said he didn't want either of these governments breathing down his neck. Getting tourists to King George Island was already an operation fraught with paperwork and governmental guidelines, and the CEO didn't want to touch our "running expedition" with a "ten-foot pole."

"Runners are apparently a different breed of tourist," Ben told me. Neither the captain nor I had known that certain words sent up red flags, and that among them were all the words I'd used to recruit other, like-minded passengers. Words such as "run," "race," "marathon," "event," and even "plan" signaled a need for special permissions. It didn't matter that I ran at most people's walking pace, or that there would be very little environmental impact, due to the course we had arranged. The words themselves were politically charged.

"Is there nothing we can do?" I asked.

"You can try to appeal directly to my boss at DAP if you'd like," the captain suggested. "It's up to him. If INACH isn't bothering him much, he might reconsider." He forwarded both the address of the airline's CEO and an investigative letter he had received from someone at the U.S. Department of State asking if Victory Adventures was an American or a Chilean company.

It was November 5 by this time. The summer season in Antarctica was almost upon us. There wasn't much time to come up with another plan. And by now I'd done enough research to realize that there really weren't many landmasses within the Antarctic Circle where tourists were allowed to land by plane or by ship, much less run. It was not a friendly environment, in more ways than one.

I felt defeated. After speaking with the captain, I took a quiet run by myself on the trails behind my house. It was a cold day, so I bundled up with gloves, a hat, and a windbreaker. The trees that lined the path I chose were almost bare, and the colors from the rotting vegetation that carpeted the ground were bright. They hadn't yet reached the muddy, mushy state they would be in within a couple more weeks. I treaded atop the crusty foliage, kicking through an occasional pile of dried leaves. The wind cut through my clothing and made me shiver. I sped up my pace so I could get warm, and breathed heavily. Then I sent a prayer to my Inner Wisdom.

"I really need to do this last continent," I said aloud. I listened to my feet. Bom. Bom. Bom. BOOM. It was a recognizable beat. I knew it well by now. How could I call up my Warrior energy, though, when everything was out of my control?

Wisdom came gently then, with another familiar refrain: May I have the serenity to accept the things I cannot change, the courage to change the things I can, and the wisdom to know the difference. Serenity, courage, and wisdom—yes, these three had been faithful companions all along this vision quest of mine. I'd learned to stay in the moment, to fight hard for what I wanted, to listen to all the wise voices inside me, no matter what their tone or message. When I was done with my run, I'd write a letter to the CEO of the Chilean airline. And then I'd wait.

The wind blew in some black clouds, and then a few heavy drops of rain began to come down on me. I switched up a steep hill to hasten my return home, rather than following the trail all the way down to the road, as I had planned.

Once I was back at my computer, with a fire going and a dog tucked under each elbow, I typed up this letter:

Dear Mr. CEO,

I am writing to you, sir, because my husband and I have just received word from Captain Ben that our vacation plans to King George Island (KGI) for March 2010 have been canceled. We are terribly saddened by this news. I believe our plans have been misunderstood. I would like to explain our situation, with the hope that I can correct this misunderstanding and be allowed to follow through with our vacation itinerary, as we had previously agreed with Victory Adventures.

I originally contacted the Captain to ask if he could fly us to KGI for the two-day trip in March, as advertised on the Victory Adventures website. I additionally asked him if there was a place where my husband and I could run. We did not want to disturb the natural environment. We hoped for perhaps a well-used road or walkway where we could run back and forth to reach a certain goal. The captain then consulted his team and was able to locate a well-used two-kilometer walkway between two points where tourists would usually walk anyhow. We would be allowed to walk/run that route over and over to meet our goal.

I think the misunderstanding arose because I was informed that we needed at least six people in order to book the flight. Since all six people would only have one guide among them, and since the guide would need to be with us for 100 percent of the time, we felt it would make sense to see if we could find some other people who would want to join us on our vacation, rather than to travel with people who had different ideas of how to spend their time on KGI. To entice people to call me, I sent out an email with the word "marathon" in the subject line. I was very clear in the details that this was nothing more than a short-distance walkway repeated over and over. I used the word "marathon" to get people to read further so that I could fill up the airplane and we would have enough passengers to book the flight.

I never imagined that the term would signal that we were planning an official "event." In actuality, we were only able to find three women who had interest in a similar vacation (later, someone completely unknown to us told Ben he wanted to join the flight as a general tourist and was willing to hang out with us while we ran—this got us up to six). Our interest has always been to live out a personal dream and never to create a planned or public event. I feel very sorry for my ignorance about the use of terms. I imagine someone saw my email and misinterpreted my intentions because they did not read further than the subject line.

As we have understood the plans we have made:

1. There will be no environmental impact because we will not be traveling in any unapproved area. We will also leave nothing behind and will not use resources beyond any regular tourist (fewer, if we can help it).

2. We are doing nothing different than exactly the same trip Captain Ben has been organizing for the last ten years. There will be no variation whatsoever from the usual activities at all. The only difference will be that we will spend some extra time on that two-kilometer walkway.

3. Your approved tour guide will be overseeing us at all times, and we will follow all of his directions without question.

Please accept our apologies for inadvertently calling attention to your airline and for requiring extra time from you to sort this through. I hope you will reconsider allowing us to live out our dream.

If it is a matter of filling out INACH forms to make sure we have covered our bases and are going through the proper channels, we would be more than happy to do so. We have always intended to follow all laws and guidelines and ethical considerations in our vacation plans to visit King George Island.

Thank you for your time.

Sincerely,
Cami Ostman

Satisfied that I had downplayed what had raised the alarm to the best of my ability, I sent this letter to the CEO of the airline, and then another, slightly altered version of it to the individual from the U.S. Department of State who had contacted Captain Ben the week before to initiate the investigation. My reason for contacting our own government was simply that I hoped I could appeal to them to take pressure off INACH, which would then take pressure off DAP.

Within a couple of days, I heard from our Department of State. Although the tone of my correspondent's email was kind and he attempted to be helpful in his explanation, his response to me confirmed what I was afraid of: He had no influence over the situation. He basically explained that he had investigated our plans because he had been notified (by whom, he did not say) that there was a "marathon" about to take place on King George Island and that Americans were involved in its organization, but that he had discovered that the tour company in charge of said Americans (Victory Adventures) was owned by Chileans. This satisfied him that he was not responsible for any further investigation. Everything was now up to the Chilean government if they had further questions, and to the CEO of the airline.

More than a week went by without my hearing any news from the airline CEO. Another half a week passed. I became more and more anxious, wondering if it was soon going to be too late to find some alternative arrangements to get to the last continent this season. I sent a message to the captain.

Had he heard anything? He hadn't, but he would contact the CEO directly on my behalf and find out if a decision had been made. He quickly got back to me with the answer: "You can come as a tourist, but you cannot run."

So that was it. We couldn't run. The trip was off.

I was at a complete loss for what to do next. Should I keep searching for a way to meet my goal, or should I give up? First and foremost, I realized, I needed to tell the rest of the team the bad news.

All of this troubled time, I had communicated only the most rudimentary of details to the other three runners. I'd said there had been a glitch in the plans and that they should hold off on sending their deposits to Victory Adventures for a few days. I did not want to alarm anyone before I had pursued all possible routes of appeal. Now I felt satisfied, or rather resigned, that there was no hope for running on King George Island through Victory Adventures, and I needed to communicate with the rest of the team.

I dispatched a humble, apologetic note to the others, explaining as best I could how our plans had fallen through and how I was back to the drawing board. I explained to Marie, Marina, and our one other runner that I had to pull out as organizer of the Bring Your Own GPS Alternative Antarctica Marathon, as we'd been playfully calling our project. For the next few days, as I waited for their angry responses incriminating me for not covering all my bases before getting other people involved, I lamented to Julie on our runs that I couldn't see a clear path to completing the seventh continent. I was too angry with Marathon Tours now, for their threatening email (and my unsubstantiated but strong suspicion that they were the ones who had alerted all the governments to look into our plans), in addition to their poor communication when I was on their waiting list, to suck up my pride and go crawling back to them. And I knew I could never afford to do the Ice Marathon at the South Pole. Maybe I'd been beaten.

Julie, a stubbornly optimistic person by nature, listened to me griping with a sympathetic ear as we traversed the trails in the frigid morning air the next few days, but finished every sentence I uttered by adding, "Yet."

"There's just no way to get to Antarctica," I said.

"Yet," Julie replied.

"Oh well. I guess I just have to live with the fact that I didn't get to finish my quest."

"Yet," Julie chimed in.

Within the week, emails from my team began to trickle in. Marina's friend simply wished me well in my endeavor to run on the last continent. She thanked me for all my efforts, and that was that. I appreciated her gracious reply and hoped the others would follow suit. But when I finally heard from Marie and Marina, I could hardly have been more astounded. In a round-robin email, Marie declared that we should follow through on our plans, go to Antarctica in March, and see what happened. In her inimitable Australian way, she said we should "can the talk of running" and take our chances that there would be a way to cover the distance of forty-two kilometers on foot, even if we had to walk it. Marina agreed with Marie and advocated we get our deposits in to Victory Adventures and buy our plane tickets to Punta Arenas.

I was bewildered. I wrote them back, reiterating that not only did we have no guarantee that we could travel the forty-two-kilometer distance on foot, but we might also be asked to stop if we tried. I didn't know if we would be able to walk freely about Villa Las Estrellas or if we would be holed up in the trailers used to lodge visitors as soon as the official tour finished the first day. Marina wrote back: "Well, they can't stop us from running around in our rooms, can they?" I honestly didn't know. Both women were so adamant about following through with our plans that I was actually brought to tears of grateful release in front of my computer screen the evening of our exchange.

Their determination made me wonder if this barrier, this final hurdle in my way, was the big test in the Hero(ine)'s Journey, à la Joseph Campbell. Every spiritual quest was meant to be punctuated by trials. Every pilgrim, real or fictional, had a mountain to climb or an examination to ace. Dorothy had to conquer the witch; Amelia Earhart had her ocean to fly over; even Jesus had to resist his three temptations in the wilderness. Due to my field of study and personal attraction to archetypal psychology, I held a hundred stories in my head of grail searches and boats looking for the mystical island of Avalon, of children triumphing over evil adults, of wives escaping their treacherous, blue-bearded husbands. Was this the final round in *my* fight to really be free of all the rules that had plagued me in my early life?

"THEY WANT TO GO anyhow," I told Bill over dinner a couple of hours later, still struggling to believe it myself.

"They what?" he asked, incredulous. "Who wants to go where?"

"Antarctica. King George Island. They want to go even without any promise that we can cover the distance. You know, they want to take a chance that the reality on the ground is different from what we're being told."

"You're kidding."

"No. I've told them there's very little chance we'll be allowed to even walk the distance, but they aren't giving up."

"What do you think?" Bill knew me, though—I'm not sure why he bothered to ask.

"Well, let me tell you a story. When I was a sophomore in high school," I started, and Bill settled back in his chair to get ready for a long answer to his short question, "I had a hard year. You know, emotionally. And my grades suffered. I ended up with a B in English, even though it was my favorite subject. So I didn't get into the advanced-placement English class for the following year, and I was really upset. All my friends were going to be in the class. I didn't give up, though. I wrote an appeal letter to the principal, but he turned me down."

Bill nodded and took a deep breath. He'd gotten really patient these past years at waiting for me to get to the point.

"I had to watch for the next two years as all my friends got to read Dickens and Austen. I sat at the lunch table with them and listened as they discussed all the greats, while I read short stories out of the big general textbook the rest of us used. I made a mental note of all the advanced-placement books so I could read them on my own someday—which I mostly have, by the way."

Bill still sat quietly, and I knew he was hoping to eventually find out how my story answered his question about whether or not I wanted to go to Antarctica under these new conditions.

"Years later, after high school, one of the AP kids was putting together a reunion and he called me to get a friend's contact information. I told him I'd give him my friend's phone number if he would invite me to the party."

Bill smiled with recognition at this part of the story. "Oh, so *that's* why you always attend the reunions, even though you weren't in the class. I always wondered how that got started."

"Yeah, and you know what? Nobody even remembers that I wasn't in the class. When they reminisce about some field trip they went on, I always have to remind them that I didn't go. Somebody usually says, 'Really? I thought you were there.'"

"Hmm," Bill considered this, but he still didn't get the connection. "So, what does this mean for Antarctica?"

"It means I'm crashing this field trip. I'm not missing out on this story, only to hear about it later. I'm going."

Bill nodded and thought this over. "Makes sense," he said. "Good for you." Then he shifted his position, returned to eating his dinner, and changed the subject. I thought his reply was somewhat curt, given my lengthy diatribe, but I dismissed it as Bill's way—he always uses fewer words than I do.

Not until the next morning, as he kissed me goodbye to head off to work, did he say more. With his hand on the doorknob, he began, "Cami, I think it's great that you want to go to King George Island with Marina and Marie, but I've decided I'm not going to join you."

My chest tightened. I hadn't expected this. I was shocked. And saddened. We were supposed to do all our traveling together. That was the rule. We didn't run our races side by side, but we always started and ended with each other there. I wasn't ready for him to bail out on me. I had taken for granted that if I wanted to follow through on our plans, he would be coming along. "Why?" was all I could get out.

"When I go to Antarctica, I want to go with the guarantee that I can run a marathon distance. I don't want to take the chance that maybe I can walk, but maybe not. But I support you."

"Will you still come as far as Punta Arenas?" I wanted to know.

"Yes, absolutely," he said. Then he kissed me, walked out the front door to his car, and drove away.

I was left standing by the front door, confused. Should I feel betrayed? Afraid? Rejected? Believed in?

I wandered back to the kitchen and poured a large mug of coffee. Taking it back to the living room, I settled into my big chair with my feet folded up under me. The dogs curled in with me, Jane on my lap, Fuji's head snuggled under my left arm. I closed my eyes and listened to my Inner Voices. *I can't go to Antarctica without Bill, can I?* I asked myself.

Very softly, I heard a gentle, reassuring murmur: *It's okay. This is your path. Nobody has to walk it with you in order to make it legitimate.* A series of images flashed through my memory at warp speed: me, entering my Seattle condominium and finding myself alone inside for the first time. And feeling safe. Me in Australia, pushing, exhausted and alone, up what felt like the biggest hill in the world. And feeling strong at the top. Me, lying awake in a guesthouse in South Africa, realizing that I was alone with my values and my inability to be faithful to them. And feeling ashamed.

These and many other instances of isolation, both happy and troubling, came to mind. Finally, inside me I heard a chorus of voices, all of them saying, *Go. Go. Go. Go. Go.* I knew my answer then. I realized that as I moved through my life, sometimes I had guarantees about the outcome of certain undertakings. Sometimes I had my partner along on the journey. And sometimes I wouldn't get to have either, but I could always have my own integrity if I listened to myself. My heart was saying, *Go!* No matter what happened when I arrived on the ground on King George Island, now was my time.

With this decided, I responded to Marie and Marina, agreeing to go with them to Antarctica. We three girls would take this leap, come what may.

NOW I COULD SETTLE down a little and focus on the here and now of my life. My private practice had been severely impacted by the economy, so I had too few clients and far too much time on my hands. To stay sane, I needed to fill my hours and days with meaningful activities. For years I'd waited to have a wide enough lull in my schedule to embark on some kind of volunteer under-taking. Now I had lots of openings in my weekly schedule that used to be filled with therapy. I knew exactly what I wanted to do: The Bellingham Sister Cities Association was looking for board members, so I applied and got voted onto its advisory board in December. For our impending trip to Punta Arenas, Bill and I would be visiting our third sister city. We'd been welcomed and treated kindly, especially during our visit to Tateyama. I was eager to return the favor by welcoming visitors to Bellingham.

In addition to joining the Sister Cities Board, I ratcheted up the miles in my running and got serious about qualifying for the Marathon Maniacs, whom I'd watched over the past few years. They were a fun group of run-ners who competed with one another for how many marathons they could complete in a year. Time and pace were irrelevant; only the number of races mattered. In October, Bill and I had run a marathon in the Okanagan Valley in Canada and then I'd continued to train with Julie for her next race: the Disney World Marathon in January. My miles were way up and I was in the right shape for giving three races in ninety days a try—what a far cry from my first three labored miles around the lake in Seattle years earlier.

Near the end of December, I began to look for the three marathons I would run in order to qualify for the Marathon Maniacs. I needed them to be local and cheap at this point. Whereas in previous years I'd wanted all of my races to entice me with fabulous destinations, now I wanted them to require very little planning. The Antarctica trip had taken all my planning energy out of me.

As luck would have it, a member of the Maniacs club was putting on a little marathon that I'd never heard of at the end of December, right in Bell-ingham. Mary's Last Chance Marathon was held on New Year's Eve on the same trails I (and everyone in town) trained on routinely. It was free and easy to get to, and both Bill and Julie could run portions of it with me.

Twenty-three days later, I was signed up for my first fifty-kilometer race: the Pigtails Ultra-Marathon, named after the Maniac who put it on. I'd never intended to run anything longer than a marathon, but cheap and simple-to-get-to races within my ninety-day window were not easy to come by. Bill insisted that an extra five miles would pass by unnoticed. I decided to give it a try, since it was only a two-hour drive from Bellingham and cost only $5, plus a food bank donation.

Bill was wrong. It turned out that an extra five miles beyond the marathon distance was an eternity. I had my first mini–panic attack since I'd tried to better eight miles in my early training for Prague. At mile twenty-two, sore, wet, muddy (it had been raining all morning), and into my fifth hour of running, I looked at my GPS, and the fact that I had nine miles left to run crashed in on me. Bill had joined me on my third loop around the lake that made up the racecourse. I told him I needed to stop. I braced my upper body on my thighs, put my head down low around my knees, and tried to breathe. I felt a sob escape from deep inside my chest as I said, "I can't do it. I can't." But somehow, I knew it was just a feeling. I closed my eyes and let raindrops hit the back of my neck as the fear ran its course. Not knowing what he could do to help, Bill lingered in the mud off to the side of the trail, waiting for my panic to subside. After a few minutes, I got my equilibrium back and made the decision to carry on.

The race took me seven hours and seventeen minutes, but I finished. Two down and one more race to go before I could call myself a Maniac.

For my third act, I ran in the Birch Bay Marathon, just twenty minutes from home. On a beautiful, clear winter day, thirty days after my first ultrarace, I dragged my fatigued quadriceps, hamstrings, glutei maximi, and all the rest of my exhausted muscles through the chilly, salty February air, feeling the lunacy of this new goal.

The race was, thankfully, uneventful. When I crossed the finish line at 5:26, I was tired and almost wondered why I'd done it, but I could now turn in my application and join the ranks of this dubiously elite group. I couldn't wait to tell Marina, when we finally met face-to-face the following month, that we were sister Maniacs.

By this time, it was near the end of February and Bill and I had only two weeks before jumping on our next plane and making our way to the southernmost location either of us had ever landed on. I was well on my way to transitioning from being a high-minded spiritual quester into being one who had completed her life-changing challenge and looked forward to the next chapter in life. But it remained to be seen whether I would run, walk, or even be able to land on King George Island so I could go that final mile.

antarctica:
THE "experience"
MARCH 2010

"Running is the greatest metaphor for life, because you get out of it what you put into it."

—OPRAH WINFREY

"It hurts up to a point, and then it doesn't get any worse."

—ANN TRASON, ultramarathon runner

13

Before I had completed my three races to qualify for the Maniacs, and before Bill and I had finalized the purchase of our air tickets for this last voyage on my quest, Marie wrote to Marina and me from Australia with bad news: She couldn't come with us. She explained that the economy had taken its toll on her and that she had to reprioritize. She was sorry, and so was I. Marie had been my inspiration, the audacity behind the decision to take a chance that meant we might be renegade runners on Antarctica in March.

Once again, I reconsidered my plans. I wrote to Marina: "You won't have three finishers even if we can run. What do you think? Is it still worth it to you to go?" I didn't personally care about the Maniacs' standards. I hadn't joined the club so I could have someone sanction my running; I'd joined for fun, and because I'd found like-minded runners among the Maniacs I'd met over the years. But Marina was among the ilk of Marathon Maniacs whose goal is to get into the group's hall of fame (Mel, from my Whidbey Island race, was inducted in 2009). One of the criteria was that members run "333 lifetime marathons or ultras," all of which must meet the Maniacs' rule of having three finishers. She wanted her runs on South America and Antarctica to count, and I didn't blame her for that.

"We've come this far," Marina responded. "I might as well go all the way."

With the decision made (once again) to follow through and touch ground on the seventh continent, regardless of whether we would get to run there or whether what we did when we got there would count in anyone's book, I took the leap and booked our plane tickets. Then, at the beginning of February, I put my guidebooks away and kicked back. I'd done what I could do. I was going to try (unsuccessfully, it turned out) not to give any more thought to running routes in Punta Arenas for Marina's South American race, or to schemes about getting in our miles in Antarctica. I needed to stick my head in the sand and take a self-imposed mental hiatus.

The one thing I allowed myself to do in preparation for our March 2010 trip was nurture my budding relationships with a few Punta Arenas residents. Bill and I had met two Chileans in Bellingham at a fundraiser for the Sister Cities Association. Mackarena and Maritza had taken six weeks out of their summer break (during our winter) to visit schools in Bellingham and observe language classes. These two women and Marcelo, a man I'd been emailing with for several months, were English teachers at the Colégio Miguel de Cervantes, a private primary and secondary school in Punta Arenas that had a long-standing exchange relationship with Bellingham's public schools.

Bill and I knew from experience that the best travel always included relationships with locals, so we took our acquaintance with these three teachers seriously. I sent them our itinerary and made arrangements to meet them as soon as we landed.

As much as I tried to keep my thinking about the trip to a minimum, Marina kicked into gear with ideas, plans, and communication. Every week I got an email from her with a new brainstorm about how to make the adventure apply to her guidelines: "Do you know how many passengers will be on the plane? Maybe they would all agree to be starters." Or "Do you know how late it gets dark on King George Island? Maybe we can just walk around the barracks all night." But my favorite (and the most plausible) was "Let's push start on the GPS the minute we hit ground. We'll just stick together and count every step toward the distance, even if we go to the bathroom. Then we'll get up early and walk in circles until we get to 26.2."

Her ideas provided some levity during this uncertain time. Unfortunately, every night I was dreaming about Antarctica, and about all the things that could go wrong. In one dream I was trying to escape from our lodgings (which looked very much like a Pacific Northwest summer camp I'd attended in the third grade, complete with log cabins and outhouses) to take a run. Paved roads wound all the way around the island, which was lush, green, and sunny, more tropical than arctic. Police guarded the camp we were in, however, and I couldn't make my way to the street to start my run. I ended up climbing over a fence and landing in a farmer's field, where I ran back and forth between rows of green beans to get my miles in, falling down every few yards because of my constant vigilance about getting caught.

In another dream, the island was icy and white, as it should be, but it was populated with a full town, complete with sidewalks and convenience stores. A large armored truck dropped me off at a service station. I stood by the gas pumps and watched as hundreds of pedestrians strolled along the streets beside a big blue bay with icebergs floating in it. I felt self-conscious about running and stood paralyzed, too afraid to take the chance.

If it hadn't been for Julie, I would have taken these dreams as bad premonitions. I recounted them as we ran. I was tapering from the three races I'd done to join the Maniacs, anticipating March and the possibility, if I was lucky, of running two marathon distances within four days of each other. Julie and I put in three-mile runs a couple times a week, and walked most other days.

It was a walking day when I told her about the second dream. She halted midstride when I told her about being paralyzed on that sidewalk. "I forgot to tell you," she said, smiling. "I had a dream, too. I dreamed that you did it. That you got to King George Island and everything was smooth and easy. And it felt real. So don't worry about it. Plus, I can't imagine you paralyzed." Her words were comforting, and a good reminder that I wasn't incapacitated so easily. She was right. Even if there were onlookers, and even if I was breaking the rules, I would still give it a shot.

I have always had a strong tendency to believe in dreams as signs. And as there was, in fact, a fifty-fifty chance that I would get to run, I decided I'd rather bank on Julie's dream than on mine. Given that no one knows the future, optimism always feels better than pessimism, I reasoned. And I never dreamed about Antarctica after that.

UNFORTUNATELY, SOMETIMES IT DOESN'T matter what you believe or whose dream you bank on—reality is what it is. At eleven o'clock in the morning on February 27, twelve days before our departure, I got an email from a friend who was out of the country. "I saw the devastating news about Chile on CNN. Will this affect your trip?" I hadn't turned the TV on yet. I had no idea what my friend was talking about, but I shouted for Bill.

"What happened in Chile?" I asked, panic brewing.

"I don't know. Why?"

"Turn on the TV. Something happened in Chile." He flipped on the television, but there was no coverage about it anywhere, so we looked online and saw that mere hours earlier, Chile had sustained the most massive earthquake recorded in recent human history. The whole earth's mass had shifted toward its center; homes had tumbled down; tsunamis were expected as far away as Hawaii; even São Paulo, Brazil, had felt the shaking. Immediately, we thought of our friends in Brazil. Lucas lived among the high-rises right in the heart of São Paulo, and if there was one place on Earth I would not want to be during an earthquake, it was that city, with its concrete and glass rising up to the heavens. We emailed Bill's Brazilian family, as well as all of our contacts in Patagonia: Captain Ben, Maritza, Mackarena, and Marcelo. Was everyone okay?

One by one that day, we began receiving confirmation that those we knew were safe. Most hadn't even felt the shaking. Maybe the situation wasn't as bad as the news was indicating. But everyone we knew was far away from the epicenter.

Santiago, Chile's capital, was close to the epicenter of the earthquake. Reports were coming in that seven hundred people had been killed in collapsing buildings there. Nearby towns on the coast were attempting to evacuate before the ocean unleashed violent waves onto their beaches. And Santiago's international airport was closed. Then we heard from Ben that his wife and children had been in central Chile for vacation and would be trapped there until the airport reopened. He was distracted by fear for their safety as one aftershock followed another, further damaging the region. I wrote Ben back, promising to pray for his family, as he had asked.

Within two more days we received another email from Ben announcing that our March 18 trip to Antarctica had been moved to March 23. A total of three flights to King George Island had been planned for March; the one scheduled for the thirteenth had been canceled because tourists planning to fly to Punta Arenas through Santiago could not be accommodated in the Santiago Airport, due to the damage the quake had caused in the passenger terminals. Aerovías DAP was trying its best to combine three excursions into one. I knew Marina couldn't go to Antarctica on March 23 because she had to get home by March 25 for a conference. With one stroke of the computer keyboard, it was over for her. And the way things were looking, I felt extremely doubtful, Julie's dream notwithstanding, that I would get to Antarctica either. Chile's infrastructure, modern and well organized as it is, was still no match for an epic natural disaster.

Before I sat down to write Marina, I gave in to a good hard cry. I curled up into a ball on my sofa and let the dogs snuffle around my wet face and lick my tears. I cried for the people who'd lost loved ones in the earthquake (and, while I was at it, for those who had died in Haiti's quake a few weeks earlier); I cried for the sweet little coastal towns that had been destroyed when the ocean sent her backlash ashore; I cried for Marina, who had held on to tiny shreds of hope these past months that we would make a wonderful memory in an icy yonderland below South America. And then I cried for myself. I was so, so tired of trying to make this thing happen.

Maybe I'd learned all I needed to learn from my vision quest and should let this go, I reasoned. When I'd trudged alongside Bill on my first marathon in Prague, I had been a woman sick of her well-behaved, other-accommodating self and tired of trying to mold life into a perfect picture of holiness and rightness. I wasn't that woman anymore. My quest had changed me: I'd met parts of myself that had been kept in the dark, and I'd learned how to be messy without feeling ashamed. Perhaps leaving the quest incomplete was a better way to conclude it. Life really can't be tied up neatly at the end, after all. I knew it might eat at me the rest of my life if I didn't get to run in

Antarctica, but so what? How many words get left unsaid in our lives, deeds (good or otherwise) left undone, goals left unmet?

The process of organizing the Antarctica trip had brought out a rebelliousness in me I hadn't let loose very often in my life. I'd refused to take the easy way and sit on a waiting list for who knew how long; I'd forged my own topsy-turvy way. The fact that an earthquake had, in the end, posed as the final, insurmountable hurdle didn't take away all the character that going down this road had built in me. This was a new kind of wilderness on the quest; it was the wilderness of going nowhere.

And as I cried on my couch, I kept in mind that there comes a time when an individual's search for meaning has to give way to the immediate basic needs of others. In this case, Chile's needs were bigger than mine. With one final heave, I stopped my tears and said, "Oh well."

I WROTE TO MARINA and told her about the change of plans. I wrote to Captain Ben and told him Marina couldn't go on the new date he'd set. Then I called Bill on the phone and explained my emotional state. He knew about the altered schedule, but he didn't know I was giving up on the dream.

"Here's the deal," I said when I heard his voice on the other end of the line. "I've had it up to my ears with this whole thing. I can barely stand the idea of it. If they do open the Santiago airport in time for our trip, and if we do get on our flight as scheduled, you have to promise not to complain about one single thing that goes wrong. I mean, if you get stuck in a center seat on the plane, you can't gripe. If somebody spills his coffee on you, you have to walk ten paces away from me before you scream in pain. I'm expecting one big catastrophe and I think you should, too."

Bill listened. "Okay" was all he said. To be fair, I hadn't left much room for discussion.

IN ANOTHER FEW DAYS, the airport in Santiago opened for business. Ben's family was home safe. Not only that, but he wrote to me and reported that DAP was working hard to accommodate as many people as could still make it down to Punta Arenas. It turned out that March 18, our original date, worked out best for the largest number of people. Marina was back in. I was glad, but I kept my distance from this news, holding it with open palms, as it were, since I knew it could change any moment. There were still large aftershocks occurring every few hours in the central region of Chile. A big enough one affecting just the wrong location could close down the Santiago airport again.

The morning of the day we were to fly through Santiago, a huge aftershock struck. Sitting at Sea-Tac Airport, waiting to board our first leg from Seattle to Atlanta, I got calls from two different friends, each asking if I was still going to be able to fly. Yes, I was, as far as I could tell, but I probably wouldn't know for sure how far I would get until I made my connection in Atlanta for Santiago. Some five hours later, we arrived in Atlanta and checked the departures screen in the terminal. The flight to Santiago was leaving as scheduled! That was good news. The bad news was that we'd arrived in Atlanta late. Our flight from Seattle had been postponed by an hour, and now we were in danger of missing our flight to Santiago, the one that leaves only once a day.

Bill and I ran full speed through the airport to try to make our plane, but arrived at the gate in time to watch it pulling away from the terminal. I had predicted this whole trip would be fraught with problems, and it looked like it was going to meet my lamentable expectations.

I crumpled onto a chair at the gate while Bill argued with the Delta attendant (who, poor thing, was also arguing with several angry Chileans trying to get home to family and friends). While he negotiated a place for us to stay that night and vouchers for breakfast the next morning, I just slumped and shook my head. I didn't think I could take seventeen days of sprinting toward things that almost happened, but not quite. It was draining. I felt the rise and fall of my adrenaline each time I got right up to the edge of meeting a goal, only to have the door close in my face.

I slept the best I could that night and simply resigned myself to not being attached to the outcome of whatever happened tomorrow. The next evening, when we did board our flight on time, I was not surprised when we ended up waiting on the airplane for over two hours for something in its hydraulics system to be repaired. We were probably going to miss our next connection in Santiago to Punta Arenas, too. After we were finally allowed to take off, I spent the entire long flight feeling defeated. I worked hard to remind myself that the final results of this trip didn't indicate the success or failure of my marathon life or my journey to grow as a person, or of anything else, really. I told myself it was only my continued grasping for this thing I longed for that was creating tightness in my shoulders and giving me a headache. Well, that and nine hours in coach.

But there was a little light ahead. In Santiago, the most unlikely place for a smooth transition, all was well. The terminal was completely closed down, due to earthquake damage, and all airport business was being conducted in large temporary tents into which seating, fans, and computers had been carted. But airport staff were available in droves, waiting to help passengers make sense of makeshift signage, and buses efficiently took people from one flight to another in a matter of minutes. Seemingly better organized than Atlanta, not only was Santiago Airport functioning, but the employees on the ground were friendly. I hadn't seen a single smile from anyone in Atlanta the day before (and I'd spent all afternoon there), even at the Starbucks counter, while the folks in Santiago, who had every right to be crabby and out of sorts, were helpful and kind. Go figure.

One uniformed man ushered us from the plane to a counter where we checked in for our next flight. Because of our delay in Atlanta, we were cutting it close, but the airline held the plane for us as our boarding passes printed. Then another staff member taxied us out to the tarmac, where we climbed up a set of temporary metal stairs onto the small jet. A flight attendant offered us candy and a smile when we took our seats and buckled up in preparation for our four-hour flight south. We made it to Punta Arenas one day late, but never so happy to be anywhere.

SINCE WE WERE A day late, I had to get straight to work as soon as we arrived. Our itinerary indicated that we were to run our forty-two kilometers through Punta Arenas the very next morning, on Sunday. Then we planned to visit with our sister-city friends in town for a few days while we recovered from that run. Marina and I were then scheduled to fly out of Punta Arenas to Antarctica on Thursday morning.

After settling into our hostel, I phoned some of our contacts. I first needed to find Marina and make sure she'd arrived safely. She was supposed to be couch surfing at Marcelo's place (I'd introduced them to each other over email). I also wanted to connect with Mackarena, who for two days had been at her parents' home nearby, waiting for our call.

With a couple of quick conversations, I settled our plans for the evening. Marina and Marcelo would come by our hostel a bit later so we could all finally meet face-to-face. Together, we would look at the map of Punta Arenas and trace out a route for the forty-two-kilometer run we had promised Marina several months ago, when we'd made our original plan to do back-to-back races in South America and Antarctica.

Bill and I freshened up as we waited for Marcelo and Marina to arrive. When I heard the hostel's doorbell ring, I felt giddy and rushed to open the door, excited to meet my two friends in person for the first time. Marcelo, about my height, with chocolate eyes and a hint of a dark goatee, greeted me with a kiss on my cheek in the traditional Chilean way. Then I turned my attention to my young collaborator, Marina. She smiled and gave a nervous laugh. I reached to hug her as she said, "So you made it? I was wondering if you'd ever get here."

"You and me both," I said, swinging the door open wider and escorting them into the living room of the hostel. "I was really worried about you, too, Marina. Did it freak you out when we weren't in Santiago yesterday?" It had been our plan to meet Marina at the airport there and take the same flight to Punta Arenas.

"A little, but I figured the only thing to do was get on the plane and hope everything turned out. But then when I got to Punta Arenas, I called Marcelo. He's been a lifesaver," she said, with a smile in his direction.

I looked her over carefully as Bill invited them both to have a seat. Marina's large hazel eyes betrayed her youth. There was an innocence, a lack of worldliness, about her. She glanced around the hostel, seeming to take in everything she saw like it was a revelation. She kept her big down coat on and her hands in her pockets while she settled into a chair across from where I sat. Only twenty-three years old, and she was about to run her fifty-second marathon on her fourth continent the next day (and maybe her fifth a few days after that). Her brown hair shimmered in the afternoon sunlight coming through the window, and when she grinned at me, her high cheeks showed rosy and fresh, almost childlike.

"So, what's the plan for tomorrow?" she asked, getting straight to the point.

"Well, why don't we look at a map and get the expert's opinion for finalizing a good route," I said, turning to Marcelo. "Will you help us?"

"Of course," Marcelo replied.

The four of us gathered around a map of Punta Arenas. We discussed a running route for the next day that had us starting our race in the town square a few blocks from our hostel. We'd then follow along Bulnes Avenue (one of the main thoroughfares through town), before turning to run along the waterfront parallel to the Strait of Magellan for about eight miles. Then we'd turn around to backtrack for five miles or so and head up a hill onto the busiest street in the city before finally cutting back downhill to return to the park. Of course, we didn't know for certain that our route would constitute 26.2 miles, so we conceded that we might have to run around the town square a few times if our GPS indicated we were still short by the time we'd completed our long, lollipop-shaped route.

After settling on our course, Marcelo and Marina stayed and chatted awhile longer, and then we all walked to the grocery store together so Bill and I could get supplies for dinner. There was a chill in the air. March is the end of the summer on the south side of the equator, but that far down, the temperature never got hot. It was windy, too, something we would have to adjust to, Marcelo told us. I wrapped my arms around myself as we strolled, feeling grateful to Bill for insisting I pack plenty of cold-weather layers.

We said our goodbyes at an intersection, agreeing to meet at the town square at ten o'clock the next morning. Bill and I were desperate to get food and get to sleep. We'd never before run a race so close to our arrival in a new country. I was weary from the journey and concerned about the next day. I was also wondering where we would find Marina's fifth starter. Marcelo had agreed to run a short distance with us and to be counted as starter number four for the race, but we needed one more.

Before bed, I phoned Mackarena one more time. She'd asked me to call her once we had decided our route, saying she wanted to show up in the morning and cheer us on. When I got her on the phone, she had two pieces of news for me. The first was that her father, Andres, was planning on running with us in the morning. The second was that she'd called the press and there would be a reporter waiting for us at our starting point in the morning.

I got off the phone and climbed happily into my single bed, looking at Bill, already snuggled down in his across the room. "Well, it looks like everything is settled for tomorrow. We have our five starters, and we're going to be celebrities," I said.

"Great," Bill said. "You'd better set an alarm. I'm likely to sleep right through tomorrow."

Within moments, I heard the rhythm of Bill's breathing telling me he was gone for the night. I lay awake for a short time, pondering the irony of the past couple of weeks. Every attempt I'd made to plan had been foiled, while now, without any effort on my part, details tumbled into place at the last moment. There was a lesson to be learned here, about trust or letting go or something. But before I could get hold of it, I was asleep.

AT TEN THE NEXT morning, even from a distance, I saw Mackarena's unmistakable head of curly auburn locks waiting for us at the little central park. We greeted one another warmly and made introductions: Marina to Mackarena, and Mackarena's father, Andres, to all of us. A reporter from *La Prensa*, the local newspaper, was there to interview us and take a few pictures as we stretched and warmed up. We showed Andres, a handsome, regal-looking military retiree in his early fifties who appeared fit and ready to go in his jogging outfit, our intended route on the map. He said he planned to go as far as he could but was certain it wouldn't be the whole way. Then Bill and Marina held their fingers over the start buttons on their Garmins and said, "One, two, three, go." Without further ado, we began running.

As long as I live, the self-made route we ran that day will remain one of my favorite marathons. For nearly nine months, I had been studying maps of Punta Arenas and making friends with Marcelo through email exchanges that mostly involved asking advice about running routes. Now, as I jogged alongside my sister Maniac, with Bill and Andres in front of us by a quarter of a mile and a homeless dog we dubbed our sixth starter (we named him Maratona el Perro) trotting nearby at an aloof distance, the first mile of the race felt like a missing piece to a puzzle I didn't think would ever fit together.

As I had many times before in my marathoning life, I savored the experience of being connected to Something Bigger. In this case, it was a network of relationships that hadn't even existed for me a little more than a year earlier. I'd never heard of Punta Arenas before I started looking for a way to get to Antarctica. Today I was going to get to see her innards and become intimately acquainted with her.

During the first mile, before Maratona el Perro left us, we stopped at a high lookout to get an aerial view of the city as she showed herself off, colorful against the Strait of Magellan. The low skyline revealed a diversity of architectural styles. Everything from nineteenth-century European buildings to very simple one-story cement-block residences mingled together comfortably.

We didn't linger; we had a long way to go. Andres stayed with us for eight kilometers, dropping out only when his shoes began to give him blisters, but he and Mackarena followed us by car, providing aid for several miles after that. Marina's pace was slightly slower than mine, but not so much that it mattered. We ran side by side and chatted almost the whole distance. She shared her favorite Kierkegaard quotes with me; I told her about some interesting research on marriage and divorce I'd read recently. She told me about her favorite race from the previous year (she'd completed twenty-eight marathons in 2009); I narrated the horror story of getting sick in South Africa exactly one year earlier.

As we ran and talked, I learned some things about Marina that would be important later on. She loved adventure and travel, but there was a very cautious part of her, too, looking out for danger and stepping with care into each new endeavor. I admired and even envied how much she'd accomplished in her life. By her age, I was already married and trying hard to fit into a prescribed role. Marina was open to the world, if somewhat wary of it, and I felt protective of that openness—in both of us. It was what brought us together.

Bill remained always within eyeshot of Marina and me. I had the map of the course in my running belt, so he didn't know where to turn without me. Besides, as he had teased, he was sure to place as the first male finisher even if he crawled the whole distance, so he ran ahead for stretches and then waited for us by walking slowly or stopping to stretch.

The sky pelted little pinpricklike drops of freezing-cold rain on us when we reached the waterfront, and a pack of stray dogs nearly attacked us once we were outside the city limits by a mile or so. In spite of those minor trials, and although we ended up overestimating our distance and running twenty-seven miles, I took pleasure in every step. My satisfaction at reaching this first milestone on the itinerary filled me with personal pride for persevering through a million temptations to scrap the whole trip.

When we finally returned to the town square six hours after we'd left it, Mackarena, Marcelo, and Andres waited there with the reporter, who had some follow-up questions. It was a glorious, absolutely perfect day! Maybe things were looking up.

WE HAD THREE DAYS to rest before our scheduled flight to Antarctica. Although I was elated to be in Chile and pleased we'd followed through on our Punta Arenas marathon as planned, a sense of foreboding shot through me whenever I thought about the next portion of our schedule. As long as we were in our sister city with our friends (who by Wednesday had loaned us a house to stay in, introduced us to their mayor, invited us to several wonderful meals, and let us come hang out in their classrooms), all felt safe and easy. In fact, we couldn't have been more comfortable if we'd stayed at home. But as soon as Antarctica crossed my mind, all the complications and changes of plans flooded forward and I was awash again in that nagging feeling that my final goal would go unmet. I continued to fluctuate between reaching a momentarily healthy state of nonattachment to outcome and grasping at it with proverbial white knuckles.

Wednesday evening at six o'clock, Marina and I had a meeting at the DAP offices. The purpose was to introduce all of the passengers who'd be going on the next day's excursion to one another, and to give us a weather report regarding conditions on King George Island. If the weather was bad, we wouldn't be flying. I was nervous, still expecting the worst.

Bill and I met Marina at the town center where we had started our race a few days earlier, and we walked the couple of blocks to the DAP building. As we entered, I could feel my anxiety rise. Would they cancel our flight due to inclement weather? Or would we discover some new piece of information that would once and for all close the door on the possibility of our running on King George Island? And what would our group be like: adventurous souls who might be likely to support our wacky dream, or fuddy-duddies who would insist we all stick together and snap pictures all day?

Walking into the DAP building, I scanned the large, white, open space with information booths and desks against the back wall. Along the wall where the entrance was, Plexiglas barriers blocked off cubicles, and behind those were windows that rose above our heads. In the center of the room was a cluster of airport seats. Bill, Marina, and I sat down to wait for someone to call us to our meeting.

We were the only customers in the place, as far as we could tell, so we whispered questions to one another about what we'd heard of other passengers. There would be three tourists besides Marina and me. I knew one of them was Yury, the Russian guy who had originally planned to come with us when we were planning our "running expedition" all those months ago. That was a comfort; I had communicated with Yury by email and already felt sure that he was flexible about how he'd spend his time on Antarctica. We didn't know anything about the others, though.

Soon enough, the door opened and two people walked in. I eyed them closely. I guessed by the fact that they weren't speaking that they didn't know each other. A petite Asian woman in her mid-thirties and a tall, young white man, perhaps twenty-five, wandered over to the seating area and loitered in our vicinity. Marina, bless her heart, was the opposite of shy. She struck up a conversation with them right away. They were both Americans. Kara was from Minnesota and was on a break from her professional life, taking an around-the-world tour, trying to hit all seven continents in eighty-one days. Alex was a premed student on an extended summer break before launching into his medical training at Northwestern University in the fall.

Marina had broken the ice, so, during the few minutes before our meeting, I told Kara and Alex about the history of our planning process and about our hopes to cover 26.2 miles while on Antarctica.

"Hey, maybe you two could be starters. You don't have to finish," Marina suggested. I held my breath and waited for their responses.

"What a blast," Kara said. "I can't wait to blog about starting a marathon on Antarctica. Nobody will believe me."

Alex, though more reserved, was equally supportive. "I've always thought about training for a marathon. This'll be a good test. I bet I won't make it very far."

At this point, a DAP employee appeared before us and asked us to follow him. As we all crammed into one of the glass cubicles together, my anxiety was slightly allayed because of Kara and Alex. The meeting was brief. Weather predictions for the morning on the island looked good. All we needed to understand before flying was that Antarctica is a protected area, so once we landed there, we had to follow our guide's directions and never veer into any area that was not approved for our presence. That was that. We were free to go. I started to put my coat on.

"Excuse me," I heard Bill say from the corner of the room. "I'm just wondering about a couple of things." I sat back in my chair and felt a bead of sweat form on my upper lip. I didn't know what Bill wanted to ask, but I wasn't prepared to hear conclusive answers to anything that would shut down my chances of running on Antarctica.

"Sure," our airline man said.

"Will they have any free time in the twenty-four hours they'll be on the ground?" Bill asked.

"Oh, yes. The sun goes down at about nine o'clock, so they will have the evening free. If there's something you all want to do, you only have to tell Alejo, your guide." He directed this last statement to the rest of us. "Alejo will help you find interesting activities."

"I see," Bill said. "And how much walking will they be doing? I mean, will they cover much distance?"

"Well, there can be several kilometers of walking. Again, they must tell Alejo what they are interested in. He can minimize or maximize the walking, as they request."

"Thank you." I craned my neck around to look at Bill. I saw a very faint smile on his face. He winked at me. I knew in that moment that if we managed to go the distance, Marina was going to have her third finisher on Antarctica.

We tumbled out of the cubicle, and Bill nudged me away from the others to get me alone. "If they have a seat on the plane, I'd like to buy it. How would you feel about that? I know you've been thinking of this as a girl-power trip."

I looked at Bill for a moment, grateful that he was the kind of man who would think to ask such a question, rather than simply move forward without regard for my feelings, but there was no hesitation for me. Bill's original decision not to come with me to Antarctica had made me sad, but I'd decided that his absence would take nothing away from my own journey. Neither would his presence. There would be no subtraction from the girl power just because there was a boy along for the ride (or the run). And having the love of my life there to share it with me could only enhance my experience, no matter how things turned out.

THE NEXT MORNING, I found myself climbing up a set of rickety steps into the cabin of a dual-propeller, eight-seat aircraft built in the 1980s. With some dismay, I observed the old levers, knobs, and switches at the controls and checked out the pilot, who gave us all a warm greeting in

Spanish. Excited but a little scared at how well used our plane appeared to be, I buckled my seat belt, turned to my companions to give them a tense smile, and then reached across the aisle to take Bill's hand. I closed my eyes as the engines fired up. I would make it to Antarctica. Or die trying, I heard a voice inside my head say.

The liftoff seemed to take forever as the plane puttered down the runway. And then, finally, we were in the air. For three and a half hours, we sailed over thick clouds, getting peeks through occasional clearings of the Beagle Channel, the famous waterway Charles Darwin sailed through as an amateur naturalist with Captain Robert FitzRoy in the late 1820s and early 1830s. Each of the passengers took turns sitting in the copilot seat at the front of the plane. When it was my turn, we were flying above the Darwin mountain range, the highest mountains on the southwest Chilean portion of Tierra del Fuego island, which Chile shares with Argentina. I peered down at the pearly blue glaciers and white-tipped mountain peaks, aware that I was among a small number of humans who had ever seen these ice fields.

I was so lost in the views below that more quickly than I had expected, we were descending through the clouds and found ourselves within sight of King George Island and the single airstrip that constituted the airport. The pilot guided the plane toward the surface of the strip and gently touched the landing gear to the ground with hardly a bump. We were here.

My anxiety ramped up again instantly. In all my efforts to get here, there was a part of me (a naysaying, negative part) that had never actually expected it to happen. I stayed in my seat as the others rustled around, collecting their belongings. I closed my eyes, trying to get in touch with what my angst was about. Until we landed and the plane door opened, there had been no guarantee we'd get here, but we had made it. So what was making me feel panicky and clammy?

Well, there isn't exactly a plan from this point forward, I heard a gentle internal voice suggest. Yep. That was it. Nothing that happened after this moment was on the official itinerary. I wasn't in charge of anything here in Antarctica. I was at the mercy of our guide. And luck. Certainly, luck had figured into everything else these past few months of planning, but at least I'd been able to feel I had a handle on certain details. No more.

I gathered my things and deplaned. This was truly a come-what-may mission. I'd worked over the years to let go of needing perfect control, and to let life come on its own terms. I was being given one more chance today to practice a lesson I never seemed to learn permanently.

As I emerged from the plane, I examined my surroundings. Laid out before us was a stark, frozen desert. Blotches of snow lay in patches over rich, dark soil—not a plant or tree anywhere in sight. The view from where we stood was like an old, faded photo. The air was gray with a light fog, and the unpaved road leading down to the Chilean community of forty, known as Villa las Estrellas, was muddy in spots and uneven. In the distance, the water in Maxwell Bay was placid and calm, a dim green color.

I turned to Bill and Marina, who were still standing near the plane. "Hurry up and push start on your Garmins. I don't want to miss a step," I said testily, the Bitch showing up without notice. If this was going to be a touring marathon, if I had to walk the whole forty-two kilometers, I wanted to start counting immediately. They obeyed me, but both reported their GPS devices were having trouble finding satellites.

In the meantime, we were greeted by a man who seemed to be channeling Santa Claus. He came forward and introduced himself as Alejo Contreras, our guide. Here was the fellow who held my marathon destiny in his hands. I inspected him. He was wild-looking, with a long graying beard, but had astute, clear brown eyes. He greeted each of us with a handshake, asking for our names. I observed him making his way down the line toward me. Alejo made eye contact with everyone, starting with Yury, and then with each American in turn.

When he got to me, I stood in front of him and dug through my anxiety to find my Inner Wisdom, source of my best intuition. Was this guy a kindred soul? Could I trust him with the concluding chapter of my vision quest? He was observing me, too, I noticed, spending an uncomfortable number of seconds on my running shoes. I had three cumbersome top and bottom layers on my body, plus a wind layer over all that, but I wore only wool socks and trail-running shoes on my feet. Alejo stared at them and then looked back at my face with a quizzical expression.

"Do you have other shoes?" he asked me.

"Only another pair like these. I never go anywhere without my running shoes." I waited to hear how he would respond.

"Neither do I," he said, in a way that made me feel we shared something, maybe a need to see the world on foot. I couldn't be sure.

Then he commanded us to follow him. He led us to our barracks, one of a number of weathered modular structures, where we left our backpacks, and then to a belowground garage, where he directed us to change into puffy red overalls like the suit he wore. He told us these would serve as wind-resistant floatation devices. We all exchanged inquiring expressions. Why did we need giant life jackets?

"We must hurry," Alejo said. "The weather is good now. You will never get this chance again." We waddled after him in our suits, down to the shore at the edge of an enclosed bay. He herded us into a Zodiac raft with a motor, and before I knew what was happening, someone on land was pushing us off into the water with one swift shove. "We will go to the glacier," he said. The weather changed so rapidly here on the island that many tourists never had the chance to see Collins Glacier, Alejo explained. We were in luck.

But as we sailed across the jade water, my thoughts latched on to the fact that we were on a boat, rather than putting in miles on foot. Bill and Marina's Garmins had finally located satellites, but we'd managed to put in only a mile and a half walking from the airstrip to the barracks and from there to the Zodiac, and we had to pause the Garmins while we were on the water.

I hadn't expected to be on a boat; my troubled expression caught Bill's attention. "Hey," he said to me. "This is Antarctica. Just relax and look around."

For some reason, his words hit me like a slap in the face, and I came to my senses. Was I going to revert to needing to control something I couldn't and lose this spectacular, once-in-a-lifetime moment to my obsession with the marathon distance? Had I learned nothing about living in the moment, about being grateful for the present? What about Prague and finishing the marathon with beer breaks? What about Whidbey Island and embracing my internal locus of celebration? The whole purpose of my quest was to lose the rigidity I'd developed in my childhood and young adulthood and to learn to take life as it presented itself. In one brief second, my anxiety gear shifted into neutral.

Here I was in a place where the environment was boss, where human life was in the hands of nature. One blustery burst of wind or rebellious swell in the water, and I could be dumped overboard with nary a chance of survival, despite my big red suit. The only moment was the current moment. Nothing else was guaranteed. Sometimes you don't get what you want, but, as the Rolling Stones pointed out, "you just might find you get what you need." I'd better pay attention. Maybe I wouldn't get my marathon done, but I was in Antarctica, inhaling the freshest air I'd ever breathed, sailing toward a glacier.

I squeezed my eyes shut and shook my head to clear it. When I opened them, we were trolling past an iceberg the size of a large house. Transparent teal and sparkly, it smelled like freshness and wonder. A little penguin swam beside us, weaving below and then above the surface.

"Hello," I said to him, "how are you today?" He ignored me and kept on his way.

A half hour later we sat with the Zodiac motor off, listening to Collins Glacier chink and crack. In the presence of a glacier of this size, you can only sit small and quiet and hope that nothing you do will disturb it. I stole a look across the Zodiac at Marina. Her cheeks were pink with the cold and she shivered as she snapped pictures, trying to capture the falling movement of a piece of ice breaking free from the mother glacier and plunging into the water.

My nose was moist in the crisp air, my eyes watery. Another penguin floated beside us, and I thought I heard her whisper, *Now, this is food for the soul.* The penguin reminded me of my conversation with the colorful Australian birds who had first taught me to pay attention to nature and to listen. What a world. What a life, I thought. Eight years earlier, I had barely been able to make it through my days, relieved to return to a five-hundred-square-foot basement apartment so I could give in to grieving the loss of a whole life that hadn't worked. Today, everything was different as I sat at the foot of the earth, beside an undomesticated glacier, just listening. My life worked for me now, as long as I didn't get in my own way. I reached over and held Bill's hand to thank him for reminding me to enjoy myself.

After allowing us to linger in mutual meditation for a time, Alejo started the motor and we puttered over to a small island to visit a gentoo penguin colony. Ten thousand couples and their offspring toddled about. Here, in late March, they had already hatched their eggs and the babies looked full grown, though they wouldn't reach sexual maturity and start looking for their life partners until they were three years old.

As inconspicuously as possible, we wandered on the island among knee-high families who nipped and brayed at one another. I didn't have any idea how long we'd been with the tiny tuxedo-clad creatures or how much light remained in the day. Time seemed to have a different meaning in Antarctica. I never glanced at my watch. I couldn't even get to it under all my layers. I just knew we'd landed on the airstrip at about one thirty, but I couldn't judge how long ago that had been. And it didn't matter to me.

At some point, I fell in with Alejo and walked beside him for a time, asking him about the penguins and about himself. My Inner Wisdom had been right: Alejo was a fellow adventurer. More than that, it wasn't long into the conversation before I realized I was getting the privilege to know a true Antarctic legend, not merely a DAP employee hired to show us around. He told me how he'd lived on King George Island during tourist season for over two decades. He loved Antarctica and enjoyed working with small groups of people, introducing them to the beauty and the wildlife here. But he was also a world-class mountaineer; in fact, he had been to the top of Mount Vinson, touted as the highest peak on the continent. He'd been the first South American to make it to the South Pole on foot. He told me how, before that, he'd followed and provided support for the International Trans-Antarctic Expedition for 221 days as the team of explorers from six countries traveled by dogsled across the white continent. Alejo was a man who understood the importance of completing an unusual goal, of following through on a quest.

While we sauntered between penguin couples, I was peaceful beside Alejo. Eventually, I felt safe enough to confide in him that I'd been living out a dream that had changed my life and the way I saw myself. He listened and nodded when I told him that we'd originally had five people planning to join us on this trip, but the group had dwindled when our expedition had been canceled.

"Ah, yes," he said when I got to this part of my story, piecing things together. "You can't advertise or plan any events or activities on King George Island."

"Well, that point was made loud and clear," I agreed.

"But," he said, "people on this island exercise. It's not a problem to take a run."

When Alejo said this, I opened my mouth to ask if we could run when we got back to the barracks, but I heard a voice in my head pipe up abruptly. Shut up, I heard her say. Just shut up and let things be. I followed her orders and closed my mouth, and remained silent. Sometimes it's important to speak up on your own behalf, and sometimes it's better to just trust. I was done trying to control my experience, at least for now.

THAT AFTERNOON, OUR GROUP took a break from touring and sat sipping coffee in the commons of the Chilean scientific base while Alejo took care of some duties unrelated to his role as tour guide. At about six thirty, he came and sat with us on one of the sectional sofas that made the commons feel cozy and homey for the scientists and staff who lived there through the dark months of winter. Alex, who had been lying down, the cold fresh air no doubt taking as much out of him as it had out of the rest of us, sat up when Alejo began to speak.

"So, we are now going to take a walk over to the Russian Orthodox church. It's very interesting. And we'll stop for some picture-taking along the way at a place where there are beautiful views of the bay." He paused and looked at me. "You can get there walking or running. It doesn't matter. I'll show you some other roads we will use, too."

"So we'll meet you there?" I asked. I wasn't sure if I was hearing Alejo properly. Were we going to get to run? Spontaneously? Right now?

"Sure. And then the rest of us will come back here for dinner and wait for you to finish."

"Will you save us some dinner?" I don't know why this mattered to me. I was afraid to ask directly if we could run for several hours, I suppose, so I was hinting that we would like to be out there for a while, checking in to see if we were on the same page.

"And drinks, too," Alejo said.

So, as Kara, Yury, and Alex put on their coats, hats, and gloves, Bill, Marina, and I rushed over to our barracks and got ready to run before the plan changed, before someone said, "Hey, you three! Stop what you're doing" and deported us for unlawful jogging. Bill and I put our headlamps on (Marina didn't have one), knowing it would be dark in about two hours. And we collected energy gels and drinks, which we left on the dressers in our rooms, deciding that our barracks could be one of our aid stations.

We had covered more than two miles on foot so far, according to our Garmins, and were assured of at least two more miles of walking in the morning before flying back to Chile, so we agreed that we would run twenty-two miles now, into the night. The others had been with us as we'd walked that day; Marina felt that counted as "starting" a marathon. As long as Bill and I finished with her, she would get credit for Antarctica from the Maniacs. And if this wasn't a maniacal thing to do, nothing was.

Coming out of the barracks, we saw the others exiting the common area. "Good luck!" they cheered. "See you on the road."

And we were off—starting what we couldn't technically call an "event," an "activity," or a "race" (I'd settle for "experience")—at seven o'clock in the evening.

We started our route by turning left off the Chilean base and heading back up to the airstrip. This was a distance of almost one mile. I noticed right away the unevenness of the path beneath our feet. We'd have to watch where we stepped. The "roads" were not paved. They were gritty, frozen dirt, forged by tire tracks, unexplainably soggy in some places, covered with snow in others.

As we turned around at the airstrip and made our way to meet the rest of our group at the Russian church, I shouted to Bill in front of me, "We're running! On Antarctica!" I felt celebratory.

Perhaps it was too soon, since a number of things could still prevent us from going the distance. Alejo could call us in for any reason he pleased. The weather could turn on us (it was twenty-five degrees Fahrenheit at the moment, beginning to snow very lightly, and the winds were picking up). There was also a distinct possibility that one of us could get injured. Twilight was setting in even by the time we caught up with the rest of the group. I wasn't convinced that once it was dark our headlamps would provide enough illumination for our footsteps. But all this considered, these first couple of miles were the culmination of a hell of a lot of brain energy; of months of dreaming, planning, giving up, and starting over; and, finally, of the generous support of a lovely Chilean adventurer and a small group of cheerleaders. I couldn't help celebrating.

After stopping in and admiring the church, we followed the route out toward the Chinese base. Here the road dipped down and then ascended up again. "This looks like my image of Antarctica!" Bill shouted over his shoulder from the bottom of the hill. The road was covered with snow and the view of the bay was obstructed, giving the sense of being lost in a vast white valley. It was a thrilling sensation, the illusion that we were the only people on a frozen planet. A snowdrift eventually prevented us from going any farther on the road, so we had to turn around and go back up toward "civilization." As we climbed, the snow flurries came straight at our faces.

I became concerned about Marina. She told me that she had run in snow only one other time in her life: the previous year in Mississippi, during a brief flurry. California girl that she was, she'd hardly even seen snow, let alone learned how to run in it. She'd bundled herself up to the point of being burdened by her clothing, and she was cautious with each footfall. I fretted over what she was going to do without a headlamp once it was pitch black.

When we reached the top of the hill, we took a left on the path that led us back to our barracks: three miles down—only nineteen to go.

Back at the Chilean base, we checked in with our group. Our loop had taken us a little less than an hour. At this rate, we would be out all night; we wanted to make sure the group understood this. I poked my head into the commons and saw Yury sitting in front of a bottle of vodka, while the others sipped red wine.

"Aw, you have to be kidding me," I said. "Save us some wine, will you?"

"Sure," Kara said. "How long till you're done?"

"I'm guessing five hours at the pace we're going."

"We will be here," Alejo assured us. Then he added, "I saw the snow, but it is just a passing cloud. We have to pay attention. It's easy to get lost if it snows hard." I knew he wouldn't let us get lost. He'd call us in if he sensed any danger. If there was ever a moment when he couldn't see our headlamps for an extended period of time, our run would be over.

I nodded that I understood and then headed back outside—there wasn't a moment to lose. Once we were out in the elements again, Bill, Marina, and I started our second loop. Marina had taken off her bulky down coat and replaced it with a windbreaker I'd loaned her. She looked less like a polar bear and more like a runner now.

Up to the airstrip, to the church, out to the snowdrift on the way to the Chinese base, and back "home" we went again. By the end of the second loop, the sun was down. By the end of the third loop, it was completely dark and snowing lightly again.

Bill was a football field ahead of me; Marina was the same distance behind me. I was worried about both of them. Bill, so prone to rolling his ankle, had better be careful on this uneven surface, especially as the snow accumulated. And Marina was increasingly tentative with her steps, now that she could see nothing. I wasn't used to considering anyone besides myself on a marathon course. But this wasn't a course. It was three people having a long-distance-running "experience" in a harsh environment without any volunteers or mile signs along the way. We had to look out for each other. I made a decision: On our next loop, I would give my headlamp to Marina. My chances of making the distance without one were much better than hers, since I was used to running in cold, wet weather and even on occasional snow and ice.

I slowed down until Marina caught up with me, and fixed the lamp on her head.

"Hey, thanks," she said.

"It's for me," I told her. "I'll run better if I'm not worried about you. Let's go." And we forged ahead.

Before we had traced our complete route for a fifth time, however, we knew we couldn't keep going the way we had started. The snow flurries, though not strong enough to call us back inside, were coming in sideways, straight into our faces, and were thick enough to cause a white-out experience in the light of our headlamps. Not only that, but Bill was mediating his pace carefully, working hard not to get too far ahead of me. I was doing the same to keep Marina within sight.

It was eleven o'clock now. We'd been going for four hours and had covered only twelve miles. This was slow work. We cut our fifth loop short and had a little tête-à-tête-à-tête).

"I think we'd better revise our plan," Bill said.

"What do you suggest?" I asked.

"We need to pick two landmarks and go back and forth. This four-point loop we're doing is getting too hard the later it gets." I agreed. The road to the Chinese base was much more difficult to navigate without light. In addition, we had ten miles left before we could stop for the night, and the Garmins were already beeping warnings about low batteries. We needed to measure out a course where we knew the distance, in case we had GPS failure.

We picked a small lighthouse near the water as one point and ran up the hill toward the airstrip for half a mile, choosing a metal pole stuck in the ground as the spot for our turnaround. Ten out-and-back trips, and we'd be done. We could all go at our own pace and offer encouragement when we passed each other.

In theory, this out-and-back routine should have been easier (if more monotonous) than the complicated loop we'd been running before. There was one uphill and one downhill—straight out and straight back. Unfortunately, what we hadn't considered was the direction of the wind. On our uphill section of the course, the wind blew directly into our faces and pushed on us hard, creating the sensation of running in ice-cold water. My body was well protected against the wind and the cold, but my face was trickier to keep warm. I wore a black running cap with a hole in the back to let my ponytail hang out. Over that, a headband did double duty on my ears and lower forehead. Then I tucked a fleece neck muffler over my ponytail in the back and over my nose in front. My eyes were the only exposed part of my face. These I squinted to keep the wet snow off my eyelashes. Each time I made my way up the hill of our one-mile route, the wind blew my muffler down my face and I had to hold it in place with my hand, which restricted my ability to use my arms to give myself momentum.

On the downhill stretches, which came as a relief with the wind at my back, I felt my shins developing the sharp, cinching pain of shin splints. I hadn't had shin splints since junior high school, but hours of slapping my feet on uneven ground without knowing how deep or short the footfalls would be were taking their toll on my legs.

Five miles into our out-and-backs, I was in bad shape. I kept reminding myself that this was the last continent on my quest, and that if I were going to get injured, at least I could take some time at home after this to heal, knowing I had done what I'd set out to do.

But on the sixth out-and-back (mile eighteen of running and mile twenty for the day, not to mention mile forty-seven for the week), I hit a wall—of pain. With every step, the muscles in my shins contracted in anticipation of the ache they would feel upon impact. Then, when the impact came, I could only wince and let out a truncated moan. It was quite a different drumbeat from the Bom. Bom. Bom. BOOM! of Tateyama.

I was glad Bill and Marina were far ahead of and behind me, respectively. Conversation would be impossible until I found some inner strength to gut through this. I felt a natural temptation to stop running, but this wasn't strong. I couldn't imagine taking a DNF (did not finish) in my Antarctic "experience." But I was developing a genuine injury that was worsening with each step.

Change your shoes, came a voice in my head.

Of course! Why hadn't I thought of it before? I'd been wearing my trail shoes, which had more grip but less cushion than my regular shoes. My old, comfy, everyday runners were dry and warm and waiting for me in my room. Sometimes it's inner strength you need; sometimes it's better shoes—every woman knows this.

When Bill came by, I told him I needed to go to the barracks. Then I waited for Marina and we all went in together for a quick break. A clean pair of socks, some acetaminophen, an energy gel, and my favorite shoes did the trick. The others were still up (though a little worse for wear), sipping spirits, laughing at each other's jokes, and waiting for us to finish. I told them we were close to being done.

Back out on the road, I was a new woman, still in pain, but much less so than before. Bill ramped up his pace and hurried to finish his laps now so he could turn his headlamp over to me. This added to the benefit of wearing my other shoes, and I was able to prevent further injury. For the last two miles, I could see where I was going.

Marina had been a trooper all this time. She kept moving at her steady, slow pace. I stayed less than a lap in front of her, unable to move any faster, though I longed to be done. Finally, at 1:30 AM on Friday, March 19, 2010, Marina and I touched the pole for the last time. Together we jogged slowly toward the lighthouse, both of us becoming more excited with each step.

Five. Four. Three. Two. One. Finished! We'd made it. It wasn't over yet, really. We had two miles to walk in the daylight in the morning, but the hard part was complete. We gave each other an exhausted hug and hobbled back to the Chilean commons. Slowly, we limped up the stairs into the trailer, where the others sat waiting for us. When we opened the door, there was a loud shout and applause from our tipsy group.

"Congratulations!" Alejo said, handing me a bottle of sparkling Chilean wine. "This is special wine for the women runners of the group! And I am your witness that you did this!" His bright eyes sparkled and his smile was knowing and radiant. I could see he was proud of us. He'd stood on mountaintops and touched the South Pole; Alejo was a man who got it, who had let adventure and hard physical activity form his identity.

I took the bottle from him and raised it in the air. I felt my tears coming, but did I get to rejoice yet? Technically, we had two miles to complete before we could say we'd done the marathon distance. In Prague, I hadn't let myself put on my medal until I'd finished the course. But here at the bottom of the world, I wouldn't be bothered by technicalities. If ever I'd been tenacious in the spirit of long-distance running, if ever I'd challenged my need for control or lived into a moment or shrugged off the rules and judgments of others, if ever I had immersed myself in what the marathon had to teach me about life and love and self, it was tonight! So I let a tear or two run down my face and completely gave in to the celebration that was happening around and inside me. Number seven! Check.

WE WENT TO BED at four o'clock, after someone who lived on the base asked us to close up shop already. After sleeping for three hours, we were up again. Our Garmins were recharged, so Bill and I got dressed and decided to amble outside together to get a good daylight look at the course we'd run in the dark. Holding hands, we walked very slowly around the roads on the little peninsula where the Chilean base was located and then hiked our way up to what is known as the E-base, the island's experiment with powering a base exclusively with renewable energy. I hobbled along beside Bill, feeling in my shins every blind step I'd taken the night before.

"Can you believe this place?" Bill asked.

"Take it in," I said. "This could be our only chance to see it."

By noon, it was time to get ready to go. As we packed up our things, our

GPS said we'd finished twenty-eight miles. Marina, who had not come with Bill and me on our walk, said hers read 26.5. But what's in a number, anyway? What really counts is the way a marathon can change a life.

Alejo said goodbye to each of us, going down the line, as he had greeted us the day before. When he got to me, he extended his hand, but I threw my arms around him and kissed him on his bearded cheek, promising to keep in touch. I was a little in love, sad to leave, and very grateful.

epilogue

After returning to Chile from Antarctica, Bill and I hiked at least another twenty-six miles through Torres del Paine National Park. I hit my limit of energy output about halfway through this trip and spent the final few days lollygagging behind Bill at a ridiculously slow pace.

I had many, many hours with myself and the mountains to let it sink in that I had just finished my self-made vision quest, completing the marathon distance on every continent. As I walked, it dawned on me that before I had started (really, before committing to run in Mudgee, Australia), I had never done anything especially spectacular. Now I'd done at least one extraordinary thing in my life. I'd landed on all seven continents and completed 26.2 miles on each of them. I had a medal from every race (or "adventure") to hang on my bathroom light fixture. (Bill had made medals for Marina and me for Antarctica, in anticipation of success.)

Running had become essential to my identity, but more important, it had provided me with a means for deconstructing, detaching, waiting, opening, listening, and trusting. What I had never been able to figure out how to do using the guidelines of my former doctrine or through worshipping a narrowly defined masculine god, I had learned to do with this practice of hours and miles and breathing.

So now what? I asked myself, as I hiked through the park and studied the shiny green glacier-made lake below me. But I was too tired from the more than one hundred miles I'd put in during the last week and a half to engage in the mental work answering that question required. It would have to wait.

I still ask myself what comes next, and there are elements of the answer that I feel certain about. First, I'll keep running. I'm shooting for the new goal of running a marathon (or longer) in all fifty U.S. states. And Bill, who has been hungry to get back to Europe to redo that continent, has suggested we start over on all seven. The most important thing, however, is not the number of miles or the time it takes to finish a race or reach a goal. The reason to keep running is that out there (on the trails and roads and through the woods or city streets) is where I meet myself. Out there running is where I tell myself stories, where I cry spontaneously, where I am angry and happy, lost and found. As long as my legs work, I'll run. When or if they stop working, I'll reassess the situation. Not everyone finds running to be a natural way to do personal-growth work, but everybody needs some way (or place or means) to do it. I'm grateful I've found one.

Second, I know I will continue traveling. Every new place or new friend offers an opportunity to rethink my particular North American assumptions about life on Planet Earth. I am confident at this point that my way of being in this world is based on nothing but a set of biases that most of the people I surround myself with have no reason to challenge. So it feels like a good thing to seek out people who will. If I hadn't met people in graduate school who asked me hard questions and taught me how to ask them of myself, I never would have wiggled free from the threat that eternity in hell posed to me. It feels important to stay curious and keep holding life's assumptions up to the question-asking process. Traveling is part of that process for me.

Finally, my relationships (with Bill and others) will continue to reflect what truths I happen to be in touch with at the moment. I think I've learned that one cannot write her beliefs in stone—or at least I can't. I expect my understandings about God and truth and all things existential to shift and change as my life unfolds. Never again will I proclaim a fixed, inflexible belief system and allow it to beat me into submission.

Aside from these promises to myself, I don't know what kind of terrain the next miles hold or what kinds of hurdles I'll face (though I'm quite sure there will be plenty of them). It has been important for me to tell my story—

the tale of a sometime jogger–turned-marathoner who truly loves herself, though she never wins any ribbons and barely ever beats five hours. When we tell our stories, we invite others to tell theirs to us in return. When we tell our stories, we create them and become the narrators of our own lives. When we tell our stories, we chart our own courses.

acknowledgments

In the fall of 2007, after Bill and I ran the Mudgee race, I signed up for a memoir-writing class with a novelist named Laura Kalpakian. It was in her class that I first tried my hand at a tentative, halting race report. Laura and the group held me accountable to keep writing and encouraged me to dream of a book. Thanks to the whole memoir class, especially "the midwives": Bernadette, Claudia, Elizabeth, MJ, Susan, and Terri. They have given me a writing community in Bellingham.

When Brooke Warner and I met, she saw something in my story that I hadn't even seen yet and helped me conceive of this book in its current form. I am more glad than I can say to have her as my first editor. She pushed me, encouraged me, and cheered me along through every slow step.

My partner, Bill Pech, has helped me give birth to, love, and discipline this project from beginning to end. Knowing him has been a grace; there's no other way to say it. He has held me up, figuratively and literally, as we traveled this road together, and, even more of a gift, he has let me do the same for him.

My agent, Pamela Malpas, from Harold Ober Associates, joined the team with enthusiasm and a commitment to guiding me through every stupid question about the publishing process with patience and good humor. My deep thanks to her for watching out for me and for caring about each race and each word.

A few of my pals need a special shout-out for their moral support, for asking me regularly how I was doing, for letting me park my car at their houses, for shuttling us to the airport, for babysitting the creatures at our home, for excusing my absenteeism from their lives. In no particular order, thank you and I love you, Christine and Ryan, Jason and Robin, Steph, Sharon, Charlene and Kn, Kevin and Renata, Deb, Benita and Dennis, Wendy and Jack, Jack and Yui, Glynn and Greg, the Other End girls, Nancy and Perry, Kakuei, Yayoi, and Koichiro, Eric and Bolor, and Temuulin.

Bill's coworkers deserve an important thank-you because they covered for him, encouraged him, and made it possible for him to enjoy our travels, knowing that everything back home was in good hands. Some of them are listed above, but I especially want Marci (and Akira) and Rosemary to know how much I appreciate their support.

My running partner and neighbor, Julie, has been my savior at times. Finding someone who runs at your pace is a rare treasure and should not be taken for granted. I never fail to be thankful. Likewise, Marie and especially Marina gave me faith I didn't know I had. Thanks to those "partners," too. Thank you to Dean Karnazes for writing me a kind note and encouraging me in my running and writing.

In addition to my running inspirations, there are people, some of whom appeared in this book, who were and are very special to us. Thanks to everyone who took care of us in our travels and invited us into their lives and homes, some of whom made us part of their families: The entire extended Lorenzato network in Brazil is a true family to us; in Tateyama, there are Mayor Kanamaru, Kenji Masako and Kinuyo, Michael, Kuniko, and Yoshitsugu, and all of the sister-city board; and in Punta Arenas, Mayor Mimica, Maria Angelica, Marcelo, Mackarena, Omar and Sebastien, Andres and Aurora, Aurora's extended family (who helped us get to Torres del Paine, the most beautiful mountains I've ever seen), Maritza and her whole family, the children and teachers at Colegío Miguel de Cervantes, and Ben are all people we treasure. I also have to send special thanks down to the bottom of the planet to Alejo Contreras Staeding, whom it is a privilege to know and who deserves a book all to himself. In Australia, thanks to Lynn from the Mudgee Tri-Club and to Don from the Mudgee Guardian. In Panama, thanks to the yellow-jacketed bicyclist and the pizza-delivery guy who brought us our post-race dinner in a downpour. And all over the world, thanks to the people who operate safe, clean hostels where individuals of all ages are welcome.

There are people who came to mean a lot to me during my writing process but who probably don't know what they did to contribute to my general well-being during the creation of this book. The members of my Barkley Starbucks "fan club," as Bill calls them, were there for me every day. They know who they are: employees (who faithfully made me my double, short, one-pump-of-sugar-free-cinnamon-dolce soy latte to perfection) and customers alike, who asked me about my progress, listened to my stories, and chose not to be offended when I told them I had to write and couldn't talk. Tracy from The Travel Team always got us where we needed to be, no matter how complicated our plans were. Shannon, my massage therapist, saved my body as I went from sitting and writing for seven hours to running twenty miles. She fixed my hip and loosened my shoulders so I could do my work. Our three local running stores all supported our efforts: Michael at Footworx never failed to listen to our tales and make us feel we were doing something really cool. Sam at Runningshoes.com inspired us on the local trails and, in the store, suited us up for running in all conditions. And Craig at Fairhaven Runners and Walkers evaluated my gait more than once when my favorite shoes were taken off the market. He calmed my despair and helped me find a new model that worked for me.

My three "clubs," which have become central to my life, all joined the project in one way or another, perhaps unwittingly. The Greater Bellingham Running Club deserves a huge thanks for making running fun. They host events, encourage runners of all skill levels, and are just generally nice people to be around. I appreciate being a part of their club. Also in Bellingham is the Bellingham Sister Cities Association. I hope when people read this book, they will find out about the sister cities of their own towns and buy an airplane ticket to go visit. The Sister Cities program, which Dwight D. Eisenhower created in 1956, is a great way to change the world one relationship at a time. And then there are the Marathon Maniacs. If you look around at any given race, they are everywhere in their yellow-and-black singlets. If they are not in their uniforms, you can still tell who they are; they are the marathoners who smile as they run. That's why I joined their group. They've met me along the way on many races and made it seem perfectly normal to run at a walking pace.

Finally, there is my family. My grandparents made a home away from home for Jane and Fuji, to the point that my dogs prefer their house to ours. They fed them (and us) to excess, laughed at my stories, and caught me up on any funny thing the dogs did in our absence. Other family members plodded through blog entries, checked in with my progress, told me they were proud of me, and endured my single-mindedness over the past few years.

I would be remiss if I did not acknowledge my ex-husband, whom I have not named, but who spent a decade with me trying his best and who taught me many things. I cheer for his happiness, as I know he cheers for mine.

Many other people in my family are very private and can't really imagine sharing their foibles or pathologies with the world. A big thanks to them for supporting me even when they didn't understand why I needed to follow this path.

about
the author

© LYNN TYLER KING

Cami Ostman is a licensed marriage and family therapist with publications in her field. She currently runs between twenty and forty miles each week as part of her own commitment to fitness and self-discovery. In her quest to run a marathon on every continent, she has been featured in several publications, including the *Mudgee Guardian* in Australia, *The Bellingham Herald* in Washington State, and *La Prensa* in Chile. She completed her seventh continental marathon by running in Antarctica in March 2010. Cami lives in Bellingham, Washington.